"Each chapter has a clear message and offers co⌐ by anthropologists' usual convoluted prose. The practice, and its internal effects, has wide implica opening the lid on that which is neglected in usual intervention-focused studies. In this sense, the book is a major cross-disciplinary bridge-building contribution. Indeed, I think the book makes clear in a way that few others have, why ethnographic research is important to getting to the heart of contemporary dilemmas in psychiatric care; especially by taking seriously the everyday experience and representational practices of patients and staff. The book avoids polarising debate around psychiatry, and taking a fresh viewpoint provides a common platform of shared concern about real challenges."

David Mosse, Professor of Social Anthropology, SOAS,
University of London, UK

"Dr Armstrong's incisive analysis of the mental health system challenges complacent and particularised explanations and presents a mature and systemic account of why mental health systems continue to struggle – harm – fail. Sharing his own lived experience of recovery and evolving agency, we see the demise of well-intentioned and highly trained clinicians to serve the structural and bureaucratic agency of the institution, be that the state, the hospital, the prison and criminal justice system. He does this through the powerful stories and voice of the most afflicted, marginalised, and excluded, providing some seminal lessons for practitioners, policy makers, legislators. Although he brings theory into to the analysis, he does so cautiously, never failing to sketch out the limitations of worshipping theory rather than testing it through real world experience and local realities."

Kamaldeep Bhui, Professor of Psychiatry and Senior
Research Fellow, University of Oxford, UK

COLLABORATIVE ETHNOGRAPHIC WORKING IN MENTAL HEALTH

Collaborative Ethnographic Working in Mental Health seeks to chart a new direction for research into mental healthcare, with the aim of creating the conditions for more productive interdisciplinary dialogue.

People involved in mental health often fail to recognise how they are described by researchers from the humanities and social sciences, which inhibits productive collaboration. This book seeks to address this problem, by including clinicians and patients in the research process and by shifting attention away from power and knowledge and towards the organisational context. It explores how clinical thinking and behaviour, illness experience, and clinical relationships are all shaped by the bureaucratic context. In particular, it examines tensions between what we want from mental healthcare and how accountable bureaucracies actually work, and proposes that mental healthcare research should not just evaluate new interventions but should investigate new ways of organising.

This book is written with a non-specialist audience in mind, as it is intended for all with a stake in mental healthcare research and practice. It is also for those with an interest in ethnographic methods, as a novel way of deploying ethnography, autoethnography and coproduced ethnography to address clinically important research topics.

Neil Armstrong is a medical anthropologist. He is a Fellow of Harris Manchester College, Oxford and Research Associate at Kings College London, UK. He is also a former psychiatric patient.

Catriona Watson is an artist and writer, based in Oxford, UK. She enjoys using the gentle but intentional colours in gouache paint, and writing epic postcards. Contributing to this project has brought together ideas and writings from the last thirty years, and it has been a joy to share these. To see more of Catriona's work, visit @banjubec on Instagram.

Hugh Palmer studied classics at Oxford university and then set off on a precarious path that led to a career a successful location photographer. He has illustrated and written many books on architecture and travel. In his fifties he answered a second calling, and is now establishing himself as an integrative psychotherapist, halfway through a degree course at Warwick University, UK.

Rowan Jones has worked in the mental health sector for fifteen years. She has a BA in Experimental Psychology from Oxford University, UK. Rowan believes talking is vital for recovery and likes to deliver trauma informed care. She uses an integrative approach with a particular focus on CBT. Rowan Jones is a pseudonym.

COLLABORATIVE ETHNOGRAPHIC WORKING IN MENTAL HEALTH

Knowledge, Power and Hope in an Age of Bureaucratic Accountability

Neil Armstrong
with Catriona Watson, Hugh Palmer and
Rowan Jones

Routledge
Taylor & Francis Group

LONDON AND NEW YORK

Designed cover image: Gustav Grube, early 1900s, from the Prinzhorn Collection, Heidelberg.

First published 2024
by Routledge
4 Park Square, Milton Park, Abingdon, Oxon OX14 4RN

and by Routledge
605 Third Avenue, New York, NY 10158

Routledge is an imprint of the Taylor & Francis Group, an informa business

British Library Cataloguing-in-Publication Data
A catalogue record for this book is available from the British Library

ISBN: 978-0-367-72293-7 (hbk)
ISBN: 978-0-367-72294-4 (pbk)
ISBN: 978-1-003-15423-5 (ebk)

DOI: 10.4324/9781003154235

Typeset in Optima
by Taylor & Francis Books

CONTENTS

ACKNOWLEDGEMENTS

This book is written in a relatively transparent way, so that the reader can see how it came into being. This means acknowledgements that might usually be found in a designated acknowledgements section are located in the text itself. For three of the chapters, authorship is shared between me and a co-author, who are Catriona Watson, Hugh Palmer and Rowan Jones. Working with each of them has been a revelation: rewarding and illuminating, and fun. However, in a world where all endeavour is collaborative, I would like to mention a few more names. This book has been guided by so many people. From within anthropology, David Gellner, David Mosse, Nanda Pirie, Keira Pratt-Boyden and David Zeitlyn. From the wider academic and clinical worlds, Peter Agulnik, Lamis Bayar, Nicola Byrom, James Davies, John Hall, Edward Harcourt. Rowan Jones provided wonderful additional feedback. Most of all, my beloved wife Nadia.

Collaborative Ethnographic Working in Mental Health is dedicated to the Steeles: Matt, Georgie, Nye and Laurie.

1

EVERYBODY KNOWS ABOUT MENTAL HEALTH

It was the early 2010s and I was I preparing to start a medical anthropology DPhil (PhD) focussed on mental health. I had just spent ten years as a mental health patient living on benefits. I had been advised not to expect to get better and not to expect to work again. But, to the surprise of all (not least myself) I completely recovered. I recovered by withdrawing from services, by rejecting treatments, care and clinical supervision. I didn't think that mental healthcare had made me ill, but I could see that it hadn't really helped much, and that I needed to distance myself from mental healthcare to become well. I wanted my research to build on my experiences of distress, care and recovery. I knew mental healthcare needed to change and I wanted to contribute to that change. So you could say that I had an agenda.

I was enthusiastic, even idealistic, and I did a lot of reading. I read piles of books and journal articles, eagerly scanning search engines and databases for more. At first, my focus was on psychiatry journals, and the anthropological literature that discusses mental health. I soon found that, despite having apparently common interests, these literatures diverged, and almost never engaged each other directly. Psychiatry publications addressed the origins, nature and (especially) treatment of mental disorders. They were written in such a way as to suggest that each publication added to a steady accumulation of data that would ultimately lead to a comprehensive understanding of mental disorders and, through that, more effective treatments. Most of the key concepts, such as 'depression' 'psychosis,' 'bipolar disorder,' were used in fairly standardised ways, and most of the important research presented evidence involving randomised controlled trials. Publications by anthropologists were rather different. They were engaged with an alternate set of research questions, thinking of mental healthcare in terms of power, narrative, or social context, or investigating the pragmatics of providing care and living as a

DOI: 10.4324/9781003154235-1

recipient of care. Anthropologists carefully positioned themselves relative to other anthropologists, but there was far less consensus about key terms. Debates were about concepts as much as evidence. In comparison with the psychiatry papers, it was striking that there was less of a sense of a collaborative anthropological venture, in which researchers sought to make progress by answering shared questions.

As time went by, I began to consult other disciplines: sociology, history, science and technology studies, philosophy, cultural studies, life writing, the creative arts and more. I was impressed with a lot of what I read. It seemed lively and interesting, well worth spending time reading and thinking about. But more than that, it seemed important. The humanities and social sciences appeared to have things to say about mental healthcare that mental health researchers and clinicians might want to know about. Together with the anthropology literature, I felt I had located a set of debates and enquiries originating outside biomedicine that had the capacity to make a major contribution to mental health research and, thus, mental healthcare itself. Anthropologists notice things that biomedical researchers miss. Philosophers investigate concepts in ways that medical researchers are not trained to do. Historians are able to analyse change in ways that draw on expertise in the archives, rather than the clinic. I was left feeling excited that the humanities and social sciences had theoretical and methodological expertise that could productively engage with biomedical research.

This potential contribution felt timely, perhaps urgent. During this period, I came across papers in mainstream biomedical mental health journals suggesting that their research had more or less stalled. Such papers typically made a sequence of claims, such as: that few advances had been made since the 1990s; that there are no truly innovative treatments, just revamped versions of existing interventions; that ostensibly newer treatments were about as effective as older treatments; that knowing which treatment might work for a particular patient was still largely guesswork; and that major problems remained. For example, in an editorial for the *British Journal of Psychiatry* published in 2013, prestigious clinical researchers Stefan Priebe, Tom Burns and Tom K J Craig wrote that although 'progress in fundamental research in subjects adjacent to psychiatry, such as genetics and neuroscience, has been considerable... It can be questioned whether the past 30 years have witnessed any scientific discoveries that have led to major improvements of practice' (Priebe et al 2013: 319). Progress can seem stalled to such a degree that some biomedical researchers think the existing research model is fatally flawed and only a 'paradigm shift' will clear the log jam (Bhugra et al 2017). For those waiting for better mental healthcare, it is a depressing story. However, sociologist Lindsay McGoey claims the inability of mental health research to advance knowledge creates winners as well as losers (McGoey 2010). McGoey argues that, for researchers themselves, stasis is a 'profitable failure.' Of course, everything in this field is contentious. Some researchers are optimistic, others pessimistic. There are clinical academics who claim that research is advancing, or (more often) will advance soon. Ongoing work on the gut biome and investigations of psychedelics are examples of possible new horizons. Others write in terms of 'postpsychiatry' and suggest we need to start again. It seems fair to conclude that at the time of writing, just as back in the 2010s, all is not well within biomedical research into mental healthcare, and there is plenty of space for input from the humanities and social sciences.

As an open-minded, unjaded doctoral researcher, I could see a clear role for multiple disciplines and approaches. The potential for a happy and productive interdisciplinarity seemed obvious. But when I arrived at an NHS mental healthcare hospital to begin my doctoral fieldwork, I was disappointed to encounter almost no interdisciplinary engagement. The mental health professionals I worked alongside showed very limited awareness of the social science and humanities literature I had found so impressive. I met excellent clinicians and some famous researchers, but few of them knew any of the works I found so inspiring. The first time a psychiatrist told me he hadn't heard of medical anthropology or the anthropology of psychiatry, I was slightly hurt. But as I heard it for a second, third and fourth time, I realised it was part of a wider pattern. You might say it became data. Some clinicians seemed to have had brushes with humanities and social sciences but framed it all as 'political' or 'antipsychiatry.' They thought that it amounted to little more than a stream of opinion and anecdote that could never really match up to, or contribute to, objective science. I was sometimes present when patients asked clinicians about antipsychiatry or made arguments critical of mental healthcare. Some patients drew explicitly from classic literature by R D Laing, Michel Foucault, or more recent figures such as Richard Bentall, James Davies, Duncan Double, Joanna Moncrieff or Robert Whitaker. However well read or articulate the patients were, it never seemed to lead to a real exchange of views. I never saw much curiosity from clinicians. More typical was a weary, occasionally impatient defensiveness. Some clinicians seemed tempted to interpret the expression of critical mental healthcare arguments as indicative of, maybe even constitutive of, a mental disorder. It is perhaps easy to confuse disordered thinking with unwelcome thinking. As time went by I started to wonder why there was such a barrier between mainstream biomedical and psychological research into mental distress and the work of other disciplines that seem to promise so much. And, just as important, I wondered how might we proceed to make dialogue easier.

When I discussed this with fellow anthropologists, we tended to blame psychiatry as a social institution, or psychiatrists themselves as responsible individuals, or mental healthcare more generally. We might have expressed ourselves according to the genteel conventions of academe, but, underneath it, we were apportioning blame. We spoke of institutional inflexibility, of rigid medical career pathways that inhibit interdisciplinarity, and of a culpable insularity on the part of psychiatry, as the least secure of the medical specialties. We expressed concern about the corrupting influence of big pharma and of a deep conceptual naivety on the part of clinicians that generates an unthinking prejudice in favour of numbers and measurement. If only the psychiatrists were as clever as we were. But, as my research went on, and, in particular, when my thesis was finished and I started to present my work to doctors, I began to see there was another side to this story. I began to see that there was something about how we in the humanities and social sciences were conducting ourselves that made interdisciplinary working more difficult.

I came to believe that the main barrier to interdisciplinary working arises out of theory. What I have in mind here are long standing associations between power and knowledge. These ideas have their antecedents in Marxist investigations of how class inequalities can be maintained by forms of knowledge, rather than just by brute force. The idea is that control of knowledge is a control of hearts and minds. Tiny minorities can dominate and exploit huge majorities if they can frame their rule as just, or necessary, or beneficial. Control of hearts and minds offers the possibility of people becoming supporters and enforcers of their own exploitation. It means that we can't just think about knowledge in terms of truth and falsehood. We need to look at how it is made, what concepts are used and how they are linked together.

The most influential and sophisticated version of this kind of position can be found in the late work of Foucault (2004, 2007). Seen through his eyes, psychiatry is, first and foremost, a kind of discipline, a way that people are controlled. Foucault calls this 'Biopower.'

Psychiatrists may present their work as purely descriptive, but Foucault suggests that this is not really the case. He argues that biomedical ideas are normative. They influence what a person might desire and what they might fear, what feels right and what feels wrong, what makes them proud and what makes them feel guilty. So scientific knowledge like this changes who we are, shapes how we see the world, how we experience ourselves and how we want to live our lives. And these changes are political. For Foucault, psychiatry is a means by which the political project of the state is interiorised by citizens, an instance of what he calls 'governmentality.'

To make ideas concrete, consider the category 'resilience.' It is common for a psychiatrist (or other mental health professional) to talk to a patient about resilience. It crops up in medical notes, forms, and case discussions. Mental health professionals present ideas like resilience as purely descriptive, the building blocks of neutral science, supported by evidence. But a Foucauldian lens, based on the association of power and knowledge, suggests something rather different. It suggests we might want to think about how the clinical idea of resilience connects to government policies that increase employment precarity, depress wages, or remove funding for community projects. This is because resilience accounts for distress in terms of shortcomings in the individual. Individuals become mentally unwell because they are insufficiently resourced. The solution is for that individual to build up their resources. Encouraging a person to build resilience is to make them responsible for problems that might otherwise be the responsibility of the state. Living without secure and remunerative employment in unsafe and unconnected communities is bad for a person's mental health. But the concept of resilience suggests that the people are at fault. If a person is distressed and fails to recover, well, that is their problem. So 'resilience' and the other categories may seem like innocent science, but they are doing political work, making individuals feel responsible for structural conditions created by policies that some see as designed to favour other groups or pursue other goals. As Nikolas Rose puts it: 'the professionalised recovery movement has flourished in so many countries because it fits perfectly with the rationalities and technologies of neoliberalism' (Rose 2019: 164). This is perhaps not so far from winning hearts and minds such that people become supporters and enforcers of their own exploitation.

These foundational ideas are developed in intricate ways by Foucault himself. However, in subsequent work by other researchers, they often become simpler and less nuanced and some of the interconnections are erased. The philosopher Ian Hacking regrets this loss of depth. He draws a parallel between research that doesn't reproduce the full complexity of Foucault's thinking and ice sculptures that lose their clean lines when exposed to the sun's rays and now sit, half-melted, in a fridge (Hacking 1998: 85). Who wouldn't prefer the un-melted ice sculptures? In some research publications, Foucauldian ideas live on as little more than conceptual debris, guiding the path researchers take yet invisible to the naked eye. However, there might be reasons to prefer less elaborated versions of Foucault. Committing to Foucault's thinking in total means committing to a wider set of claims about government and the state that can be seen as intellectually cumbersome, and leave a limited role empirical work, which can do little more than confirm and illustrate a predetermined picture.

In any case, these ideas have powered some impressive research. At risk of oversimplification, we might say that mental healthcare emerges as an encounter between dominating knowledge and a hapless individual. Knowledge can seem to be the main, even the only, active ingredient. Mental healthcare staff become vectors of knowledge, whose agency is limited and whose intentions, independence and integrity all fall under suspicion. Dominating knowledge is presented as reshaping individuals, transforming their understanding of distress and thus their experiences of distress and exerting disciplinary control, so that their goals and ambitions are the goals and ambitions of the state.

But this is just one interpretive lens, a single take on how to analyse mental healthcare. However convincing or helpful it is, it leaves questions in its wake. Can an account of power and knowledge derived from an analysis of class domination say everything we want to say about mental healthcare? How well does it capture and illuminate experiences of power inequality in mental healthcare? How recognisable is this framing to the participants, the patients, mental health professionals and others with first-hand experience of mental healthcare? This last question is probably least frequently asked but is most important for this book. The mental health professionals I spoke to were sceptical. They tended not to find visions of dominating psychiatric knowledge and dominated psychiatric patients to resemble their day-to-day experience. Neither knowledge nor power play quite the role that these approaches assume. Far from being the authoritative bearer of biopower, psychiatrists said they felt harried and constrained, their attention scattered, forced to respond to multiple pressures as best they can.

My own ethnographic impressions confirmed this response. The social world of mental healthcare described in the pages below seems to be so much more than a grand Foucauldian plot. Sometimes small details show this best. In my doctoral research, having picked up fairly mainstream Foucauldian assumptions, I expected the Diagnostic and Statistical Manual (DSM), sometimes called the 'bible' of psychiatry, to figure prominently in healthcare settings. As the authoritative repository of knowledge in a healthcare system that I thought of mainly in terms of knowledge and power, I expected to find copies everywhere. I thought that wherever psychiatrists and patients were gathered together, it was liable to be close to hand. It wasn't. Copies were very difficult to locate. When I asked clinicians they struggled to find one. Usually they couldn't. In one case, after about fifteen minutes of looking, we found what seemed to be the only copy the clinic possessed propping open a window. It made me reflect that if it was valued primarily for its physical properties, the categories of knowledge located within the DSM are less central that they might appear.

As my fieldwork went on, I began to see that a lot of what mental health professionals do arises out of ad hoc deliberations that reflect institutional pressures. Clinicians struggle to deal with intense and multiple pressures and a constant sense of how their conduct might look to outsiders, to line managers, to senior staff members, to care quality monitors. These sorts of concerns rarely make it into humanities and social science publications, although there are valuable exceptions to this. An early monography by Lorna Rhodes called *Emptying Beds: The Work of an Emergency Psychiatric Unit* vividly describes mental healthcare professionals as hard-pressed and over-worked, continually placed in difficult, almost impossible positions (Rhodes 1995). In Rhodes' account, doctors are forced to somehow balance patient interests with the needs of the ward, ensuring enough patients are discharged quickly enough to free up the beds for the continual flood of new arrivals. Rhodes suggests that staff respond to these pressures by talking about care and making records of care using terms from a range of sources to create what she calls a 'patchwork quilt':

> The staff...were bricoleurs of psychiatric and social theory, using what was available according to whether it would fit a particular context... at any moment, and sometimes all in the same moment, a staff member might be a biological empiricist, a Freudian or a Laingian antipsychiatrist.
>
> *(ibid.: 4)*

This doesn't sound like dominating knowledge. More recently, in a commentary on ethnographic approaches to mental healthcare, the psychiatrist Elizabeth Bromley remarked: 'I do not recognise my work in these descriptions' (Bromley 2019: 110). This matters. It is difficult to see how productive dialogue between the biomedical sciences and the humanities and social sciences could be promoted without more agreement on what mental healthcare looks and feels like.

When I spoke to service users, many said they felt disempowered, and wanted mental healthcare to be more inclusive and equitable. This sounds quite Foucauldian, in that expertise and authority create problematic power imbalances. Service users find themselves defined in ways they object to. Being forced to describe a life crisis in mental health terms can feel oppressive. Experiences that seem valuable (and which, in later chapters, we show to be life-changing) are reduced by healthcare professionals to meaningless misfirings of neurons. But service users also told me about aspects of their experiences that didn't fit the Foucauldian model so well. Rudolph Klein, in his *New Politics of the NHS* famously describes how the NHS used to be like a church but is now more like a garage (Klein 2013). What he means is that patients used to be respectful and trusting, but are now like customers seeking a service. In mental healthcare at least, things seem to have progressed further still. The way some patients described care made it sound less like a garage than a production line. They talked about how care was impersonal, almost automated, running according to its own needs and logics and having all sorts of unintended and unnoticed consequences. Clinicians engage with patients in standardised ways, demanding the disclosure of intimate details, sometimes humiliating personal secrets, whilst following standardised protocols. This creates an extraordinarily rigid, asymmetrical relationship that I call 'routinised intimacy.'

What all this suggested to me was that there are a number of reasons why it might make sense to write about mental healthcare in a less Foucauldian manner. Thinking in terms of knowledge and power might have some purchase on this social world, but it leaves a lot unsaid. The social world of mental healthcare seems messier, less ordered, more haphazard. Relaxing the grip of Foucault seems to open up research to new themes and questions. In particular, it enables research to be directed towards questions that are more directly related to patient health. For example, it allows us to ask: Why is it so difficult for psychiatrists to really listen to patients? How should healthcare be organised to maximise effectiveness? This book is intended as a response to the concerns that I first felt at the beginning of my doctoral research. We look to foreground how mental healthcare is organised and use the critical literature on bureaucracy to think through the problems of staff and patient discontent. Knowledge and power still pop up as important themes, but it is organisational dynamics that hold most explanatory power and occupy most of our attention. This book is expressly intended to be relevant, an attempt to think through how anthropological and ethnographic research might be conducted so that it becomes more useful to clinical work. We hope to create the conditions for more productive interdisciplinary dialogue and to consider how contributions from the social sciences and humanities might address the lack of progress in biomedical research in mental health.

*

As I finished my doctorate, I discovered the work of the philosopher Miranda Fricker. I was already convinced that anthropologists and others investigating mental healthcare needed to work in a less Foucauldian style, and I wondered if Fricker's ideas about epistemic injustice might provide new theoretical resources. The notion of epistemic injustice suggests a way investigating patient discontent regarding clinical relationships by framing it as a variety of unfairness. Epistemic injustice gives us a new way of unpacking why patients feel disempowered, why clinical relationships can feel unsatisfactory and what happens when psychiatrists don't listen. Thinking of mental healthcare in terms of epistemic injustice suggests that clinicians behave unjustly because many of their routine ways of thinking about mental distress and behaving around mentally distressed people are, ultimately, an indefensible and culpable intellectual error. Fricker's work has been very influential.

For Fricker, there are two forms of epistemic injustice, testimonial injustice and hermeneutical injustice. Testimonial injustice occurs when someone is wronged because prejudicial stereotypes have undermined their credibility as a truth teller in an unwarranted fashion. The 'central case' of testimonial injustice Fricker provides is from Harper Lee's novel *To Kill A Mockingbird*. The novel is set in 1935 in racially segregated Alabama. A young black man, Tom Robinson, is accused of beating and raping a white girl, Mayella Ewell. The accusation is false, and there is plenty of evidence to support Robinson's innocence. But the jury don't think so. They are unable to evaluate the evidence or even really listen to Robinson. They believe that 'all negroes lie,' that black men are immoral and untrustworthy, especially around women (Fricker 2007: 25). This, of course, is racism. Systemic prejudice leads them to truly believe Robinson is guilty. The moral and epistemic coincide to replicate and reinforce deep injustice. When the idea of testimonial injustice is applied to mental healthcare, the argument made is that clinicians disbelieve service users in an unwarranted and harmful way. Clinical knowledge is not the solution, but the problem, because diagnostic categories encourage stereotypical thinking. Clinicians are unable to listen to the patient because they are like the racist jurors who thought 'all negroes lie.'

The second form of epistemic injustice, which Fricker calls hermeneutical injustice, occurs when a significant area of experience is obscured by a lack suitable words and ideas. An absence of the right vocabulary means we are unable to articulate or even think about certain experiences. As the 'central case' of hermeneutical injustice, Fricker discusses Carmita Wood, as described in Susan Brownmiller's memoir *In Our Time*. According to Brownmiller, Wood had worked for eight years in the Cornell University nuclear physics department, first as a lab assistant and then administrator. Throughout this time male colleagues would behave in an unprompted sexualised way with her. They would 'jiggle' their 'crotch' or 'brush up against her breasts.' At a Christmas party she was cornered in a lift and had kisses forcefully planted on her lips. The resulting stress led to ill health, and ultimately, she had to quit her job. She wasn't entitled to unemployment benefit because she was regarded as having left voluntarily. But in conversation with other members of a consciousness raising group, she found immediate recognition of her experiences, a realisation that they were not rare, and a sense that her response was understandable and justified. They came up with a term they hoped could capture these experiences: 'sexual harassment.'

For Fricker, Wood experienced hermeneutical injustice until she attended the consciousness raising group and found a way of making sense of her experiences at Cornell. The category 'sexual harassment' filled a gap in her (and our) collective hermeneutical resources, linking events together so they are intelligible and articulable. The concept of sexual harassment brought crotch jiggling and unwanted kisses under a single description and framed it as misbehavior. Wood didn't simply leave her job because she was sick, she left because she was the victim of harassment. She deserved redress, and her colleagues should be held to account. If Wood had tried to convey her experiences without the category of sexual harassment (or anything like it) complaints would be likely to have been met with trivialising framings that further undermined her credibility, compounding the injustice. So for Fricker, Wood faced a specific kind of disability, because a

> cognitive disablement prevents her from understanding a significant patch of her own experience: that is, a patch of experience which it is strongly in her interests to understand, for without that understanding she is left deeply troubled, confused and isolated…and this, in turn, prevents her protesting it, let alone securing effective measures to stop it.
>
> *(Fricker 2007: 151)*

According to Fricker, to enjoy autonomy, and liberty, we need to be able to make sense of what is going on around us, and that requires the right conceptual resources. Ironically, the absence of a concept of epistemic injustice might itself be an instance of epistemic injustice that leaves people cognitively disabled. Fricker's understanding of the harms of epistemic injustice is illuminating. She argued that epistemic injustice undermines people, causing them to lose confidence, whilst an absence of the expressive tools impairs the development of self-understanding and personal agency.

So how helpful are these concepts in understanding patient discontent? Can they provide theoretical resources to a post-Foucauldian investigation of mental healthcare? Most current work on epistemic injustice in healthcare addresses testimonial injustice. It is easy to see why. There are striking resemblances between the experiences of Tom Robinson and accounts of patient frustrations. Service users often talk of a sense of being the victim of discrimination, that they are undermined by their diagnostic status. Patients describe a lack of real dialogue in conversations with clinicians as being the norm, even in an area of healthcare where relationships are deemed to be central. Carel and Kidd argue that epistemic injustice is 'structural' in mental healthcare because ideas like 'delusion' encourages clinicians to see everything a delusional person says as false, bizarre and irrational (Carel and Kidd 2014). Kyratsous and Sanati describe how 'popular heuristics' of borderline personality are shaped by identity prejudice that a 'Borderline' person is manipulative (Kyratsous & Sanati 2017). Once a person is deemed manipulative, a range of reasonable actions and legitimate requests can be dismissed.

There are clear moments of testimonial injustice in mental healthcare. I remember during my doctoral fieldwork a man on an acute ward insisted that he was a linguist and translator. I'll call him Jon. For more than a week, Jon spent a lot of his time explaining to nurses that he knew many languages. He was able to talk very precisely about his working life and how he had built a career out of his language skills. The nurses were having none of it. They evidently disbelieved him. In the nurses' room they even joked about it. But then, one day a new patient was admitted. He was Japanese and appeared to speak no English. An interpreter was requested, but no-one was immediately available and in the meantime communication was difficult. Jon offered his services. He proved able to speak fluent Japanese and act as a very competent interpreter. The staff were amazed, and, I thought, a little ashamed. Some made a point of apologising to Jon.

This seems like a very clear, real-life example of testimonial injustice. Jon's diagnosis of schizophrenia undermined his credibility as a truth teller in an unjustified way. Some people with a schizophrenia diagnosis sometimes make false claims. But not all claims made by people diagnosed with schizophrenia are false. And there really is no justification for not listening. Let's explore this with a small thought experiment. We might compare Jon with, say, a (notional) delegate attending a linguistics conference. The delegate might have a name badge describing them as a Professor of Linguistics Emily Smith. And if you look Emily up online, you'll see she is featured on the staff page of a notable university. In contrast, when we talk with Jon, we have none of this supporting evidence. And we might recall that Jon also claimed that the police installed bugging equipment in his flat, which we take to be false. Compared to Emily Smith, it might have been reasonable for the ward staff to be less sure Jon was a linguist; to entertain some proportionate doubt about his claims. Such a stance appears warranted. But there was no reason to be wholly convinced that Jon's claims were false and no reason to not listen to his description of his career.

I felt Jon's rickety self-presentation played into the diagnosis of schizophrenia and distracted staff from what he actually said. At best this is lazy from staff whose job is to be alert and aware. And it is worth knowing that many patients on the ward took his claims seriously. We might speculate that staff members were quick to disbelieve, and ultimately mock, Jon because he was claiming competencies, even excellences, that they themselves didn't have. Jon's expertise undermined the order of things on the ward. In any case, it is easy to see parallels between Jon and Tom Robinson. Being schizophrenic in a mental health setting appears to be in some ways like being a black person in a 1935 Alabama courtroom. Fricker's work is helpful because it shows how staff behaviour was not just mistaken (and not just infuriating). It was unjust, and that injustice appears to be connected in some way with professional expertise and working lives. Just as important, Fricker's work forms a framework for us to articulate how staff harmed Jon.

In the ethnography below, we find a considerable distance between representations of distress in medical notes and ethnographic accounts of distress. Psychiatrists sometimes talk of 'agreeing to disagree' with patients, but in reality, their interpretation is the only one that counts. A patient will struggle to convince staff that they are having an existential crisis, or an epiphany of any kind. Staff don't hear accounts of the value of episodes of what they think of as mental illness. Instead, they insist on their medical categories. It can be undignified. It can be infuriating. At very least, it is a variety of inattention that carries something of the flavour of epistemic injustice. Nonetheless, we don't particularly think in these terms. We don't challenge Fricker's theory, but we take a different direction of travel. The reasons are threefold. First, we don't seek to challenge medical framings of distress, which we see as perfectly attuned to their institutional environment. We merely argue for the viability of alternative framings and suggest that these framings may be preferable in certain circumstances. Second, we differentiate between being listened to and being believed. Careful, respectful, open-hearted attention does not require agreement or belief. We argue that it is an absence of real listening, not an absence of being believed that is behind patient discontent. Thirdly, we find that the reasons why patients are not treated as epistemic equals has more to do with institutional pressures than identity prejudices. Clinicians struggle to listen because it makes it more difficult for them to do their job.

The ethnographic material in the chapters below illustrates our case. In chapter six, we describe how Hugh Palmer told a psychiatrist that he is Barrack Obama. Staff didn't believe him. But they did appear to listen quite well, and to provide a safe place. Hugh didn't feel unheard, and, anyway, it sounds warranted not to take at face value a claim to be the ex-president. It was later in his trajectory as a patient that problems about being listened to became apparent. Similarly, in chapter five I describe my own patient life. My care team thought I had a mood disorder. They wanted to give me drugs to change how I felt. My own take was different. I saw myself as having a life project, a response to some difficult events, in which mood played a role, but was not more important than ethical commitments. I was never really able to articulate this to staff in such a way that they engaged with what I said, despite multiple attempts. Whatever I said, it was poured into the mental disorder mould. Staff always knew best. As a result I eventually learned to talk like them and suppressed my own account.

Experiences like this are common in mental healthcare. But, I don't think clinician prejudice or stereotyping played much of a role. Rather, clinicians dismissed my version because it was irrelevant, in a setting where there is little spare capacity to deal with irrelevancies. The institutional surround impinges on clinical attention and exposes mental health professionals to scrutiny. Staff members have responsibilities and need to consider how to represent their work in documentation in such a way that it is legible and defensible. Thinking in terms of mood disorders really helps this task. Mood disorders have recognised symptoms to which there are established treatments. A person with a mood disorder can be represented in notes in a clear, concise and familiar way, and these notes can form the basis of predictable, defensible decisions. So if I found clinicians to be bad listeners, it was because they understandably wanted to stay within the bounds of this limited, defined universe. Had they seriously engaged with my take on what was happening to me, it would have required personal judgements and decisions that are harder to evidence or otherwise support. This exposes them to reputational risk. So the barrier to epistemic equality wasn't prejudices about people with mood disorders, but pressures to keep on the clinical straight and narrow. It is clinical responsibilities that make genuine dialogue difficult.

The notion of epistemic injustice is helpful, but I don't think it will clear the log-jam in research. In the pages below, we borrow some elements from the epistemic injustice literature. We suggest that biomedical understandings of distress have expressive limitations. They deal with some things better than others. Like any single account of human distress, they have strengths and weaknesses and open up some areas of experience at the expense of others. If patients only think in biomedical terms, they are likely to find themselves to be like Carmita Wood at Cornell, cognitively disabled by the limitations of the available vocabulary, because biomedical terms are not designed to make sense of distress as an experience. If they are to overcome this obstacle, patients need different takes on distress, accounts that accommodate them as actors, that make sense of links between distress and relationships, that are truly personal. In the absence of this, mental health patients are undermined as epistemic subjects. If it imposes a single, exclusive account of distress on patients, mental healthcare makes its patients victims of hermeneutical injustice. Fricker's account of the harms of this is uncomfortably close to home. She describes how hermeneutical injustice leads to a loss of confidence and agency, leaving people confused, alienated, and passive. A loss of agency is sometimes seen as part of mental disorder. And sometimes it is associated with becoming 'institutionalised,' or developing 'learned helplessness.' But we might also want to consider if it is the understandable and predictable result of the way medial discourse thins out our collective expressive resources and leaves critically important experiences inexpressible.

*

In the first section of this chapter I described how I became dissatisfied with the way social scientists tended to understand mental healthcare, and I argued that the problems arise from the influence of Foucault. In the next section, I considered whether Miranda Fricker's ideas about epistemic injustice might be a substitute. I concluded that, despite their merits, I was still left looking for a way of making sense of the way that mental healthcare patients feel unheard and misunderstood and clinicians feel overextended and overscrutinised. How can it be that both feel disempowered? How can we arrive at a more consensual model of healthcare, so that we can start to work collaboratively to make collective progress on clinically important questions? The solution, I suggest, is to foreground the institutional setting. It is by attending to mental healthcare as an accountable bureaucracy and thinking through some of the consequences that we can reduce the distance between anthropological accounts of mental healthcare and lived experience. How mental healthcare is organised sets priorities, determines what is and isn't possible, shapes perceptions, directs what we call 'attentional triage.' It is the setting that explains why clinicians feel pressured and why patients find healthcare to be impersonal and uncaring. Less concrete, but not less important, the bureaucratic organisation of mental healthcare has a certain ethical character, and produces a certain atmosphere, which colours experiences of giving and receiving mental healthcare.

Directing ethnographic and analytic attention to the institutional context of mental healthcare enables us to make some specific arguments. The humanities and social sciences literature on accountable bureaucracy is vast and hugely informative. I do not contribute to debates in this literature, but draw out key ideas and insights as a way of directing our attention. I find that certain kinds of effect are common in accountable bureaucracies in general. These institutional effects result from the way that accountable bureaucracies define work in terms of responsibility, which must be dealt with through particular documentary procedures. My claim is that these effects can also be seen in mental healthcare. Organising mental healthcare as an accountable bureaucracy promotes some aspects of care at the expense of others. Put simply, making decisions, taking responsibility, producing papers trails and enabling institutional competition is promoted. But other aspects of care that have to do with relationships, listening and openness, are sidelined, even undermined.

When we think of bureaucracy, we think of rules and regulations, boxes to tick and forms to complete. Working in a bureaucratic setting is repetitive and constrained, because bureaucracies attempt to replace the vagaries of personal preference, judgement and taste with standardised, predictable, even machine-like, procedure. Bureaucracy has emerged as a rich area of enquiry in anthropology. In a key early publication, Marilyn Strathern remarked that: 'The concept of audit... has broken loose from its moorings in finance and accounting; its own expanded presence gives it the power of a descriptor seemingly applicable to all kinds of reckonings, evaluations and measurements' (Strathern 2000a: 2). Since then, the process of breaking loose has continued to such an extent that the expanded presence of bureaucratic accountability now seems to cover more or less all work environments. It is remarkable. We are now so familiar with bureaucratised working that we expect any workplace to have targets, metrics, policy statements and accountability procedures. The power of bureaucratic accountability can appear almost limitless. In the post war period, it was assumed that fairness and social equity required a more equal distribution of social, cultural and economic capital. Now we have such confidence in bureaucratic working that we expect institutions to be able generate fairness, even justice, however inequitable the social environment. There isn't a single type of bureaucratic organisation and the effects of organising this way are not simple. But if the literature on bureaucracy teaches us anything, it is that we shouldn't be surprised that the institutional setting of mental healthcare is not neutral or irrelevant, but, rather, has its own impact.

A bureaucracy that is accountable produces documentation of everything it does, to create paper trails that record (or purport to record) sequences of standardised actions. When applied to institutions, this holding to account has a particular meaning. An accountable bureaucracy can be audited. A lot of worker time is spent producing documentation that represents work and that may be scrutinised according to specified standards. Comparison with expected outputs is possible, and conformity to defined standards can be assessed. Documentation makes it possible for failings to be described with apparent precision. Actions that are not routine stand out, and require additional justification to protect individuals or their organisations from reputational or other damage. In addition, documentation allows institutions to compete in market mechanisms. Documentation can be used for tendering, enabling bodies that buy services to compare competing providers. In his seminal work on bureaucracy, written at the turn of the twentieth century, Max Weber thought of bureaucracies as efficient and called them an iron cage of rationality. But, as Cris Shore suggests, it may be more apt to think of them as a 'transparent glass prison of accountability' (Shore 2017: 111). In the ethnographic chapters below we see this transparent glass prison from a number of perspectives. The question we need to ask is whether this is the best way of organising mental healthcare.

Just as importantly, bureaucracies are a space where values play out. Max Weber tried to capture this ethical quality by describing office work as a 'vocation' with its own 'ethos.' Paul du Gay describes the ethical attributes of the good bureaucrat as being methodical, detached and disinterested (du Gay 2000: 120). It is the ethos of the office, internalised and reproduced by each official, as much as the rules themselves, that makes bureaucracies capable of being fair, efficient and transparent. When we talk of bureaucracies as being corrupt or having institutional problems, such as 'structural racism,' what we often mean is that staff do not follow this ethos of fairness and impartiality. The rules may be the right rules, but that is of little value if officials fail to implement them. The question for us is how appropriate these values are to the world of mental healthcare. Do we want mental health professionals who are detached and disinterested? Should we at least consider the impact of these values on practice?

Bureaucracies are better at some tasks than others. In particular, aspects of work that are difficult to quantify become problematic. Marilyn Strathern showed how importing bureaucratic technologies from accounting into higher education had subtle but far-reaching effects. Examination results and performance indicators reconfigured notions of student excellence and teaching philosophy (Strathern 1997, 2000c). These observations are pertinent to mental healthcare, where managerial instruments like KPIs (key performance indicators) appear to be superseding clinical impressions. This transition can have drastic consequences. In *Seeing like a State*, James Scott describes the sometimes disastrous aftermath of state bureaucracies organising forestry, farming and town planning (Scott 1998). In Scott's account, bureaucracies use replicable, impersonal schematic categories to make aspects of the world 'legible' and manipulable. This is how bureaucracies work. But according to Scott, it 'necessarily entails collapsing or ignoring distinctions that might otherwise be relevant' (ibid.: 81). Bureaucratic simplification has led to widespread harm, even, on occasion, catastrophes, including famine.

David Graeber expresses concerns with the epistemic limitations of bureaucracies in his characteristically trenchant prose:

> Bureaucratic knowledge is all about schematization. In practice, bureaucratic procedure invariably means ignoring all the subtleties of

real social existence and reducing everything to preconceived mechanical or statistical formulae. Whether it is a matter of forms, rules, statistics or questionnaires, it is always a matter of simplification.

(Graeber 2015: 75)

For Graeber, bureaucratic simplification is a kind of 'structural stupidity' that creates 'dead zones' in our imagination. He suggests that we can trace its spread by following changes in language, in the arrival of a distinctive idiom full of 'bright, empty terms like vision, quality, stakeholder, leadership, excellence, innovation, strategic goals, or best practice.' According to Graeber, the terms are vacuous. Unsuited to epistemic work, they are not the building blocks of serious thought. This is clearly concerning. Structural stupidity is not what distressed people are looking for when they engage with services. Distinctions should not be collapsed but be maintained. Isn't mental healthcare about unique individuals who deserve to be understood and treated with compassion? Don't we need the building blocks of care to be serious and substantial?

Some commentators add a further complexity to this picture. They note that the documentary failings of bureaucracies are not always failures of capacity. Rather, they are ways of getting things done. Michael Herzfeld presents bureaucrats almost as stage actors, concealing their true selves and presenting their work as a sequence of necessary, inevitable, impersonal decisions (Herzfeld 1992). Bureaucracy emerges as an ambiguous world of irony and secrets, in which documentation conceals as much as it reveals. In his ethnography of development organisations, David Mosse shows how the work of representation becomes detached from the events on the ground, such that the difference between success and failure becomes wholly a matter of rhetoric and documentation (Mosse 2005). Similarly, Nayanika Mathur's investigation of state bureaucracy in India finds that bureaucratic expertise consists precisely in learning how to represent work such that it appears that rules have been followed and the job done (Mathur 2016). This literature raises concerns about the role of insincerity and even dishonesty in the running of accountable bureaucracies. We might assume that mental healthcare should be located in a settings where trust and openness are valued. But if this literature is right, then organising as an accountable bureaucracy may make this more difficult, because a degree of deception is part of how accountable bureaucrats get the job done. We are left with questions. Are mental healthcare institutions places where staff need to be evasive, even dishonest, to get the job done? If so, would we know about it? And how does this impact on care?

Some writers note that the softer, more human aspects of bureaucratic working come from what Daniel Lipsky called 'discretion ' (Lipsky 1971, 2010). According to Lipsky, many bureaucrats have the freedom to decide which rules to enforce and which to ignore, how to prioritise cases and what can be put on the back burner. The exercise of this discretion may be seen in a positive light. It enables bureaucrats to adapt their work to meet the needs of individual cases. However, it is also the means by which bureaucracies might consistently favour some populations (such as articulate and assertive middle-class people) and disadvantage others (such as marginalised people). Very often, discretion allows bureaucrats to deal with an excessive burden of work, inadequate resources and limited time, and may be the locus of considerable informal expertise. In an influential early monograph on organisations Mintzberg suggested that some kinds of bureaucracy have more space for discretion than others. 'Machine bureaucracies' restrict discretion because the work is highly standardised (Mintzberg 1979). But in a 'professional bureaucracy', where the work is more complex, workers need a greater degree of autonomy. In this case standardisation is achieved more by training and professionalism. Mintzberg and McHugh later coined the term 'adhocracy' to refer to bureaucracies that are designed to be flexible and responsive by giving considerable autonomy to low level operatives (Mintzberg & McHugh 1985). This can be seen as a way of making the bureaucracy more humane.

Do mental health professionals have enough scope for discretion? Do they work in a professional bureaucracy, that gives them the liberty to see patients in their uniqueness? Harrison argues that this used to be the case across medicine: 'the ostensible indeterminacy and uncertainty of medicine, along with the excess of demand over supply in the context of a non-marketed system, have historically prevented the bureaucratization of medicine, and have established physicians as street-level bureaucrats' (Harrison 2015: 65). However, for Harrison, over the last two decades, the adoption of Evidence-Based Medicine and the introduction of market mechanisms to NHS healthcare have, together, enabled increased bureaucratisation and restricted the space for discretion. This is because Evidence-Based Medicine and marketisation: 'share an underlying logic that treats medicine and healthcare generally as capable of explicit specification, rather than esoteric, indeterminate or dependent on tacit knowledge' (ibid.: 73–74). Harrison suggests that this transition, away from professional instinct and personal judgement, and towards propositional knowledge and instrumental rationality is characteristic of contemporary healthcare. The reader might be left wondering how suited these organisational forms are to mental healthcare. Why do we value paper trails so highly? Why do uneven or non-standardised treatment seem so terrible? Has the cost of accountable working ever been weighed against the benefits?

*

We don't suggest a single way of understanding mental healthcare organisations, but, rather, deploy a range of ideas – habitus, moral injury, institutional affordance, bullshit – to address aspects of the phenomenon. We note that many clinical tasks sound like bureaucratic tasks: recording data, documenting risk, presenting care as a sequence of defensible decisions. In some cases, we find clinical knowledge is a way of justifying decisions made for purely institutional reasons. On other occasions, we find clinical reasoning and institutional logics to be so entwined as to be inseparable. We suggest that clinician intuitions about service users might well change if the clinical setting were changed. Indeed, the plausibility of some clinical concepts, particularly the more contentious ones such as 'personality disorder' are likely to be challenged by a change of ways of organising. In some respects, the institutional setting of mental healthcare is mental healthcare.

In the ethnography below we provide plenty of examples of how crude and reductive clinical thinking can be. David Graeber's dead zones of the imagination cut through every clinical encounter, every instance of notetaking and clinical reasoning. This is how audit cultures work. The transparent glass prison that Cris Shore described is familiar to mental health professionals. We might want to say that mental healthcare as a whole takes place in a transparent glass prison. But the literature on bureaucracy suggests something further: that this is inevitable. An accountable bureaucracy is not a place for subtlety and nuance. Its technologies come from finance and banking. In the ethnography below there are instances of discretion. Staff members find ways to be kind. But they are described as transgressive, something that not only doesn't contribute to professional progress, but exposes the staff member to censure. More recent commentators on bureaucracy query how meaningful accountability procedures really are. In some cases at least, they appear to be insubstantial, misleading, acts of documentary misdirection. Bureaucratic working harms clinical relationships. It makes healthcare less caring, less compassionate and harder to personalise.

In a sense, bureaucratisation demystifies the world by eliminating expertise that is not accessible to common sense. Accountability means we do not need to wholly trust experts, as we can use managerial techniques to monitor and evaluate their work. Just so long as we accept the descriptors that have been taken from finance and accounting and extended to almost all forms of work, that is. This was Graeber's point. Bureaucracy can reassure just so long as we can invest in its 'bright, empty terms like vision, quality, stakeholder, leadership, excellence, innovation, strategic goals, or best practice.' If we can't, if we worry that this means 'ignoring all the subtleties of real social existence,' then we might have to live with our fears, accept that we can't really know how well mental healthcare works.

Some of the conceptual apparatus that mental health professionals use can seem outlandish. How can we talk of mental disorder if we don't know what mental order is? Why is it a good thing to regulate moods? This outlandishness is recognised by staff members, who sometimes struggle to contain their scepticism. But all of these concepts make sense in the context which formed them and in which they function. They are pieces of a larger whole, in which mental healthcare is constructed as an accountable service, in which staff act in ways that can be recorded and shown to be routine and defensible. If we are to have services provided by experts, and we want to hold those experts accountable according to the kinds of bureaucratic instruments currently in use, mental healthcare has to coalesce around the things that accountable bureaucracies can handle. In practice, this means mental healthcare is primarily about dealing with responsibility. This emerges strongly in chapter seven below. The job of the clinician is to handle responsibility for patients through appropriate decisions and appropriate documentation. In the pages below, we see multiple ways in which these institutional arrangements shape care. Our claim is not that medical accounts are faulty, or inferior. But we see that have limitations and we might speculate what kinds of concepts and ideas might be generated by a different organisational context, a context that were more tolerant of uncertainty and messiness and which was more focused on personalisation than paperwork.

Mental healthcare doesn't have to be like this. It doesn't even have to take the form of an accountable bureaucracy providing services. It doesn't have to consist of interventions being delivered by experts. Mental healthcare could be reciprocal, or dialogic. It might be focused on empathy and insight, or on community building, or, even, remaking the self through psychotropic ordeals. Care for people in distress takes all these different forms today, but these activities are pushed to the fringes, so much so that we don't always think of them as real mental healthcare. The problem isn't one of efficacy. The alternative forms of mental healthcare may be equally effective, conceivably they might be more effective. We just don't know. And they might have fewer of the relational problems that attract so much criticism. The problem is that none of them is fully compatible with how healthcare is currently organised. To be incorporated into mainstream mental healthcare would demand a different way of organising and a different regulatory universe. This is because neither dialogue nor empathy nor community are easy to record or measure or standardise, and make it much more difficult for professionals to be held to account.

We recognise that these arguments are sensitive, particularly to service providers. To do their job, mental health professionals need to represent their observations and reasoning as objective and unpredetermined. Professional authority, and what Kathleen Montgomery calls 'the performance of certainty' rests on precisely not representing reason as a contextual rationalisation (Montgomery 2006: 199–201). Clinicians have good reason to find our argument challenging, and perhaps provocative. However, we suggest that it is a price worth paying, because the resulting ethnography and analysis captures something important about mental healthcare institutions. Currently institutional effects are largely uninvestigated. If we want to conduct research that is organised around improving mental health, it is essential to address these issues.

The way mental healthcare is organised should be a central focus of research. If the way accountable bureaucracies work makes it harder for clinicians to really listen to patients, if organisational features impair dialogue and sets up asymmetries between professional and patient that can create distrust and resentment, we might wonder how this plays out in terms of patient health. It is quite common to think of relationships as central to mental healthcare. Indeed, research on the therapeutic relationship suggests that better relationships predict better outcomes and may even be a major part of the cause of better outcomes (McCabe, Preibe etc). If we want mental healthcare to be more caring, or more compassionate, we need it to be organised differently. We might need to ask the public to accept higher levels of uncertainty about the effects of mental healthcare, and we might want to disaggregate mental health, so that care and responsibility, listening and deciding, supporting and treating, might not occur in the same place, or be enacted by the same individuals. These are arguments I return to in the final chapter of the book. In the next chapter I discuss methods.

2

WHAT DOES IT MEAN TO KNOW ABOUT MENTAL HEALTHCARE?

This book can be seen as a methodological experiment that evolved to address the challenges of investigating mental healthcare bureaucracies. Our methods are notably unbureaucratic in style: flexible, open, improvised, personalised, spontaneous. Some of the chapters are by me alone, and others are co-authored. We juxtapose our writing with benefits documentation from the DWP and medical notes obtained via Freedom of Information Requests. And we attempt to use theory in a distinctive way. Each of the five empirical chapters reflect a unique way of working. The first uses ethnography and analysis from my doctoral research. Following that is a chapter coproduced with a patient, Catriona Watson. Next comes a chapter of autoethnography, in which I explore my own experiences as a service user. After that comes a second chapter coproduced with a patient, this time with Hugh Palmer. Finally comes a chapter coproduced with Rowan Jones, a clinician who is also a service user, who writes under a pseudonym. In the previous chapter I tried to set out the larger arguments of the book and discuss some of the background literature that later chapters reply upon. This chapter explores our methodology. How did we arrive at this way of working? Why does this seem to be an appropriate way of addressing our research questions? And what have we learned about collaborative ethnographic working along the way?

Research can seem like a comfortingly straightforward process. We need new knowledge because we want to improve mental healthcare. As far as I can tell, nobody wants mental healthcare to stay as it is. Everybody wants it to change. Amid the many disputes about the meaning of distress, the status of diagnosis, and the effectiveness of particular treatments (amongst other things) everyone agrees there are problems with current care provision and everyone is calling for improvements. It can seem like common sense. There is also something close to a consensus that research is a part of the required

DOI: 10.4324/9781003154235-2

process of improvement. It may also be the case that more resources are needed, increased levels of staffing or more training, but, at least as important as any of that, new knowledge is required. A typical view might be that some of the problems of mental healthcare arise out of knowledge deficits and that the production of new knowledge is necessary, if not sufficient, to diminish these deficits and thus make substantial improvements to mental healthcare.

Many examples could be provided, but to give just one, the website of the Wellcome Trust, a charitable body that uses its £37.8 billion portfolio to fund health research says:

> Depression, anxiety and psychosis are holding back millions of people every day. We still know far too little about how and why these conditions develop, and how they can best be resolved.
>
> But it doesn't have to be like this.
>
> We want to create transformative change by finding better ways to intervene early so that people experiencing these mental health challenges can thrive.
>
> To do this, we fund a diverse range of researchers, and collaborate with others, including policy makers.
>
> *https://wellcome.org/what-we-do/mental-health*

The Wellcome Trust suggest that the problem is that we know far too little, but that if we fund more researchers, we can produce more knowledge that might improve, perhaps even transform, mental healthcare, making it more effective, perhaps safer, or more efficient. So at least some of the problems of mental healthcare are understood to be problems of knowledge, of knowing far too little about distress and what to do about it.

This book is based on similar commitments. We take it that research is essential if mental healthcare is to improve. We hope that this book contributes to the process. However, we retain some caution, even scepticism, about the current state of mental health research. This is for two reasons. First, not all research is emancipatory, or even helpful, for everyone. Even if it is part of the solution, research is also part of the problem. Some of the difficulties are obvious. Why does so much mental healthcare research take the form of clinical trials of pharmaceuticals? The research agenda can feel skewed towards comparing products, blurring the line between academic research and marketing, and leaving other research questions unanswered. We might begin to wonder who this research is really for. There are also questions about who conducts research. Why is it that researchers without lived experience get to conceptualise distress, and what are the consequences? In most fields of medicine, we are accustomed to hearing expert descriptions of ill health that are far more subtle and complex than anything a lay person might come up with. But the reverse is often the case in mental healthcare, where simplistic clinical accounts can stand in stark contrast to nuanced and sometimes beautiful patient narratives. How would research change if patient experience were made central to research activity?

Second, at a more conceptual level, it isn't clear that this book is primarily an exercise in the production of new knowledge. When I chatted with research clinicians and attended their lectures and seminars, I found they talk as if they see research as a process of uncovering independently existing facts intended to fill absences in our collective knowledge. Gaps in research were opportunities for future empirical work, and shortcomings in published research were seen as failures of methodological rigour, cases of 'bad science' that disrupt otherwise blameless knowledge production. In contrast, this book is an attempt to tell people something that they already know. We don't expect our insights to be completely new or a complete shock. It would be a worry if they were, at least, if they were new to all readers. We anticipate, rather, that our descriptions and analysis are familiar.

This might sound odd. The reasons lie in how mental healthcare institutions work. To illustrate, let me provide an ethnographic example. I was required to take some training sessions offered by an NHS Trust as a condition of ethics clearance for my doctoral fieldwork. Nothing is quite so revealing of an institution as its trainings. The trainings I undertook were mandatory for everyone with a contract with the trust, whether or not that contract was honorary, like mine, or part of paid employment. Trainings covered various topics, including self-defence and operating the electronic medical records system, but it was noticeable how much time was allocated to confidentiality and data security. This was deemed important for me because it was expected that patients would divulge intimate and highly personal information about themselves. I could see that some sort of preparation was needed. I lived in the same area as many of my interlocutors and our paths were bound to cross, both during the fieldwork and afterwards. But that didn't seem to be the end of the story. I had already noticed some odd priorities regarding data security in the NHS. Clinicians seemed more exercised by lapses in data security than almost anything else. It seemed to outweigh even treatment efficacy. The prominence of data issues made me think of Weber's remark that 'the concept of the "official secret" is the specific invention of bureaucracy, and nothing is so fanatically defended by the bureaucracy as this attitude' (Weber 2009: 233). Although it perhaps fell short of fanaticism, confidentiality certainly occupied a lot of time.

One thing I learned in training is that demonstrating good practice regarding confidentiality is not the same as actually maintaining confidentiality. I didn't want to break confidence with my interlocutors. That was something I took very seriously. But I learned that I was obliged to be able to document good practice about confidentiality to protect myself, and this only partially overlapped with actually maintaining confidentiality. It was like a Venn diagram. I knew how to go through the motions. But I also knew that it would be possible to protect informant confidentiality without conforming to best practice, and that it would be possible to conform to best practice without protecting informant confidentiality. So the training inducted me into a world of meta-secrets, secrets about secrets. But that itself was a secret, to be shared only with great caution. Anthropologists are said to be experts in secrets. There is a recognition within the field of anthropology that the sympathetic outsider ethnographer often finds himself or herself drawn into what Paul Dresch calls a 'trade in secrets' (Dresch 2000: 109). Secrets like this form the heart of much anthropological analysis, and enable an analysis that cuts through assumption and presupposition. So I felt fortunate to have training in anthropology. But I could see that it made the production of knowledge a rather complex business.

Once my ethnographic research began, I found that although patients did tell me very sensitive things, by far the majority of secrets I heard were told by clinicians. I was amazed at how many psychiatrists, psychologists, nurses, social workers, occupational therapists and health care assistants had secrets they wanted to tell. Almost all were guilty secrets. I heard doubts about the efficacy of clinical work, dissatisfaction at feeling coerced into styles of working that result in low quality care. Several psychiatrists told me they didn't believe in clinical trials and didn't bother to read the latest research. One said that evidence-based medicine was a con. Another said that it is was damaging. Community psychiatric nurses talked about how ineffective mental healthcare can be and how they try to dissuade people from becoming patients. Two nurses told me in confidence about how they each had a child who they thought could be diagnosed and treated for a mental disorder, but that they were adamant that this would never happen. One said her son 'would become a patient over my dead body.' I was told by many clinicians in various roles that many of the patients currently being treated for mental disorders aren't really mentally ill. Some psychiatrists told patients things that they explicitly rejected when talking to me. None of these views could be expressed openly. It sometimes seemed to be a relief to tell me.

It wasn't immediately clear to me why this was happening. One way of beginning to think it through is found in the work of anthropologist Michael Herzfeld. For Herzfeld, bureaucracy is a form of 'secular theodicy' (Herzfeld 1992). Religious theodicy refers to attempts to explain how evil exists in a world created by an omnipotent and benevolent deity. For Herzfeld, secular theodicy is less lofty, a 'social means of coping with disappointment' (ibid.: 7). The role of a bureaucracy is to reassure, to help the public deal with anxieties generated by our painful lives. They reassure the public that mental illness is being treated in an appropriate way, that healthcare is effective and efficient and safe. Managerialism is an antidote to our neuroticism, our inability to trust. Thinking in terms of secular theodicy may seem shocking. Surely the real work of mental healthcare institutions is to care for the mentally ill? But there is plenty of ethnographic support for the claim below, especially in chapters three and seven. Being a clinician means producing documentation that enables the performance of secular theodicy. In a sense, the job is to manage appearances. Staff members become documentary experts, devotees of representational pragmatism. The ultimate audience for this performance is the general public. It is us.

Over the course of my research I began to see that dissembling is a characteristic part of the clinical repertoire. For example, I once chatted with a social worker who told me he didn't believe in schizophrenia but, whilst he described to me his doubts about schizophrenia, he was also filling in a form saying a patient on his caseload had schizophrenia. He explained that this was the only way of securing an inpatient bed. It was a necessary compromise. The requirements of paperwork forced him into strategic insincerity. Sometimes medical notes look evasive, or tendentious, or limited. Sometimes they look like spin. Occasionally, when you know the back story, they are more like outright acts of concealment. Risk management is conducted in vague, opaque and self-serving terms that protect staff. Notes mention 'significant suicide risk' and then stress that 'safety planning was discussed' or that the patient is 'aware of out of hours support.' This language has huge representational strengths in virtue of its vagueness and unclarity. It is possible to represent risk as successfully addressed, as long as you don't look too closely or ask too many questions. Richer or more comprehensive characterisations of suicide risk would undermine these efforts. The dead zones and recurring faults embedded in mental healthcare documentary practice are part of the means by which public anxieties are contained. In a sense, the job is to manage appearances. Staff members become documentary experts, devotees of representational pragmatism. Recognising complexity undermines theodicy, whilst structural stupidity gets the job done.

For these reasons, mental health institutions are places where it is very difficult to establish what people really think. What professionals said depended on context. In a confessional moment with a concerned but marginal anthropology student like myself, many members of staff were critical, sceptical dissenters. When making decisions about patients, writing notes or discussing patients in team meetings they were far more conventional. And who knows what they thought on the drive in to work. I wondered if the radical social worker's scepticism towards schizophrenia was also conditioned by circumstances in some way. Perhaps it created links with colleagues or endeared him to people diagnosed with schizophrenia. All that was speculation, but it was instructive to begin to think about how opinions and views are contextual. I started to see that, even if 'clinical judgement' is a key way of authorising care, it wasn't really clear if thinking of judgements in terms of beliefs was the right approach.

Because this book concerns the social life of a bureaucracy, with all the complex layers of secrecy, dissembling, strategic insincerity, and meta-secrecy, that this entails, it doesn't feel like the production of new knowledge, at least not in the conventional sense discussed above. Rather, we are trying to find ways to articulate things that are already known, but are to some degree made secret by the institutional context. A lot of what we have to say should be familiar to service providers or service users (and, sometimes, both). There is a sense in which everybody knows what we have to say, even before we've said it. There are two senses in which is the case. First, we wish to honour multiple understandings of mental distress. Everybody featured in this book, not just the authors of the text, but all the clinicians, patients and onlookers know something about mental health and mental healthcare. We suggest that, rather than arguing for a single account, it is preferable to embrace polyphony. But we also want to honestly engage with the dissembling at the heart of bureaucratised mental healthcare. Everybody involved in mental healthcare knows that it is not as it appears in official documentation. Everybody knows that care is flawed in multiple ways. Everybody knows mental healthcare is reductive and simplistic and impersonal and the documentary reassurances of efficacy and safety are flimsier than we might wish. We can't let go of this.

When we gave talks based on sections of this book to audiences of patients or mental health professionals, we found high levels of recognition, at least when the presentation went well. People were familiar with how we described mental healthcare, and the arguments we make. It wasn't new to them. So we see this book not so much as an attempt to generate new knowledge as a project to attend to things that people already know. Our intellectual contribution (if we are making a contribution) is to use anthropological and other literatures to find conceptual resources to describe this accurately, and frame it, so that it might be counted as evidence, and be brought into interdisciplinary research. If the following chapters appear to be both familiar and unfamiliar, obvious and unexpected, we might be making progress.

*

Something that was brought home repeatedly whilst interacting with clinical researchers is that ethnography is an unrespectable research method. One reason for this is that ethnographic methods are improvised and unstandardised. We relish the haphazard. Ethnographers like to tell stories from the field in which an unwanted encounter is like an epiphany, transforming research priorities, leaving carefully designed plans hatched in distant libraires and seminar rooms to be discarded in favour of new, improvised research initiatives hastily put together leading to more productive lines of enquiry. As Hazan and Hertzog put it, 'serendipity is an engine, pulling anthropology forwards' (Hazan & Hertzog 2012: 9). Negotiating the unanticipated and the indeterminate is a central feature of ethnographic expertise (Rivoal & Salazar 2013: 3). The unexpected is an opportunity, whilst sticking to plans and protocols smacks of fearfulness, and is said to be likely to lead to unimaginative, uninspiring work of diminished value. It is a point of principle, perhaps a point of pride, that the way one ethnographer describes a given social world will not be same as another, equally competent ethnographer. For this reason, ethnographers do not try to delink findings from method. After all, they reason, what you see depends on how you look. All this can seem unsettling to biomedical and psychological sciences with more fixed methods, where reproducibility is seen as an essential feature of knowledge. It can make ethnography look like anecdote. Unrespectability can form a barrier to interdisciplinarity.

Our argument is not that all research should be ethnographic, or that all research that uses measures and scales should be rejected. But we want to argue for the value of ethnography and the potential role it has in interdisciplinary efforts to improve mental healthcare. And we note that the production of knowledge inevitably entwines methods and results. This is as true of clinical trials as much as anthropological investigations. The findings of ethnographic work build on happenstantial events and on relationships. That is how ethnographers proceed. But the scales and measures used in more mainstream research do not fall from the sky: they have a particular history which also includes happenstantial events and relationships. Scales and measures may look impersonal and acultural, but they necessarily introduce assumptions into findings. For example, the outcome measures used in clinical trials of psychiatric pharmaceuticals currently blur together phenomena such as: a loss of delight in former pleasures, a sense of dread regarding the future, impaired sleep, and shame, transforming them all into examples of low mood, a measurable, subjective feeling in the individual that may be accurately quantified by a questionnaire. Other scales are possible. There are other ways of constructing depression. For example, in chapter three I explore how experiences of dread and shame might be tied to structural, relational or cultural factors rather than located in the individual. Or, as I discuss in chapter five, the same feelings of shame and dread might be read not as emotions felt in the moment, but as part of a moral project, developed by an individual in response to life events. No single approach is likely to be exhaustive or exclusive or have the final word. But once these assumptions are made, they are difficult to extract from research findings. For this reason, we are cautious about thinking of research as a single, unified entity. We need to examine what research is being conducted, and attend to which questions are being asked and how they are addressed methodologically, rather than focussing solely on whether the research is well designed or if the findings are accurate or true.

We hope to illustrate how the social worlds of mental healthcare may be understood in multiple, or polyphonic ways. We try to be faithful to lived experience, rather than build a theory or master narrative that might unite them. We are critical of the dominance of any single, unified theory to deal with the social world mental healthcare, we do not ourselves want to commit to a single theoretical vision. At various points in the pages below we draw on anthropological theory, ideas from philosophy, sociology, literary theory, social psychology and theology. Not all these ideas sit comfortably together. This might sound like an intellectual vulnerability or defect. However, David Zeitlyn suggests it might be seen as a strength:

> The approach I am advocating evokes the early cubism of Braque or Picasso, rather than the single viewpoint of photography or perspective-based painting…the facets of a cubist painting show different aspects of the object portrayed, which may not be simultaneously visible in reality (such as the forehead and the back of the head) but which conventionally we infer: when we are shown a face, we suppose a skull behind it. By combining elements from mutually exclusive perspectives, cubist painters made us aware of our unceasing and unconscious attempts to fill in the invisible armatures that hold together the little we see at any one moment.
>
> *(Zeitlyn 2022: 4)*

We aspire to be, in Zeitlyn's terms, theoretical cubists and not photographers or perspective-based painters. We regard theoretical ideas to be in service of ethnography, to bring out features of lived experience or show links between individual lives and structures.

Thinking in these terms cuts both ways. If we want to adopt a more pluralistic understanding of distress, this demands epistemic humility of the ethnography in this book as much as the accounts found in the medical notes we use. This text is intended to be a withdrawal from representational competitiveness. Sometimes ethnographers or others from outside biomedicine favourably compare their own rich, personalised accounts of service users with the sketchy, schematic action-oriented accounts made by clinicians. It isn't a fair fight. Ethnographers have few responsibilities towards patients, and have both time and more sophisticated theoretical resources. But more than that, representational competitiveness misses the point. The work of an ethnographer is not the same as the work of a clinician. Each representation is produced for particular purposes. These are issues we return to in the next chapter, which discusses methods and methodology.

The central purposes of our collaborative ethnographic approach is to produce knowledge that helps us think about the impact of the institutions that house healthcare interventions. This impact has been neglected in research, in part because it is invisible to clinical trials of interventions. We believe that the impact of the institutional setting operates on people in multiple ways, in how they experience themselves, in their ethical, aesthetic and pragmatic lives. These are by no means abstract issues. We think that the institutional setting impacts on quality of care, effectiveness, efficiency and safety. Our intention here is not to measure these effects but to show that they are real and indicate how they might be theorised. This does not reflect a hostility to measurement, but a recognition of how little we understand. Adequate theory is the pathway to measurement, but we are not far down that path.

*

The odd thing about describing a piece of research as collaborative is that it is difficult to conceive of research that isn't collaborative. Ethnographic working, in particular, is based on relationships. There isn't a single way of conducting ethnographic research, and there can be a value placed on individual ethnographers finding their own personal style. But whilst 'in the field' or 'conducting fieldwork' (as practitioners sometimes put it), all ethnographers necessarily conduct their research relationally. Ethnographic research is interpersonal. It relies on, or, sometimes, consist of, communication, empathy and trust. In their widely read textbook *Ethnography: Principles in Practice*, Hammersley and Atkinson say 'ethnography usually involves the researcher participating, overtly or covertly, in people's daily lives for an extended period of time, watching what happens, listening to what is said, and/or asking questions through informal and formal interviews' (Hammersley & Atkinson 2019: 3). Alpa Shah describes ethnographic work as 'living with and being a part of other people's lives as fully as possible' (Shah 2017: 47). It is an unambiguously collaborative task.

There are further collaborative ties involved in ethnographic working that might be less apparent. Ethnographers do not live with others naively. Ethnography is a research method, not merely everyday curiosity (even if the two may not always be separable). Ethnographers forge connections with the people they meet (people in ethnographic research are sometimes called 'informants,' or 'interlocutors,' less often 'research participants') in the light of beliefs and expectations about how ethnographers should behave. These beliefs and expectations reflect the work of earlier ethnographers (who, in a sense, become informants too) and the ethnographic literature. In other words, ethnographers learn how to become part of other people's lives (if, indeed, they do learn) by relating to an emerging, fluid tradition of skills, approaches and techniques developed by generations of ethnographers. In addition, research activity is always developed in relation to themes or questions or lines of enquiry, themselves formulated in relation to debates and currents in the literature. Which research questions to ask, and how they should be asked are both developed relationally. So even when an ethnographer is trying to be a part of other people's lives, and letting those lives shape their sensibilities and lifeworld, they are also communing with ethnographers and other researchers that lie offstage.

It doesn't stop there. Ethnographers typically complete their 'fieldwork' and then come home, or to the library or office, to analyse their research materials (typically written notes, audio recordings, visual representations and sometimes material objects or artefacts, that is collectively sometimes called 'data'). But their work continues to be collaborative, in several senses. To view the worlds they've lived in and been part of, and to produce relevant and interesting analyses, ethnographers draw on earlier work. Often this involves making explicit comparisons with other ethnographies or applying theory to try to draw out or illuminate the data they have. This means collaborating, albeit in an asymmetrical way, with other ethnographers. And as they start to write their own ethnography, the process continues. As well as drawing on published sources, they are likely to test out ideas, both formally in seminars, supervisions and academic events, and informally.

If the idea of an isolated, asocial researcher is an oxymoron, it shouldn't come as a surprise to ethnographers. At the heart of ethnographic working is a commitment to understanding the contextual, communal, interpersonal nature of human lives. A huge part of the potential of ethnographic working in mental healthcare is to push back against the methodological individualism of dominant research disciplines such as psychology and psychiatry. These disciplines have distinct strengths, but they are not really equipped to analyse social, systemic or cultural effects (and are not always able to acknowledge or even detect the epistemic gaps where the effects may be located). The role of ethnography is not to supersede these disciplines or negate their findings, but to complement them with evidence and theory that considers causal effects between persons, or systems or structures or cultures. So ethnographers should be amongst the first researchers to notice and analyse the collaborative nature of research, and to feel comfortable with the suggestion that all ethnographic working is collaborative.

Even if all ethnographic working is collaborative, one reason to call this book collaborative is to call attention to our particular relational background. To do so might be seen as an exercise in transparency. One way to tell the story of this book is of chance events occurring in a network of collaborative relationships. In July 2019 I was invited to give a talk at Auto (ethno)graphy, a symposium at the Royal College of Art convened by Susan Young. At the time Susan was PhD student at the RCA who I had got to know via the service user led research project Re:Create Psychiatry. My talk for the symposium, 'Why Don't You Listen To My Story? What Do You Know About My Heart? Ethnography, Autoethnography and the Fruitless Desire to Get Epistemic Satisfaction' drew on a fragment of ethnography from my PhD research and used Miranda Fricker's work on epistemic injustice to think about power relations in mental healthcare settings. Some of the themes of the talk are picked up in this book, but the ethnography is not used. I had earlier been introduced to Fricker's work by a philosopher, who had included me in an unsuccessful funding bid. Whilst working on the bid I had become interested in Fricker's ideas, and I organised a panel on epistemic injustice in mental healthcare at an anthropology conference, and then took the panel to an event at a service user organisation. Feedback from both was instructive and stimulating and contributed to my talk at the symposium. After my talk I spoke to a commissioning editor at Routledge, who asked if I had a book contract. I didn't, but I wanted one and I had some ideas about the book I'd like to write. I wanted it to be a development of my PhD thesis, but with a new, collaborative methodology. The reason for the change was that I had become uncomfortable with conventional ethnographic working, because it seemed to replicate, albeit in reduced form, some of the epistemic problems of biomedical research that I wanted to address.

Ethnographic working may be sensitive, flexible and personalised, but asymmetries and power imbalances persist. However attentive and open-hearted, the ethnographer is a participant observer amongst participants. An ethnographer may join in seamlessly with people's daily lives, but they do so for reasons that are external, possibly alien and may even be incomprehensible to those people. These differences, which may be accepted, or go unnoticed or unremarked upon during fieldwork deepen when the ethnographer leaves the field. Once the ethnographer starts to represent their work in academically credible ways, (which mainly means writing ethnography, but can also include curating visual representations, or holding events), the rich relationships that characterise immersive, holistic ethnographic research start to change. What used to be something direct and unmediated, spontaneous and reciprocal shifts into a very different kind of relationship, asymmetrical, considered, instrumental. People who were once friends, supporters, confidantes and allies become objects of analysis, redesignated as informants or interlocutors, illuminated by theory they do not know and related to debates in a literature they have not read. Shared experiences that might have been meaningful, consequential or precious, become data. Subjects become objects. 'I's become 'its'.

Martin Buber explored the way that genuine dialogue can be profoundly illuminating and mutually transformative. He calls these I-thou relationships. But he warns that the shift from this to a subject-object relationship entails huge losses:

> Now with the magnifying glass of peering observation he bends over particulars and objectifies them, or with the field-glass of remote inspection he objectifies them and arranges them as scenery, he isolates them in observation without any feeling of their exclusiveness, or he knits them in observation without any feeling of universality.
>
> *(Buber 2019 [1923]: 21)*

For an anthropologist working in mental health and striving to produce research that might capture personal patient experience, this makes for difficult reading. What Buber calls peering observation and remote inspection seem critical parts of the ethnographic methodological armoury. However much I might believe myself to be a corrective to psychiatry and psychology researchers, and however committed I am to seeing people in their uniqueness, if I conduct business-as-usual ethnographic research, I am still the one making the decisions about how to represent people, using them to make my arguments or tell my story. There is a further tension here. Even if it is little more than epistemic custom, good analysis is often seen as relying on, and arising out of, the coolness of distance. Objectification might be seen as a critical part of the process, which might also rely on retaining some sense of people as subjects. There is something uncomfortable about this. Is ethnographic working necessarily deceptive because the openness and candour of the research process is reversed once the ethnographer starts to write? Does the authority of ethnographic knowledge rest on covert objectification? What would ethnographic research look like if the process of objectification were curtailed or interrupted?

*

Coproduced ethnography, also known as co-created ethnography, has emerged as a way of addressing problems like these by making research more open, equable and democratic. Coproduction is not a precisely defined method, but is seen as including the people being studied in research design and planning, in the construction of analytic concepts, in the activities associated with data gathering and in representing the results of research (Boyer & Marcus 2020: 1). For an ethnographer, coproduction appears to be an opportunity to extend the open, reciprocal, responsive research style into the process of writing (Marcus 1997, 2001; Fabian 2014; Gay Y Blasco & Hernández 2020). It often introduces a further layer of openness or indeterminacy into the already flexible anthropological research process. Boyer and Marcus write about 'the revelry of collaborative anthropology' stressing the creative and even transgressive potential of this way of working (Boyer & Marcus 2020: 18).

The supposed benefits are both ethical and epistemic. In a number of publications, Eric Lassiter has demonstrated the political power of such public, collaborative ethnographic working (Lassiter et al 2004; Lassiter 2005). There is currently a large and apparently almost unanimous demand, even a 'participatory zeitgeist,' for coproduction in medical research (Palmer et al 2019). Some say that all medical research should contain some patient input. However, there are others who query the value and feasibility of this kind of working. For example, Oliver et al point to a 'dark side' of costs and risks and a lack of evidence to confirm the hopes and aspirations are being fulfilled (Oliver et al 2019). Some feel that the ubiquity of coproduction should arouse suspicions that it is little more than an empty form of words, a sham procedure that facilitates a continuation of the status quo.

Nonetheless, coproduction continues to advance. The demand is particularly strong in mental healthcare research. This is because including service users in the production of knowledge is seen as the only way to correct historic power imbalances and discontinuities between service provider and service user, such that knowledge production includes lived experience and responds to patient needs (Sweeney & Beresford 2020). Coproduction is said to have a potential for higher quality, more relevant and more impactful knowledge that, because it is produced in a more democratic way, has the potential to be 'transformative' (Flinders et al 2016). For example, Williams et al argue that coproduced knowledge has the potential to resist pressures to produce only highly routinised, management-friendly forms of knowledge, this looks like it might be a hugely valuable asset (Williams et al 2020).

Collaborative ethnography is a particularly appropriate method for this study because it appears to have special powers when investigating bureaucratic institutions. This is critical to our project. One of the challenges of conducting this research was to distance our analysis from the way that bureaucracies represent themselves. Anthropologists sometimes talk of 'methodological agnosticism' as a way of describing their stance of sceptical curiosity, neither completely buying in to a set of beliefs nor rejecting them out of hand. Methodological agnosticism is not always easy. Anthropological studies of bureaucracy face particular challenges. To explore the issues that animated us, we needed the interpretive space to query official forms of knowledge that in many contexts are deemed expert or authoritative. This demands that it is possible to interpret medical notes, exchanges between clinicians, or between clinicians and patients, as reductive or misleading, sometimes duplicitous or deceptive at a structural level, indicating higher level patterns, not personal bad practice. Refusing to take expertise at face value is an exercise in active but qualified disbelief. It can demand a certain kind of emotional labour. This is because if we are critics of bureaucratic medical representations, we are also consumers. Some of the authors of this book continue to be users of mental healthcare services. All are consumers of healthcare. When I visit the GP, I might find myself wanting to trust their reasoning and accept the documentation they produce. At a time like this, when I might be worried about my health, I don't want to be agnostic, but a believer, able to buy in to the reassurance offered by evidence-based medicine, and the performance of doctorly expertise. I am likely to be reluctant to produce a critique that argued, for example, that the biomedical concept of evidence is empty rhetoric, a language game designed to enable clinicians to perform accountability.

At the same time, I am also a bureaucratised worker. I teach in a university that requires me to produce documentation that is very similar to medical notes in that it carries the flavour of professional expertise but is shaped by institutional needs. I have learned how to deploy forms of words that dispel responsibility, and show I perform my role professionally and I recognise that this comes at the cost of full candour. I suspect that some of this sounds familiar to many readers, even those who don't work in healthcare or education. Many, perhaps most, readers of this book work in a bureaucratised setting. Even the events that led to the production of this book have traces of the same processes. In a sense, we are all under the spell of bureaucracy. In our day to day lives we tend to veer between belief and doubt. As a producer of such documentation, I am sceptical, worldly, sometimes cynical, at times perhaps untrusting; yet I know that as a consumer, I find myself prepared to suspend my critical faculties, and put my faith in systems, in the hope of the cessation of anxiety.

The power of collaborative working in investigating bureaucratised work settings lies in the way relationships maintain candour and resist pressures to accept tidier and more reassuring bureaucratic representations. Research methods that seek more routinised, reproducible forms of knowledge tidy away the messiness and ambiguity of lived experience. Collaborative ethnographers can recover this complexity. Personal connections promote solidarity and highlight evasions or lapses in candour. Together, we find the courage to be honest and to resist inclinations to overlook the partiality and evasions of medical self-representation. In other words, collaborative working helps researchers to resist secular theodicy. My sense is that our collaborative ethnographic method harnesses relationality, bringing I-thou relationships, and all their radical potential, from the field to the desk. We understand our method to be an instance of what Clarke and Wright call 'tactical authenticity' (Clarke & Wright 2019). The indeterminate, relational and creative collaborative methodology becomes part of the message. Coproduction offers a means of producing knowledge in such a way as to resist the same epistemic pressures that we describe as shaping clinicians. It is thus ideally suited to the empirical work we are attempting.

However, this book cannot be seen as pure coproduction, if that means that all four named authors had a equal role throughout. The concept of the book, which I verbally pitched to the publisher at the symposium described above, is a development of my PhD thesis and so took shape in advance of meeting with the named co-authors. My initial plan was to coproduce the life of a single service user. I was approached by a service user who was interested in my work, and we began talks to figure out how we might work together. The thought was that a single life explored in depth would provide the granular detail and nuance that clinical knowledge lacks and so be an excellent foil for an exploration of the institutional context of mental healthcare. We planned to use a Freedom of Information request to access medical notes, and then use the contrast between coproduced ethnography and medical notes to demonstrate how institutional factors impact the clinical gaze and how illness experiences might be understood otherwise. For a number of reasons, we didn't take this plan forwards.

For one thing I felt uncomfortable working closely with a service user without my own extensive mental health history being part of the text. It felt dishonest. How could I engage with the interpersonal authenticity of collaborative working whilst concealing my own past? I felt that if I wanted to coproduce with others I was obliged to introduce autoethnography. This was quite a change of direction. When I planned my PhD I had initially intended to be open about my past whilst conducting ethnographic fieldwork. I had thought of it as an asset. I started my doctoral fieldwork having already experienced first-hand many of the phenomena I was investigating. In her pioneering ethnography of life amongst people with severe and enduring mental health problems in the US, Sue Estroff describes the challenges of understanding service user experiences without having personally experienced them. She relates how she didn't realise that in mental healthcare settings, different forms of clothing indicate different roles, such that an observer can tell who is a patient and who is a member of staff. Estroff even wanted to take medication:

> The decision to take medication was a difficult one, and it caused much consternation among my family, friends and colleagues. Interestingly, the psychiatric professionals had the most reservations, not the social scientists. The staff members whose opinions I sought strongly advised against it, saying they would never take medication.
>
> *(Estroff 1981: 30)*

Estroff clearly learned from this response. The reader is left wondering if the doctors would be as cautious about medication, and worried about adverse effects, if Estroff had actually been a patient. Ultimately she does take meds, and keeps a six week journal to record the experience, noting how meds caused self-doubt, restlessness, and numbness which she describes as 'instructive' (ibid.: 106).

But, like anyone in my position (and like all the authors of this book) I already knew that doctors and patients dress differently, and that meds can cause experiences that, in other circumstances, might be classed as mental health problems in their own right. The consternation among family members that Estroff recounts is ethnographically illuminating, but the ethnographic record would surely be incomplete without also including lived experience of the impact of illness experiences on family dynamics, roles and expectations. Estroff had lived amongst people she described as 'making it crazy.' I myself had made it crazy. It felt like I had something extra that I might bring to my research.

I had intended to be open about my past in all my research. However, this turned out not to be possible. To prepare for my doctoral research, I conducted a pilot study in a mental health team, I gave a talk which explained what I was doing but also who I was. I tried to suggest that my mental health history, although now ended, might help me do my work. The result was unexpected. I found that because I was a former patient, the mental health professionals were highly uncomfortable with my presence. Several mental health professionals made phone calls to the project manager in the university psychiatry department, indicating their dislike of the arrangements. I remember how surprised the project manager was. She knew I was attached to a prestigious university, through the anthropology department doctoral programme and my membership of the academic psychiatry department. The mental health professionals didn't have anything to say about me personally, but expressed discomfort in having a patient working alongside them. They appeared prejudiced against mental health patients. I was fully supported by the academic department of psychiatry but it was agreed I couldn't really continue working with the team. But as this was only a pilot project, I had room for manoeuvre. It was better to go underground. When I approached other mental health teams, I concealed my medical history. This certainly worked from a pragmatic point of view: there were no calls made to the department. Indeed, many teams were very welcoming and went out their way to assist and promote my work. So I ended up in a biomedical closet. This continued until I began collaborative ethnographic working with service users. Continuing to conceal my past seemed untenable and unethical. Coming out as a former service user ultimately felt like a relief, a cessation of the active concealment of my past but also an opportunity to re-evaluate my experiences.

To start work on this book, I first approached Catriona Watson and Hugh Palmer. I had known Catriona for years, after we met in a group organised by the local NHS Trust. Hugh I met during my PhD fieldwork and we became friends. With each of them, I explained the basic outline of the book and asked if they wanted to contribute. We decided we would share authorship for each coproduced chapter, such that we each agreed on content and each could veto things we didn't like. The content of each chapter was not pre-set and would be arrived at collaboratively, but the chapter had to contribute to the larger argument. Catriona introduced me to Rowan. It took time to figure out how best to engage with Rowan's dual positioning. We gradually put together a proposal for an eight chapter book, with one chapter of ethnography from my PhD, three chapters of coproduced ethnography, and one chapter of autoethnography. With an introduction, a chapter examining methodology and a conclusion, that made the eight chapter book you are reading now.

Rowan, Catriona and Hugh each discussed ways of narrating their lives and at the same time I suggested ideas from the ethnographic literature and from theory that might illuminate the narrative. After discussion, the next step was for my co-author to produce text about themselves, written in the first person and in their voice. We then discussed this text and edited it together in the light of ongoing conversation and reflection. Next I produced analysis, written in my voice, which again was formed by earlier discussion and was co-edited in an ongoing, iterative process. Over time, adjustments were made to both texts, until we were both satisfied with the chapter. The text in my voice and the text in my collaborators' voice are thus both coproduced. I couldn't really tell if this counted as 'ethnographic fieldwork' or 'writing up.' It seemed to have elements of both. The events described are mostly drawn from memory and so do not constitute findings from a demarcated period of fieldwork. But the process of discussion becomes part of the memories themselves, guiding what events to select, how to express them, and what to miss out.

Chapter three might be considered conventional ethnography, but there are many hidden collaborators: not least my doctoral supervisor, my examiners, plus friends and colleagues who read versions or with whom I chatted about the ideas. I also gave a version of this chapter as a talk to The Oxford Uehiro Centre for Practical Ethics, and gained some helpful feedback. In addition, I rewrote the chapter to fit the style and objectives of the book as a whole. This meant reducing the amount of space given to positioning my work within the literature, and using theory in a different way. The aim of this chapter is to use detailed ethnographic material to highlight the impact of the institution. I select two pieces of ethnography from my doctoral work, using them to show how institutional rather than clinical pressures (or more abstract forces like Biopower or governmentality) play out in mental healthcare, such that clinical work is transformed, even to the point where a psychiatrist might change a diagnosis when pressured by a patient.

Chapter four is coproduced with Catriona Watson. We draw on DWP paperwork and anthropological theory to discuss how powerful institutions can impact individual patients, forcing them to engage with various framings of distress. Catriona's ethnography stresses her own hermeneutic autonomy. She is not discursively colonised, but weaves her own narrative account of her distress, including the moral injury associated with benefits documentation. Chapter five is autoethnography. I draw on my own medical notes, and use anthropological concepts – especially 'habitus' – to point to the limitations of bureaucratically expedient biomedical narratives in understanding and shaping personal change. Chapter six is coproduced with Hugh Palmer, who writes about his experiences in terms of mythic archetypes, includes illustrations as well as excerpts from his medical notes, to draw out the ethical dimension of his experiences. Taken together, these chapters suggest a potential harm of relying solely on biomedical narratives. I suggest that the kind of narrative a mental health professional needs to behave appropriately in an accountable bureaucracy may differ in important ways from the kind of narrative a person needs to make sense of their distress and effectively work towards recovery. Next is a chapter that explores the frontier between mental health service user and provider. Rowan Jones (writing under a pseudonym) is a mental health professional who is also a service user. Her account of working in mental healthcare is shockingly candid and paints a picture of layers of attentional triage and strategic insincerity on the part of healthcare professionals, and how this is reflected back by patients.

*

The choice to work collaboratively has far-reaching consequences. If we work together, then who are we writing for? What do we hope to achieve? It seemed wrong to solely address an anthropological audience, or academics interested in technical aspects of ethnographic working. Collaborating is time-consuming and emotionally demanding. Why should my collaborators expend intellectual and emotional labour, and expose their lives, to contribute to debates that are of no consequence to them (or, even worse, be designed largely to advance my career)? So we wanted to produce a book for all concerned with mental healthcare that makes an argument that is directly relevant to current debates in mental healthcare. The goal is to contribute to change. Throughout, we place less stress on locating this work within published literature, or commenting on arguments made by other scholars. As a result, there are fewer refences, or digressions into other debates, than in a conventional anthropology publication. Similarly, inaccessible or obscure prose feels self-indulgent. We have tried to write in prose that is clear and comprehensible and doesn't require training in anthropology (although that can be a struggle). At times we even risk attempting to make our writing enjoyable to read.

For each coproduced chapter, we wanted to find what worked. None of the chapters is intended to the final word. Other chapters could have been written. We hope that they demonstrate how, by adopting a distinctive research methodology, we produce distinctive data. Once we started working together, I found myself less receptive to the allure of largescale intellectual schemes and more inclined to see efforts to organise ethnography around single theories as reductive. Theory offers exciting, even bracing intellectual projects, but they can end up riding roughshod over the messiness and complexity of the lives of my collaborators, and myself. For example, it isn't that I rejected the notion that power imbalances are found in mental healthcare settings. But I found myself more convinced that power is diffused, chaotic, relatively unpatterned, radiating out as staccato bursts.

There are ethical consequences to collaborative working that are jarring because of the current institutionalisation of research ethics. The unplanned nature of all ethnographic work tends to get lost in the documentation of ethics. But these effects are greater in collaborative or coproduced ethnography. Once laid out in the tick boxes and leading questions of ethics forms, ethnographic research can appear a solemn undertaking, demanding specific expertise, planning, and focus. This implies that research is a distinct activity, separable from everyday sociality. Research might be fun, but it is also structured and goal-oriented. According to this vision, a person will always know when they are conducting research, and so those being researched should always know about it and have agreed. On this basis, it is recognised that research activity demands ethical scrutiny in a way that day to day social life does not. These thoughts guide bureaucratic representations of ethnographic research in funding applications and in university research ethics processes. For example, the Association of Social Anthropologists of the UK (ASA) Ethical Guidelines 2021 for good research practice state:

> Whenever reasonably practicable, participants should be made aware of the presence and purpose of the researcher. Researchers should inform participants of their research in the most appropriate way depending on the context of the research… Inquiries involving human subjects should be based on the freely given informed consent of participants.
>
> *(Association of Social Anthropologists of the UK (ASA) Ethical Guidelines 2021: 2–3)*

This advice sounds sensible. Why shouldn't participants be made aware of research purposes and be given a chance to consent or nor consent? And doesn't it make sense to have formal bodies to assess proposed research to check it fulfils basic criteria?

The experience of producing this book has heightened my sense of the importance of taking research ethics seriously but has given me reason doubt this framing of the ethics of ethnographic research. Humans are social creatures, constantly relating to others, reflecting on and sharing experiences. The moments of connection and intersubjective understanding that drive ethnographic working are valuable in day-to-day life as well, forming part of our essential repertoire as social creatures. Ethnography seems to be a magnification of sociality. Ethnographic fieldwork involves a heightened awareness, an open-ended intersubjective attentiveness, reciprocal and undetermined. It means taking the time to really listen, to relate to and understand other people. Since we do this anyway, in our day to day lives, the frontiers of what counts as ethnographic research are blurry.

The story of how this book came to be produced reflects this ambiguous process. The larger argument emerged over several years. Becoming a mental health patient can mean having a lot of time and little to do. These are fertile conditions for extended social exchanges that might count as ethnography. During my time as a patient I spent hours chatting with fellow patients, describing and comparing experiences, and embarking on angry denunciations of services, furious accounts of being unheard, or misunderstood, or mistreated. Some of the basic ideas that structure the book draw heavily on these exchanges. But I did not, of course, inform any of my fellow patients that I was a researcher, because, at the time, I didn't know either. It was only years later that these exchanges were reframed as ethnographic work when they were incorporated into my PhD thesis.

The process of writing a PhD required research ethics clearance from the NHS. However, as an ethnographer, it wasn't possible to forget or exclude earlier conversations. During fieldwork I soon learned both that a few happenstantial remarks made by a disgruntled social worker in a car park could be far more useful than carefully phrased responses to interview questions. So I continued my open, inquisitive research style, learning both from the recorded interviews that were described in my ethics applications and from the impromptu conversations that continued to take place as I moved around hospital premises.

I did not always know when I was conducting research. Some ethnographic material in this book is taken from my experiences as a patient and some from unplanned experiences as an ethnographer. I don't think it is possible to tell which is which.

Collaborative ethnographic working means listening, being open-hearted and attentive. It isn't easy. I found that the mutually supportive, and mutually influencing relationships formed during the writing of this book felt like the antidote to the routinised intimacy of my earlier clinical relationships. By sharing authorial responsibility, by working together in an unplanned, flexible way, always open to the potential benefits of happenstance, we found that our method was part of our argument. Humane, mutually respectful dialogue is empowering. It builds self-understanding and self-respect. The institutional conditions that mental health staff work within makes genuine dialogue more or less impossible. The result is stilted, one-sided talk. We hope that this collaborative work helps us understand why this is the case, and points to new ways of organising that put human relations at the centre of mental healthcare.

3

NO MENTAL HEALTHCARE WITHOUT MENTAL HEALTHCARE INSTITUTIONS

In this chapter I describe in some detail a period of about an hour in the life of a woman called Viv. Amongst other things, Viv is a service user. During this hour, Viv has a series of encounters with service providers: first with Rebecca, a CPN and then Giles, a psychiatrist. At first, Rebecca and Giles appear to be certain that Viv doesn't suffer from a mental illness. Sixty minutes later, they appear to think she does. But they don't seem to change their mind about Viv herself. They don't come to some new insight into her suffering. Rather they change their mind about how to deliver care for Viv. Thinking of Viv as having depression helps them deal with the responsibility and risk she presents. In other words, the reason for the change appears to be institutional.

I don't suggest that this narrative represents typical care, or is somehow representative of clinical life. Rather, this is a relatively unusual moment, in which institutional pressures are amplified and so more visible (and analysable) than is usually the case. This is a story in which power imbalances play out and where clinical thinking is deployed. But it isn't a story of biopower or subjectification, or, even, biomedicalisation. In this case at least, theoretical constructs like that take us away from lived experience and estrange us from the ethnographic moment. They also set up expectations that are false. Rebecca and Giles are not the powerful ones, wielders of hegemonic knowledge that constrains Viv and transforms her subjectivity. It is Viv who is able to pressure Rebecca and Giles into doing what she wants, imposing her preferences.

This is a chapter about how a person might come to be diagnosed with depression for institutional reasons, what this reveals about mental healthcare and how ethnographers and other researchers might need to respond. It is difficult to make sense of the impact of institutions. No single forms of words or theoretical model seems to capture it all. Before we get to Viv's story (or is

DOI: 10.4324/9781003154235-3

it: Rebecca and Giles' story?) it might be useful to introduce some of the ways clinicians (primarily a CPN called Claire) an anthropologist (Annamarie Mol) and a political theorist (Bernado Zacka) have unpacked the impact of organisations as a way of contextualising and opening up the discussion. I discuss each of these in the light of my ethnographic and autoethnographic knowledge. I both borrow from the sources and draw some contrasts to better understand mental healthcare.

*

Community mental healthcare services are organised around multidisciplinary teams. These teams include psychiatrists, psychologists, community psychiatric nurses, social workers, occupational therapists and support workers. Given the complexity of the problems teams deal with, and current low levels of understanding of those problems, this seems like a very sensible institutional design. Healthcare that draws on several distinct professional perspectives and styles is surely superior to care that is reliant on a single disciplinary approach. A psychiatrist who notices that a person meets the criteria for a mental disorder may fail to spot troubling family dynamics that are more obvious to a CPN who makes home visits. An occupational therapist might see signs of recovery in a patient and connect them to activity and social contact, but have less sense of how a mental disorder might help or hinder progress. Psychiatrist and anthropologist Robert Barrett takes this argument a step further. He sees a relationship between a multidisciplinary team and the components parts of a person: 'Psychiatric casework involved deconstructing and reconstructing a person; alternating between parts and whole; disassembling them into bits and pieces and then putting them back to together into a "whole person" again. For patients, this was the most powerful effect of being treated by a team' (Barrett 1996: 106).

It sounds rather optimistic, a polyvocal paradise in which different specialities combine in a complementary way to address different aspects or components of the human. But when, during my PhD research, I started to visit mental health teams and listened to team discussions of their caseload, what I encountered was rather different. In place of distinctive perspectives and methods, I was surprised at how difficult it was to differentiate professional roles. Most talk was uniform or generic. A social worker could sound a lot like a psychologist. A support worker could be hard to differentiate from a CPN. I was puzzled by this at first. Somehow, disciplinary distinctions that seem so important in academic publications are dissolved by the institutional context. Of course, there are moments when roles do become clear. Only a psychiatrist can prescribe medication, for example, and this can be raised in team discussions. Psychologists offer formulations of individual psychopathology that raise eyebrows amongst social workers more attuned to structural problems. But it was remarkable what a small role multidisciplinarity played in day-to-day discussions. This prompts some unexpected questions. How should we understand the relationship between mental healthcare institution and professional practice? If one impact of mental healthcare institutions is that they tend to erode disciplinary perspectives, what other effects may they have?

Each mental healthcare specialty is usually understood as an autonomous body of knowledge housed in a fairly neutral institutional setting. As discussed in chapter one, to Foucauldian social scientists that feels ominous, because expert biomedical knowledge is really about power. Put crudely, mental healthcare is said to enforce the disciplinary project of the state. According to this view, what is presented to the public as care is really a means of control. The aim of this book is to argue that this is not the best way of thinking about mental healthcare because it misunderstands the relationship between mental healthcare institutions and mental healthcare itself. Mental health professionals should not primarily be understood as vectors of knowledge, or, even, as being particularly powerful. Rather, their activities are largely shaped by the setting in which they work. They are bureaucrats at least as much as they are clinicians. This chapter is the first of five empirical chapters in which we use ethnographic evidence to illustrate this case.

The odd erasure of disciplinary distinctions described above is just one instance of institutional impact. Staff members talk a lot about how they feel compromised by the institutional setting and can end up feeling a bit disingenuous and at times even fraudulent. It is difficult, though, to know quite how to conceptualise institutional impact. Institutional pressures are often seen as simplistic and superficial, delinked from clinical priorities, a distorting lens that misrepresents the work of mental healthcare. It can be an emotive topic. Institutional pressures are sometimes described by mental health professionals as an external constraint, like Weber's iron cage, that limit what clinicians can do. At other times they are seen more like a diversion, taking clinicians away from what they think they should be doing and towards less valuable activities, such as writing notes and filling in forms. There is a third framing, in which care and institution become so interwoven that they are inseparable.

How can we start to dig deeper into the impact of the institutional setting? Anthropologist Annemarie Mol's work suggests one line of approach. She locates tensions in healthcare between what she calls the logic of care and the logic of choice (Mol 2008). Her claim is that because Biomedical healthcare is increasingly understood as if it is a commercial transaction, in which medical practitioners provide services to customers, increasing choice is seen as desirable, a way of improving services. This, according to Mol, is a problem. Markets are built around the logic of choice which is importantly different from the logic of care: 'in one way or another a market requires that the product that changes hands in a transaction be clearly defined. It must have a beginning and an end. In the logic of care, by contrast, care is an interactive, open-ended process that may be shaped and reshaped depending on its results' (ibid.: 23). Better health does not necessarily result from more healthcare products, and the quality of care cannot be deduced unproblematically from the results. For this reason, according to Mol, simply promoting choice is not a good way of promoting patient interests or improving the quality of care or care outcomes.

For Mol, the problem arises out the way freedom is conceptualised. We are familiar with an association between paternalistic medical authority and disempowered, passive patients. But Mol argues that making patients into consumers may not be the best way to counter disempowerment. Choice and freedom do not map onto each other as simply as the logic of choice suggests:

> If you have a potentially lethal disease and there is a drug like insulin that is likely to allow you to live for quite a while longer, what do you do? When they talk about this, most patients say: 'I have no choice.' But this lack of choice does not call for emancipation. That they feel no freedom is not because they have been submitted to the force of authority. Something else is going on...In that context, their first concern is not with who is in charge, but with what to do.
>
> *(ibid.: 46)*

In other words, in many clinical contexts, the freedom of choice that seems constitutive of being a consumer is irrelevant to both clinician and patient. To provide the best care, clinicians might need to give advice that contravenes patient preferences.

Mol's thinking about these two logics, and the kinds of institution that might serve them, seems helpful. Institutional priorities towards consumer choice redirect the behaviour of clinicians away from the logic of care, and impact healthcare as a whole. Mol's work gives us reason to question organising mental healthcare around the logic of choice. However, as I got to know mental healthcare, it seemed like other logics were in play. Both clinicians and patients told me about how care is organised according to institutional logics that seem to be neither about care or consumer choice.

These topics were on my mind one day around the midpoint of my PhD fieldwork as I drove out to meet with Claire, an occupational therapist I had got to know quite well. Claire was an experienced member of staff, having worked for several years as a support worker before qualifying as an community psychiatric nurse. She was articulate and confident, and I felt able to ask her quite direct questions about her working life. In response she suggested a particularly crisp way of understanding the impact of the institutional context. Her remarks were forthright, but they echoed comments made by many others, both in recorded interviews and (more often) made off the record.

We met in a clinic room used for outpatient appointments. It was a clear wintry day and the room was uncomfortably chilly. The low sun got in our eyes, but there were no curtains and we shuffled our chairs around so we could avoid the glare and see each other. After we had been talking for about twenty minutes, our conversation took an interesting turn:

CLAIRE: 'Services, as you know, have changed so much in the Trust in the last ten to twelve years...part of what I don't like, personally, is...Payment by result, very target driven, very data quality-esque shaping of services, it wasn't, to my feeling, really based on individual need, it all looked very good on paper, and it all looked like it would meet the needs of any given individual, but actually people are so unique, in what they want and what they need and the kind of support they find helpful, and I think that when you introduce these very target driven services, I worry that that gets lost a little bit.'

NEIL: 'Yeah.'

CLAIRE: 'Part of what happens when services get that way, and I see it happening within all aspects of the NHS, is that services change.' ... 'There is the job I would love to be doing, the job I'm expected to do...and the job that I actually do, and,'

NEIL: 'Could you tell me about each one of those?'

CLAIRE: 'The job I would love to be doing, is, I would love to, and this is very idealistic, but this is my ideal, blues skies, ideal, I would have a much lower caseload.'

NEIL: 'OK.'

CLAIRE: 'I would have a caseload that predominantly consisted of people with significant mental illnesses, and that's not excluding people with depression and anxiety because they are incredibly debilitating illnesses, but people who I feel are actually going to benefit from my interventions, again, in an ideal world my caseload would be a lot lower risk.' [Laughs]
   'But I would actually have a caseload of people who are actually unwell, you know, there's always going to be a bit of a mix, from the people we in an un-PC way call the lifers.'

NEIL: 'Yes.'

CLAIRE: 'But also people so I can do very very short term focussed intervention work, with a real recovery focus to try to get them well, to a point where they feel more stable and able to continue to implement what we've done. I, again, this is personal feeling, but I feel ... from a promotional perspective, that would be the job that the Trust would say I should be doing. In reality I think the job I'm expected to do is to, yes, do those things, but with a high caseload and making sure my paperwork is up. For me, particularly recently I think, there has been a huge emphasis on data quality.'

NEIL: 'Yeah.'

CLAIRE: 'And I'm not negating, I'm not negating that their needs, er,'

NEIL: 'It's got to have a role.'

CLAIRE: 'It's got to have a role and always will do, but [pause] with the introduction of payment by results and target driven outcomes, I feel that they don't really match what someone may be asking for or what I think they need.'

NEIL: 'Yeah.'

CLAIRE: 'So, I feel that part of the job that I'm expected to do is a little unrealistic.'

NEIL: 'OK, yeah.'

CLAIRE: 'Umm, and the job that I want to do is a little unrealistic in the current climate and the job that I actually do is that I attempt to do both and feel that I'm not doing either well enough.' [laughs] 'Does that make sense? If I'm being honest.'

NEIL: 'OK, yeah, be honest.'

CLAIRE: 'If I'm honest I feel I'm trying to combine the two…We all work late, we all come in at weekends, occasionally, to catch up on things because it's not just that, there are casenotes to do, supporting letters to write, medication to get sorted, if people are high risk you need to see them a lot, there are safety plans to negotiate, there are referrals, you know, with a caseload of more than thirty people, that's a lot of work in the week, and the unfortunate result is, yes, I feel split in the middle and I feel I'm like I'm doing a half-baked job of both…it's a compromise, the two don't marry up as they should.'

Claire worries about internal contradictions within her professional role, but these are not Mol's tensions between the logic of care and the logic of choice. Rather, she is concerned about the logic of the institution, which fractures her working world into three jobs. The job she would like to do is one in which her clinical work more closely matches her expertise. That would mean seeing fewer patients but also having a different kind of patient caseload: fewer people with relatively minor anxiety and depression, and not too many 'lifers' who are unlikely to get better but who represent risk. This is because she would like to focus on people she regards as having real or significant mental illnesses, who are likely to benefit from the care she can offer. The job she is expected to do is rather different. It is based on making services look good on paper. In her words, it is 'promotional.' This means producing documentation, managing risk, dealing with patients that she is unable to help or who are not really suited to the kind of care she can provide, whilst participating in a care system that she believes fails to match the individual circumstances of her patients. The job she actually does seems like an unhappy compromise that splits her in two, because, despite working additional hours, she is unable to fully meet the informational needs of her managers or the healthcare needs of her patients.

All three jobs are unrealistic. The smaller caseloads required by the job Claire would like to do would be too expensive. In addition, focussing on patients would diminish Claire's capacity to produce the documentation the NHS Trust needs, both to participate in market mechanisms and (although she doesn't mention it in the extract above) as required for external scrutiny. The job Claire is expected to do is also unrealistic in that it is simplistic and reductive. This lack of realism includes both the kind of patients Claire sees and the care they receive. The idea that the wrong kind of patient has infiltrated services was – to my surprise – widely expressed by members of staff. I was repeatedly told throughout my PhD fieldwork by staff members that people who aren't really mentally and who don't really benefit from the kind of care services can provide were making up an ever greater proportion of clinical caseloads. Staff were angry but powerless. It felt a long way from dry academic debates about the meaning of mental illness categories and frontiers between health and illness. Claire was insistent that many people on her caseload are not really suited to the care she can offer, with the result that she spends a lot of her professional life with service users she can't help.

There is another way of understanding tensions in bureaucratic environments. In an influential book, political scientist Bernado Zacka (who we met in chapter one) suggests that it is in the nature of bureaucratic working that staff members face competing and inconsistent demands (Zacka 2017). Members of staff are expected to be fair, to be efficient and to be responsive to client needs. Properly understood, according to Zacka, that isn't a problem. To do their job well, he argues, they need to hold these demands in tension and not focus on a single one. Zacka calls this 'a healthy pluralism' (ibid.: 221). He knows that it doesn't always work. But, when it fails: 'The problem is not that bureaucrats lose their capacity for sound moral reasoning, but that the moral perception and role conception that feed into such reasoning become overly narrow and specialised' (ibid.: 12).

Zacka gives us reasons to question Claire's account. Claire thinks that she would do her job better if she was free to do what she wanted, because that is the best way of matching care with individual need. But from Zacka's perspective, this would mean Claire was getting overly narrow and specialised, neglecting the goals of fairness and efficiency. Really doing her job well means accepting the tensions between competing goals and finding ways to reach accommodations. For Zacka, compromises are signs of doing the job well. So might we characterise the job Claire would like to do as wanting to be responsive to a client's needs and the job she is expected to do as a combination of this with the need to be fair and efficient? I think the answer has to be no. We might agree with Zacka that it isn't necessarily desirable for Claire only to do the parts of her job that most appeal to her. Services should be organised around patients, not staff. But Zacka's model doesn't really correspond to Claire's three jobs. The problem with the job Claire is expected to do isn't that it is a mix of her personal efforts to meet the needs of individual service users combined with diverging pressures to towards efficiency and fairness. Rather, in Claire's view at least, the job she is expected to do is oriented towards producing documentation that her employer needs to participate in market mechanisms. This makes it inefficient and unfair. It is an unsatisfactory compromise that wastes staff time, and leads Claire to treat people unsuited for the care she can provide. There is also a kind of ambient effect as well. Because the job she is expected to do is so problematic, it imposes a kind of disingenuousness in a setting where trusting communication between service providers and service users is seen as a critical aspect of care.

*

Whatever way you choose to represent social inequality, Viv and her family are located somewhere towards the least privileged, most disadvantaged end. They have limited economic, social and cultural capital. In the phrase widely used, they are 'well known to services.' This includes social services, mental healthcare services, and the police and criminal justice system, as well as a local charity. Viv recently came to the attention of the local mental health team following the arrest of one of her sons for a string of very serious violent sexual offences. The case was locally notorious, and received extensive media coverage. Viv was briefly admitted to a psychiatric ward as an 'informal' or voluntary patient. She was discharged a few days later and was due to come and see a CPN, Rebecca.

I asked Rebecca about Viv. What kind of person is she and what kind of care do the team provide? Rebecca said that Viv was depressed and anxious. She's feeling guilty about her son and his crimes and hated by other members of the local community. She talks about wanting to kill herself (which, Rebecca explained, is known as 'suicidal ideation') and, in the view of the team, she presents a substantial suicide risk. But, Rebecca stressed, they want to provide 'the minimum care possible' for Viv. I asked why. Rebecca replies that 'we don't believe Viv has a mental illness.' She explained that they think that Viv is depressed, but she doesn't suffer from a depressive disorder; she is anxious, but she doesn't suffer from an anxiety disorder. The reason for this is that her distress is seen as broadly proportionate to the environment. Rebecca describes it as 'normal depression.' She added that Viv has plenty to feel depressed and anxious about. 'How would we feel' she asked 'if we were in her position?' I could see what she meant. I could imagine something like a perfect storm of distress: intense guilt and shame made worse by social ostracisation. Rebecca articulated this in terms of stressors. The level of stressors is very high, and so the level of distress is also high. At the time this struck me as odd. Thinking of guilt and shame as stress removes the specific meaning of the experiences. It makes them instances of general problems, lumped together with work pressures, precarious living arrangements, high levels of background noise and concerns about climate change. At the time I wasn't aware of why an expert might want to do this.

Rebecca also explained that Viv's personality is 'being taken into account.' She said that the team feels that Viv has 'personality issues' and 'definite personality traits.' According to Rebecca, the team takes the view that these personality issues are important when thinking about appropriate treatment. This is because: 'Mental illness is something that could happen to anyone, to me and to you. Who you are doesn't make any difference. It can come and take your life away. But with personality, it is who you is the problem.' She went on to say that personality problems have their origins in childhood, either in abuse or neglect, and go on to shape character such that the patient finds it hard to lead a functional or fulfilling life. So Rebecca said that like many people with personality traits, Viv is poor at self-soothing and has poor coping skills, at a time when she has a lot to cope with.

I notice that Rebecca is reticent when talking about these issues. She talks in a cautious way, almost like a politician in a tricky interview, choosing her words carefully. I wondered if it was because she felt uneasy apparently criticising or blaming Viv. After all, Rebecca was claiming that Viv herself is the problem. This didn't feel like an entirely kind way to talk about a person in distress. However, I also felt unsure how sincere Rebecca was. I couldn't tell what her real views were. Was this talk of personality traits and poor self-soothing part of the job she'd like to do or the job she is expected to do? If Rebecca believes Viv is experiencing normal depression, why talk of personality at all? She was able to talk convincingly, in the way that would be required for team meetings or medical documentation, but I thought her heart wasn't really in it. This gave some of the words a slight ironic edge.

Frequently during my PhD fieldwork when I listened to healthcare staff members I noticed subtle shifts in tone and register, qualities that are hard to record but critical to meaning. For example, during a team meeting in which a female CPN described how a male patient had been sexually aggressive towards her, I noted how she used phrases like 'he really had a poor sense of personal boundaries' and 'I did detect some impulse control issues.' These anodyne, non-judgmental, bureaucratised terms acquired rhetorical force through understatement. They were immensely effective. With Rebecca, I suspected we are in the grey area described by Claire when she says that the job she actually does is a half-baked mix of her ideal and expected roles. Rebecca didn't entirely believe in what she was saying about Viv, but neither did she completely reject it.

Rebecca went on to say that Viv might already have 'become dependent on services.' What she meant is that Viv wanted to be in contact with Rebecca each day, either by phone or in person. This made Rebecca wary. She didn't want Viv to have too much contact with services, or, possibly, any contact with services. She said she thought that this might lead to Viv losing skills, in a situation where she might benefit from improving them. 'I know it is hard' said Rebecca, 'but life is hard. You have to learn how to cope.' She said she didn't want Viv exaggerating her distress to secure attention. 'Manipulative behaviour' like that is expensive and it 'diverts us from our real job.' In the section above, Claire said she wanted to focus her attention on patients with real, substantial mental illnesses because they are the ones who can really benefit. Here, Rebecca makes a similar point, but with more emphasis on potential harms rather than the absence of benefits. According to Rebecca, Viv could easily 'become a burden on services,' whilst, in the same process, losing her autonomy and self-reliance. This was something the team had discussed. They had decided that in their dealings with Viv, they would limit contact to generic 'support' offered by Rebecca to restrict the scope of any dependency they might create. In addition, Rebecca said the team had made sure not to prescribe Viv any medication. This is beginning to sound a lot like Claire's ideal job. The team as whole don't want Viv on their caseload, or, at least, too many people like Viv. If left to Rebecca's clinical judgement, we might expect to see very limited contact with Viv.

Before we go to meet Viv, Rebecca steps into the waiting room to introduce me and ask if it is ok for me to be present in the appointment. I stand behind her as she introduces me as a researcher in medical anthropology. Viv is sitting with her sister. She seems alert, expectant, slightly excited. Rebecca stresses that I don't have to be there; that the appointment can go ahead without me, but her tone suggests that there is no reason why not. But Viv seems pleased I am there. She asks what medical anthropology is. As I explain I am a research student, I sense she is a little disappointed that I am not more senior, but that she is nonetheless pleased.

Having established that I will join them, we walk together down a corridor and enter a tiny room. It seems too small for an appointment and is made worse by my presence. Airless and cramped, there is barely enough space for a table and three chairs. We are forced into a physical proximity that belies the unspoken social discontinuities between us. Rebecca sits on the other side of a table and I sit with Viv. Rebecca begins by talking quite neutrally about 'how have things been going?' Viv starts to talk about how depressed she has been. She says that she can't sleep and that she finds it 'painful to be alive.' Rebecca nods, listens, and asks simple questions. Is Viv in contact with her son? She says no. Is she in touch with her other children? Viv says yes she is. Rebecca is supportive, but without offering opinions or advice. She tends to repeat back what Viv says or make remarks such as: 'that must be very painful,' and 'I can see how difficult that is.'

Viv starts to discuss how she feels that her husband is 'supportive, but doesn't understand' and that she is becoming forgetful at work. She presents herself as overwhelmed by her feelings, and baffled by them too. As she talks, she glances at Rebecca directly. She describes how she comes down-stairs in the night, unable to sleep and tormented by intense, overwhelming feelings. She says it is too much to cope with. Hours go by sitting alone on the sofa. She doesn't know what to do. She was thinking of killing herself, that she wanted very much to do it, but was held back by concern for her younger children. She's circling the topic, at times sounding closer to suicide and then further away. There is a pause, as Rebecca offers reassurance and comfort. Viv goes on: 'I know drinking doesn't help, I know that, you've told me that and I don't do it when I feel terrible.'

As she talks she begins to cry. She says: 'I can't manage...it's all too much.' Hunched over the table, her body tenses and shakes. She hugs herself and gasps for breath. Rebecca hands her the box of tissues. She waits for Viv to compose herself, sitting perfectly still. 'Take your time, Viv, its ok, there's no hurry. Just take your time.' Viv returns to the topic of medication. She says she doesn't want tablets because they don't help, but she knows she needs something because nobody could bear what she is bearing, nobody could go through what she is going through. Might there be some tablets that could help? Something to help her cope, to take the pain away? Otherwise, suicide is always there.

Rebecca asked if Viv might want to speak to the doctor about antidepressants. She said yes. We got up and went to find Giles. As we were leaving Rebecca said: 'You'll be alright, won't you, for a few minutes, while I speak to the doctor?' Viv agreed that she would be fine. Giles' office is further down the corridor, but he's not in his office and we find him in the staff kitchen making tea. Rebecca explains to Giles what is happening. It was more or less the same as how she had described Viv to me earlier that day. She said that Viv seems to be very depressed and is talking of suicide. The risk seems to be real. Nothing had changed. There were no new developments. But this time, Rebecca went on: 'might it be worth giving her antidepressants?' Giles says he can see that 'there might be a justification for prescribing antidepressants.' He asks me what I think. I'm out of my depth and don't know what to say. He then talks through a possible rationale: that she is very distressed, that antidepressants 'might help a bit,' that she is at risk of both suicide and of 'developing a depressive illness' and, anyway 'antidepressants won't do any harm.' Giles finds several ways to justify prescribing antidepressants. But his tone is slightly flippant. I don't think he has any expectation that the medicine will be effective, perhaps, even that she will ever take the pills. He went on to say that the notoriety of Viv's son's crimes make her 'a very high profile case' and the team 'needs not to take unnecessary risks.' They will be looking after Viv for the next six months at least, during the wait for the trial. It might be safer to put her on medication.

So the three of us return to the room. Viv seems much calmer, and visibly brightens when she sees Giles. There is no room for another chair, and he crouches down in front of her. 'You're a very tall doctor aren't you?' she says. When, later, he writes down her date of birth on the prescription she jokes coquettishly about her age 'I shouldn't be telling you that should I?' Giles is undeflected and impassive. In any case, Giles gets some leaflets about medication down from a binder located on a high shelf and talks Viv through 'the options.' He says that there shouldn't be any side-effects, but that you can never be sure. This all seems formulaic. Viv didn't look like she was listening, but Giles words were perhaps more for me than her anyway, He hands over the prescription, and the meeting is finished.

*

So what just happened? How could Rebecca and Giles be so clear about what they want to do, yet make a U-turn without a second thought? How could the U-turn be so smoothly and speedily achieved and then so effectively concealed? And why did Rebecca want antidepressants anyway? Making a link between knowledge and power offers limited insight here. Giles and Rebecca are in discursive control, yet seem powerless. Viv seems to hold all the cards. The institutional context makes Rebecca and Giles responsible for Viv, and eager to maintain good relations, and this emerges as being more important than providing care.

Claire's three jobs jostle and collide. Neither Zacka's nor Mol's work take us very far. Rebecca and Giles start out with a clear sense of the job they would like to do. They want to minimise clinical input because they believe that it may be unhelpful to Viv. In particular, they seek to avoid prescribing antidepressants as they say that instead of being depressed, Viv has 'personality traits', and so is an unsuitable patient, as if she is one of the wrong kind of person who Claire, in the section above, describes as infiltrating caseloads. Then, during an appointment, Rebecca and Giles apparently change their minds, increase input and prescribe antidepressants. They prioritise documentation over care, because it helps them do the job they are expected to do even though this contradicts the job they would like to do. However, in discussion, both Giles and Rebecca are adept at making the U-turn sound clinically sensible, as if this is what they had wanted all along. They can produce a clinical justification for either course of action. Clinical reasoning emerges not as a means of making decisions, but as a way of justifying decisions made for institutional reasons.

When Rebecca and Giles engage with Viv, they do so in ways that are perfectly attuned to the institutional context. The language they use looks medical, a set of independent, objective, scientific tools, perhaps, that can be used to make good decisions about care based on an accurate description of distress. They are not primarily oriented towards producing the best possible description of Viv. They need to describe her such that they are able to document responsible clinical behaviour whilst achieving their organisational goals.

It is striking how performative everything is. When I chatted with Rebecca before we saw Viv, I felt unsure about her true beliefs, or, even, that she had true beliefs. She seemed to want to treat Viv as a vulnerable person under a lot of pressure, who could gain little from services and might be harmed. Her account of personality disorder was shaped around this narrative. It sounded like Rebecca thought that more well-balanced people would find it hard to cope, and that Viv was less robust than most. The talk of personality in particular didn't really sound entirely honest. Rebecca needs to talk about personality to enable authoritative note-taking that enables a defence of doing very little. It is a way of justifying inaction at the cost of full sincerity. At first, when Rebeca listens to Viv, she sticks to this plan, but something changes her mind. When we chat in the kitchen, Giles is slightly ironic, far from being fully serious. He can make out rationales for various courses of action. The decision he makes is not based on the logic of care or choice, and does not reflect the overarching power of biomedical discourse. My sense was that Giles thought that Viv was trying to flirt, perhaps reading this as attempted manipulation. But to me, she seemed to be trying to be nice, not really flirting but going through the motions, sensing, perhaps, vanity in Giles. Like Giles and Rebecca, Viv is aware that this is a performative space, where candour or sincerity are out of place. Like them, she is a skilled performer, because she too has learned the unwritten rules of mental healthcare.

The role of the category of personality is revealing. Personality emerges as a quintessentially bureaucratic category. As used by Giles and Rebecca, its meaning is determined by their institutional needs, not research papers or diagnostic manuals. It forces them into a stance that falls short of full sincerity, but allows them deal with responsibility and risk without constraining the possible decisions they can take. Talk about her personality pathologises the way that Viv relates to services and justifies limiting treatment without actually committing to a diagnosis or producing a fixed plan for the future. In terms of Claire's three jobs, talk about Viv's personality blurs distinctions between the jobs, so that the job they are expected to do sounds like the job they'd like to do.

Historically, the notion of personality has been used within Biomedicine to describe people who displayed patterns of abnormal behaviour, but had normal intellect and seemed not be suffering from acute psychiatric symptoms (Crocq 2013: 149). In the DSM 5, 'Personality traits are enduring patterns of perceiving, relating to, and thinking about the environment and oneself that are exhibited in a wide range of social and personality contexts' (American Psychiatric Association 2013: 647). Within academic and clinical psychology the concept of personality is seen as having predictive power: 'Personality traits are clearly central in predicting a wide array of important life outcomes, such as subjective well-being, social acceptance, relationship conflict, marital status, academic success, criminality, unemployment, physical health, and job satisfaction…even mortality years into the future' (Widiger 2012: 13). Personality disorders are understood to be wholly distinct from mental disorders, with their own independent origins, mechanisms and symptoms. Sometimes personality traits can be used as an explanation for why pharmaceutical remedies have failed. This can be a topic of joking amongst staff and patients. One patient told me he was on his fifth combination of medications for Bipolar Disorder. He said, with a smile, that 'I can try one more combination before they say I'm PD.'

In the DSM 5, personality disorders are grouped into three 'clusters.' Cluster A includes paranoid, schizoid and schizotypal disorders. Individuals with these disorders are said to often appear 'odd' or 'eccentric.' Cluster B includes antisocial, borderline, histrionic and narcissistic personality disorders. These people are described as 'dramatic,' 'emotional' or 'erratic.' Cluster C includes avoidant, dependent, and obsessive-compulsive personality disorders. Individuals with these disorders are said to appear 'anxious' or 'fearful.' In the DSM, people may have features of several PDs, both within and across clusters. In much talk about PD, the cluster or type of PD is not mentioned.

During my PhD fieldwork, I noticed that care staff would often talk about personality. It could lead to heated disagreements. One psychiatrist told me he was a specialist in personality disorder, whilst another said 'how can a personality be disordered? We don't know what an ordered personality is.' Clinicians don't talk about healthy personality traits. They don't, for example, write notes about hope, courage or prudence, even though they might be seen as having a direct bearing on distress. The language around personality is distinctive and unflattering. People with personality are described as 'emotionally unstable,' 'volatile' and 'manipulative.' They are said to be 'extremely responsive' to various triggers such as 'perceived slights,' 'threats of abandonment' and 'signs they're not being taken seriously enough.' It can become 'habitual' or 'entrenched.' When a clinician uses phrases like this, they are implying personality problems, even if this is not made explicit.

There is a huge difference between how staff talk about personality on and off the record. Shaheen, a CPN, told me how frustrating it can be to work with people with personality traits: 'you talk to them, you discuss how a certain way of behaving is unhelpful, is making them depressed, they agree, they say they'll change, then they walk right out the door and continue exactly the same...it can feel like an endless cycle.' I was told by Katie, an experienced psychiatric social worker and AMHP that neither staff nor patients are really comfortable with personality. For patients it is because 'it isn't nice to be told you've got PD traits.' For staff the reason is rather different:

> We all have PD traits, we all manipulate to get our way, or need to feel needed, so it can be hard to refer a person you like to complex needs [the personality disorder clinic]...I don't mind being woken by the police at 2am when it's a bipolar person because you know they're really unwell, there is really a chemical imbalance. Mania is preferable, is best of all, because treatment is obviously necessary, there are clear steps and rapid effects, more effective for mania than for depression.

Tracey, another social worker, was even more forthright. She said that she: 'can now spot a PD a mile off. You can tell within ten or fifteen minutes from their attitude...everything is not right, they're complaining about everything, can't sustain employment or relationships...and they want things from you, they want stuff, you feel that in your gut.' None of this, of course, is written down. But it isn't possible to understand medical documents that refer to personality without having a sense of this unrecorded hinterland. When

Rebecca told me that Viv has definite personality traits, I knew that we were treading on delicate ground.

Talk about Viv's personality sounds like a set of claims about independently existing qualities in Viv. I don't think that is the case. When Rebecca speaks about Viv's personality, she is really talking about a relationship between Viv and the healthcare team.

More specifically, Viv's personality traits are a way of referring to a relationships between service user and service provider that is deemed (by service provider) to be problematic. It isn't that Rebecca is wrong in suggesting that Viv's distress cannot really be separated from her as a person. As I hope the ethnography in this book shows, as soon as you get to know a person, links between distress and character, habits, values and tastes always emerge. It might be said that the adequacy of the concept of mental disorder rests of not knowing people very well. Rebecca and Giles do not use the concept of personality to elucidate the nature of Viv's distress. They appear fairly unconcerned about the nature or meaning of Viv's distress, focussing more on its scale and the risk it presents. Personality problems are supposed to be wholly distinct from mental disorders in their origins, causes and phenomenology. There is no sign of that here. Instead, Viv's personality defects are selected not because they impact her health, but because they impact services. If services were changed, then which patients were problematic and what made them problematic would change too. One implication of this is that it is difficult to keep Claire's three jobs apart. Even when trying to do the job she'd like to do, we should expect that Claire finds herself viewing the world through categories designed for the job she is expected to do.

A few days after the appointment with Viv, Giles told me that his policy to minimise contact with patients with personality is a personal preference. He said he aims to offer short-term support and treatment, with an eye to referral to a specialist team, but not all psychiatrists see things the same way. Some teams, he said, were more willing than him to treat personality, sometimes because of scepticism about the distinction between mental illness and personality. When Giles told me this, I recalled a team I spent some time with who as a whole appeared to be less Biomedical or biological than most. Team members were vocal about their scepticism towards diagnostic categories and the 'medical model.' In team meetings, even where a patient was diagnosed with schizophrenia, there was discussion of life events and external circumstances rather than just 'the illness.' A psychiatrist on that team told me he liked to use certain antipsychotic medications as 'psychic glue' for patients with personality traits. He said psychic glue was helpful to people who were trying to get their lives together.

Giles went on to describe how some teams refuse to treat personality patients at all, even in moments of crisis, because they think that delivering mental healthcare to people who don't suffer from mental illness only makes things worse. For Giles, this is very risky: 'If things go wrong, it looks bad if we haven't offered any treatment' he said. However, he thinks it is better for the team if they limit their contact in a judicious way and 'carry the risk.' The clinical case for him was clear: patients like this don't have mental illness. In Giles's view mental illnesses are real, underlying, pathologies that are independent of the person and intrude, harmfully, into otherwise healthy lives. So the rationale for treatment is negated. In addition, treating people with personality traits as if they suffer from mental illness is liable to have unintended adverse effects, making them less autonomous and more needy, and this can 'create a lot of stress for the team' as well as taking up a lot of time that could be much better used in other ways.

The idea that personality might be disordered is widely seen as stigmatising and this might be expected to be a bruising experience for Viv. We might speculate that Viv has a lifetime of indignities and humiliations to draw upon. Rebecca suggests that Viv's distress is proportionate, given the difficulties of her situation. If Viv is coping about a well as a person could in such demanding circumstances, then why did Rebecca go on to talk about personality? We can see the answer to this in how Rebecca talks about Viv. It is because Viv is burdensome to services. Rebecca says that treating personality traits as if they were mental disorders is expensive, and is a diversion from the team's real work. Note that these two qualities are relational: they are dependent not just on Viv herself but on how services are constituted. Viv is a problem to services because her distress is not the kind of distress that they are set up to deal with. Services are for a different kind of person, a person who benefits from pharmaceuticals, for example. We might speculate that if services were organised around the needs of people like Viv, then some other patient group, such as pharmaceutical responders, might emerge as problematic.

Staff members recognise that the institutional context shapes how they go about their work, but are perhaps less aware of how patient experiences and agency are similarly shaped. Rebecca told me that Viv felt guilty and was hated by her community because of her son's crimes. We might expect the conversation to focus on these painful experiences. But shame and guilt falls outside the remit of mental healthcare teams. The NHS does not provide forgiveness and atonement services. Redemption is not a recognised treatment outcome. So when Viv and Rebecca talk, it is about painful feelings, mood, self-soothing, coping, and risk. They treat shame and guilt as forms of low mood, resulting in risk for which appropriate steps can be taken. Rebecca and Giles thus find a way to respond clinically such that they actions are legible and defensible. This is why antidepressants emerge as a viable treatment option. It takes them a long way from the phenomenology of Viv's distress, and could leave Viv feeling unheard or disempowered. But Giles and Rebecca are acting on the basis of institutional pressures, not medical logics. In other words, Viv is not being medicalised or bio-medicalised, but, rather, bureaucratised.

The clinic emerges as transactional setting. It is a site for deal making, in which a patient's distress and risk may be exchanged for various kinds of care. In the style of a true healthcare consumer, Viv knows how to be maximise her receipt of healthcare services however adverse the environment. My impression is that Viv, Rebecca and Giles all understand this intuitively. Viv's institutional positioning leaves her with few other forms of agency. Viv is a skilful player of what might be seen as a bureaucratic game. She was genuinely very distressed, but I sensed a certain directionality to the expression and manifestation of her emotions. The distress was real, but not unmediated or uncurated. It was, in a sense, being offered to Rebecca. I began to see that Viv wanted something in return. A kind of deal is being done. The exchange is predicated on the moral commitment that Rebecca has towards Viv. As an accountable clinician, Rebecca has a responsibility for her patients. Viv seemed to be handing over distressing feelings. The feelings are intense and painful and they give Viv leverage. It is as if Rebecca is obliged to reciprocate. Viv's distress, once articulated in the clinic, became a bargaining chip, which might be exchanged for a certain kind of support, and for medication. The prescription for anti-depressants is relational, in that, in this setting, it is the best she can do. It is a bureaucratised goal in a bureaucratised setting. Securing a prescription like this could mean many things: being strong, learning from experience, doing the right thing for yourself, winning against the doctors. If, as seems likely, Viv didn't take the meds, that doesn't suggest that Viv is capricious, or feck-less. Getting access to meds is the only kind of institutional response that she might elicit. She is neither more strategic nor less candid than Rebecca and Giles. Both service provider and service user are forced into a performative role that is strategic more than it is sincere. To adopt a metaphor, Viv plays the cards she is dealt.

*

So what are we to make of this lack of sincerity? What is it about mental healthcare that inhibits candour? How should we deal with this in our research about mental health? Rebecca's careful, elusive phrasing, and Giles casual levity left me not just uncertain as to their true views, but facing a research problem. How should I represent clinicians and patients if they appear not to be wholly candid? Clearly, neither official definitions in the DSM, nor studiously defensive phrasing in medical letters (or, sadly, careful chats with curious anthropologists) directly or unambiguously reveal what Rebecca and Giles really believe. Over time I began to wonder if asking what Rebecca or Giles *really believe* is the most helpful framing. Perhaps they don't really believe anything, but adopt shifting, contextual stances according to felt need in the moment. The problem with that is that these are consequential opinions, reflecting professional judgement. This was a source of confusion throughout my doctoral fieldwork. It seemed to be important to think about why service providers aren't consistent, or open, or honest when working.

After all, it is hard not t thin that this might impact clinical outcomes. The problem, of course, is that this isn't usually how clinicians describe their work. To some extent, professional expertise includes actively concealing this. These topics reoccur at points through this book. I don't have a single, comprehensive answer. In this chapter I want to suggest that, at least as regards how Rebecca and Giles deal with Viv, consistency or sincerity are obstacles to good practice. To be professional means developing an exquisite sensitivity to the demands of the job. To think about this, I draw on Heywood's ethnographic work on queer activism in Italy (Heywood 2018).

Heywood suggests that people relate to moral codes in complex ways that are difficult to handle ethnographically. We shouldn't, he suggests, ignore cases where people fail to adhere to ethical injunctions. As he puts it: 'to fall short is to fall short of something in particular' (ibid.: 44). To illustrate, he cites cases where people adhere to one morality in public (for example, to be a loving and faithful spouse) and another in private (to have multiple affairs). It would be possible to dismiss a person who upholds spousal fidelity in public but cheats in private as a hypocrite, whose public commitment is false, a lie to go alongside the cheating. But Heywood suggests something more subtle: that people may adhere to moral codes whilst expecting to also break the code, and that hiding moral failings like this might be seen as a way of maintaining a kind of fidelity to the code. Heywood calls this a 'double morality.' An unfaithful spouse might exhibit a double morality is she or he breaks the rule in the right way, by keeping the infidelity secret. The thought is that an equivocal relationship with an ethical code is still a real relationship.

We could say that Giles and Rebecca both adopt something like a double morality regarding biomedical knowledge. They do not expect to fully adhere to clinical reasoning, but know that whatever decisions they make, they should create a rhetorical smokescreen in which institutional considerations are concealed. This is what it means to be a competent clinician. It isn't that Giles and Rebecca simply reject medical reasoning, or don't believe it, or are hypocrites. Rather, they recognise that, behind the scenes, a variety of considerations have to influence the decision they reach, but this should be concealed. So their relationship to medical knowledge are is equivocal and contextual, and, up to this point, resembles the relationship Heywood's cheating spouse might have to an ethic of monogamy. Similarly, when Claire describes her three jobs, she stresses that there is a 'promotional perspective,' in which she presents herself differently from the job she actually does. Heywood's work teaches us that professionalism might not mean following the rules, but in maintaining fidelity to the rules by means of concealing diversions and transgressions.

This book tries to take the institutional context of mental healthcare seriously. The ethnography in this chapter shows how clinical work is shaped by institutional needs and priorities. This shaping might be seen in part as external constraint and in part as diversion, but, most of all, as a kind of intertwining. It isn't that all clinicians respond to institutional needs in the same way. We can see divergences and even contradictions in how concepts like personality are used by different clinicians within the same institution. But we can see that in each case, the institution plays a decisive role. Organisational needs shape how clinicians see patients, how they frame distress and what they do in response. Rebecca and Giles might approach Viv in very different ways if the institutional setting were changed but Viv remained the same. If they weren't responsible for Viv, but could simply offer her a service she could take or leave, then perhaps they would be more honest. Equally, Viv might behave very differently towards Rebecca and Giles if the institutional setting were changed but her predicament remined the same. Imagine, for example, if they talked to her about shame, rather than imposing the bland categories of low mood. In other words, the way that patient distress is understood, recorded and treated by clinicians can depend on how services are constituted. This prompts further questions. For example, to what degree do epistemic movements like evidence-based medicine, and clinical projects like patient self-management and the recovery model arise out of the institutional setting of mental healthcare?

In Claire's account, the impact of the institution on care is not trivial or benign. Claire's three jobs suggest that the gravitational pull of the job she is expected to do negatively impacts the job she actually does and thus harms patients, even if the harm originates outside the medics themselves. This suggests that organisational factors are a source of iatrogenic harm. The job Claire is expected to do appears to be of growing importance, exerting an ever stronger force. If Claire is right, that is likely to reduce the quality of care, but increase the quality of the documentation that represents care. We are more accustomed to thinking of iatrogenic harm as undesirable pharmaceutical effects or disempowering clinical relationships. I suggest that we should recognise the need to further investigate the costs and benefits of bureaucratic accountability in mental healthcare. However, before we return to these questions we start to examine how these effects play out from the patient's point of view.

4

BIPOLAR

The Beautiful Opponent

with Catriona Watson

I was a bright middle class teenager who undertook a gap year. It was an experience (laced with a reaction to anti malaria medication) that triggered latent bipolar illness, which runs in my family. I was nineteen. My psychoeducation and fascination with bipolar, and a big chunk of luck, have helped me find a place where I feel much more at peace with my genes and whatever metaphysical force brings us here in the first place.

I first became unwell whilst teaching in China. I approached my travels with half an eye open to concerns regarding an intrusive and inhumane state presence in the lives of my students, and this theme rather ballooned as I learned more about the society I found myself in. Western ethics and Chinese sensibilities have always been in a cautious relationship – as I grew more tired, frustrated and lonely in a new teaching role it became impossible to see reason from distortion. The Dean of the school I worked for complained when he found out I had quoted the lyrics to Silent Night to my students. The distress this caused me was huge, and it was hard to identify what a 'reasonable' reaction would have been. I feared for the wellbeing of my students. I declared profound homesickness for my mother country, which while being true was also an immensely politic thing to say. No-one would get into trouble. Back in the UK, my family nursed me at home until I declared I felt 'as broken as a china doll'. My Mum, who was a GP at the time, strongly believed that hospital was necessary. I agreed to go to hospital, recognising it as necessary and appropriate, and was admitted immediately as a 'voluntary' patient. No other options had felt appropriate, given the state of disconnect I was in. Being allowed to be the willing one who 'triggered' a voluntary admission that first time, has given me a sense of confidence in my own reasoning that has endured throughout my entire psychiatric career. My family reached in to me, building bridges in

DOI: 10.4324/9781003154235-4

vocabulary, family stories where I learned new things about my family, and offering many opportunities to make my case myself. All my admissions since have been voluntary – this has been important.

At first my diagnosis was uncertain. I was afraid that I was being followed by Chinese government spies and this seemed unlikely, but as a psychotic experience it didn't immediately indicate bipolar. I welcomed the fact that they admitted they didn't know straight away – it suggested that care was being taken to get it right. It took several years before we reached a point where bipolar seemed the best fit, and rather than being 'pure', there was a sense that something else was involved there too. My consultant explained that diagnostic categories of bipolar and schizophrenia aren't absolutes necessarily – some people think they are on a continuum. As a treatment goal we wanted the illness to stay away, and insisting on a 'pure' model wouldn't have helped us. My diagnosis remained that of bipolar (unclassified) and antipsychotic medication (a major tranquiliser) was introduced at a low dose.

Nursing staff also spoke openly about the limitations of meds – describing them as blunt instruments and introducing me to the phrase 'chemical cosh'. My psychiatrist also shared uncertainties about treatment decisions, taking time before introducing major tranquilisers to the existing mood stabiliser. They described 'following the course of the illness' as if it were a river, an image I have always liked, suggesting that to learn about my own personal river, and wait to see what the river would do, was the best approach at that point. Anthony Clare writes that madness is best aligned with medicine, rather than elsewhere, as that is the most compassionate place to keep it. I found this to be so.

In appointments with a psychiatrist I talked about relationships (especially with those important to me and my stability), and medications, (trying to weigh up desired effects against undesired side effects). I also raised questions about myself and my capabilities, and whether experiences (such as problems with sleep) might count as a symptom or a side effect. Here the doctor drew on wider experience and on the latest evidence. He could bring to bear knowledge of evidence but not a discussion of matters of personal taste, although bipolar in its extremes can impact on these. Sometimes the knowledge base brought a kind of hope: 'a euthymic period can last up to sixteen years, maybe even more. So it's really worth doing a good recovery and getting out there again' said one ward consultant. He helped me envision an experience of bipolar that wasn't bringing my life to a complete standstill, as it was at that point. It was easy to agree with, even though I was very down at the time. Having that possibility in front of me has made me adopt a 'make hay while the sun shines' approach – I became much more strategic about how time in between episodes was spent in terms of its long term impact.

Doctors could segue from the domain of evidence into the wider culture and social landscape. One recommended I watch Woody Allen's 'Everybody says I love you' and another, that I read Ian McEwan's novel 'Enduring Love.'

Actually I didn't do either. For me the magic was seeing them enter very genuinely into my experience in a caring way, recognising that life can be hard to navigate for the best of us, and very full of hope and respect for me. Naming everything as pathological didn't feel a solution and I felt their warmth as they proposed an alternative lens to explore my struggles. I felt a rich understanding and valuing of what it is to be human.

At a certain point I was prescribed a PRN dose of a major tranquilliser to accompany the small dose I was already taking routinely (PRN means pro re nata, indicating to be taken when I deemed necessary). I had a small stash I could take when I needed to cool my overheating mind. This was a nego-tiated learning process. I would inform the psychiatrist or CPN that I had done this. Gradually we learned to trust each other with this treatment approach – it developed in sophistication over about ten years, ultimately resulting in my discharge from secondary care. Other long-standing bipolar patients in my friendship network were doing something similar, and between us, we created a secondary network of well-informed, very caring peers. When it seemed someone was becoming unwell, we could offer each other timely advice and support. I call this 'spotting,' borrowing from termi-nology used by circus stilt walkers who use various strategies to protect each other in crowded public places. It's a lovely thing to do for someone you care about, to apply in caring for their bipolar all you have learned about caring for your own. 'Veteran' patients are an incredibly useful resource when I am living with an ongoing mental health vulnerability.

I can now pick up on 'temperature' changes before anyone else becomes aware of them: identifying independently an 'overheating' or 'acceleration' that might benefit from extra meds. The experience is sensory and internal. There is a clinical expression, 'pressure of thought' which precedes 'pressured speech' – these capture the experience beautifully, rather like water coming out of a hose. I can feel overstimulated by life in the public domain and concerned in private by my wishes to achieve things in my preferred way. I might realise I have more thoughts, they are faster and more wide ranging. Sometimes they are more allied to the imaginary or potential, than the real and actual. Sometimes I can make myself laugh out of nowhere – that's one of my bipolar upsides which some people envy. Alongside rest and peace and quiet, meds have a cooling effect, slowing down an overheating engine. Or like turning down the gas underneath a boiling pan. Alongside medication, nursing and therapy helped me learn to see myself in a realistic way, correctly identifying what I am good at and where I need to learn more, acknowledging my actual psychometric shape... This all leads to good, ultimately antipsychotic, decision making, and the creation of a personal reality that works and nourishes me.

Medical language describes 'mixed state', but actually all moods are mixed, and this is one of the things that I think makes bipolar interesting. Nowadays, during euthymia, my moodscape looks as if it falls into five dis-tinct moods: hungry, sad, tired, cross, and 'need for my own headspace'.

These are five basic colours that can blend together like paint to form a subtle variety of hues. These hues are variable like the weather, my mood being distinct from any ambitions or beliefs I hold, or decisions that arise from those beliefs. Certain intense and enduring colourways I would identify as being 'low' or 'high' in medical speak, but knowing my own personal moodscape gives me forewarning long before these subtle blends are apparent to others. Bipolar in euthymic state makes me think of a metaphor of a sleeping pet rat in my pocket. I know she's quietly there breathing, and by misadventure or an absence of care she could be disturbed, frightened, and pee on me. Undisturbed, no one is any the wiser. But it's not a freedom or an absence of illness.

I find 'my bipolar' fascinating. That could sound like a bad thing, to be so thoroughly interested in myself. But in fact, it is a capacity to find myself interesting that has made my recovery possible. Perhaps it is simple extraversion. The shifts and storms of bipolar have never been boring, although occasionally I bored myself with the endless recital of my woes, and I have not regretted having a vivid inner life at all. A bipolar friend of mine was part of a group show for her art foundation diploma. Apparently bipolar was a common theme among the students. My friend laughed – 'it's practically a prerequisite module for the course.' I glowed with pride that I was one of Them. I felt special, part of a vein in society I admired. A diagnosis of bipolar seemed to be a hallmark of some essentially wonderful strangeness, a quality many strive for and fail to achieve. And I had It! I had arrived. My bipolar course would play out in an extraordinary unfolding – all I could do was to show up, be in it, be this thing.

Bipolar is fascinating because of the nature of the suffering, and the assets generated as a result of it. My suffering is a precious birthplace where my survival, growth, recovery, my pulse... beats stronger, a formative process I am proud of, although I can't say I'd wish it on anyone. Surviving multiple bereavements by suicide made me wise and compassionate. Being in therapy showed me to be linguistically creative, and funny. The sensory nature of mania creates an impression on the mindbody that is unforgettable, a memory of being physically audacious and embodied that never leaves. Social exclusion left me with less to lose and made me more entrepreneurial. I can't help but be socially sensitive, but sensitivity has its advantages. And my strong sense of politics and fairness is deeply nourished by the compost of living in institutional care.

But feeling special has had its down sides. My internal world can include such dense metaphors that people can perceive me as unreachable, or unrecognisable. But also, I developed better PR skills, acknowledging that I needed to make allowances for my confused audience. I accepted a responsibility to make myself more understandable, if I was to live in the world as an 'out' bipolar person. A negotiation must be had between my unique strangeness, and the needs of the wider social world. I strongly believe that within all the hurt of bipolar, as we live with a kind of wild, untamed quality of being - this is our beauty. We have no alternative, so we must allow ourselves that small thing. Just as nature throws up birds with astounding plumage, or people with a stronger ability to distinguish smells, or produce twins, ... we have a quality of feeling, noticing, experiencing, minding... that is nothing less than fascinating.

I also feel a kind of political endeavour, an important call to action, to avoid being a 'victim of the system.' I explored my mad identity very deeply in the first few years of my illness. I was initially uncomfortable displaying a concessionary bus pass because it was bright orange and said 'certified disabled'. I didn't initially feel ready for the disabled label, and had my own prejudices about being associated with physical disability stereotypes. But I felt my hidden disability to be a real thing. There are strategic advantages to being able to 'pass as normal' but it can feel like a denial of an important personal truth if things are always sanitised and cleaned up, nothing challenging ever presented. It feels unfair to keep things under wraps, and unrealistic. There is so much more to be gained from owning my personal demons and riding with them. Later, I took the orange pass on.

When I used the orange bus pass, I got odd looks and it felt like people saw me as using it fraudulently. I felt awful. It invited prejudice, offering me no space to express myself as I would like to. Years later, I made the decision to get my driving license reinstated, and lose the formal concessionary pass. I now pay £600 a year for a standard bus pass, the freedom to not use that hated piece of plastic... but to use a near-identical pass to do exactly the same thing. I like carrying my driver's license as ID even though I never felt safe as a driver. 'Normal' paperwork works in my favour, a chance to discuss bipolar on my own terms. When I use my 'normal' pass, I get to dictate the timing, language and context of a conversation about bipolar that affects me. To me, having a handle on the conversation in this way is easily worth the money.

Because I started getting ill at 19, the impacts of bipolar experience played out more severely than they would have done if I had spent more time living as a healthy adult in my early twenties. I didn't achieve a degree after several attempts. To my family a degree was a badge of adulthood. Instead, institutional relationships dominated my social space, and my childhood friends struggled to understand the impacts of my hospital admission - some begged me not to go into hospital and later broke contact. Others felt very differently and put a lot of energy into embracing 'the new Trio.' Hurtful misrepresentations of mental illness in the tabloid press made my experience even more painful. A programme aired on TV about bipolar and stalking, implied that stalking behaviour was a typical bipolar feature. I internalised this message of social distrust and it played out in my thinking, distressingly, for years. I believed the programme to be spreading inaccurate information, but feared others would believe the TV and not me. From that time onwards, I discovered the media had more power than I did over my relationship with the wider public, almost like an inverse celebrity. On the plus side, living in a therapeutic community in my early twenties laid down some excellent foundations that have strongly supported my life with bipolar – as an alternative to higher education it was successful in making my home life more functional, and ultimately made employment more sustainable. But it never goes on my CV, as it doesn't make me more socially recognisable and relatable in the wider world, but less. People haven't thanked me for seeking appropriate and helpful solutions to my mental health problems, and haven't acknowledged when my efforts were successful, other than to lessen exclusion.

During my time in higher education I studied modern languages, sociology, and educational theory, and was especially interested in deviancy theory. It felt very helpful to see how the idea of deviancy played out in an unspoken way in many areas of my life, and how 'unacceptable' stories of self are created about me, without a contribution from me. Learning the sociological and political theory about deviancy and disability has given me a greater understanding of the social codes we are all governed by. This has helped me take some of this stuff less personally.

I don't think I would be able to keep going if I didn't have a sense that nature brings riches to people who are prepared to pay attention. I think it's important to keep an eye open for these observations as they are unsung heroes. Perhaps it's like bird-watching. I strongly believe that within all the hurt of bipolar, we live with an enormous, wonderful, wild beauty. We have no alternative, so we must allow ourselves that.

*

The moment of diagnosis tends to be understood as a decisive discursive event, a moment when the freshwater of self-understanding meets the overwhelming seawater of biomedical knowledge. This framing foregrounds knowledge. The interpretive focus is on knowing, understanding and believing, and shifts in a person's subjectivity through redefinition and reframing. 'Feeling blue' becomes 'having depression.' The 'hunt for meaning' becomes a 'struggle for health.' Common sense is displaced by 'the medical model,' personal intuition by professional expertise, guesswork and informal estimation with evidence and dispassionate judgement. Classifying distress in medical terms might offer patients the comfort of experts who can understand and take responsibility. Equally, the arrival of biomedical knowledge might be ominous, an unwanted intrusion by big pharma and its untrustworthy clinical henchmen.

Social scientists have been concerned for some decades by the properties of medical discourse. Illich saw medical labels as a kind of alien incursion that resembled colonial occupation, redefining and degrading some of our most important human experiences (Illich 1990). Scheff argued that mental health labels are self-fulfilling and self-maintaining (Scheff 1966). Goffman showed how mental health labels stigmatise, 'discrediting' the labelled, 'spoiling' their identity (Goffman 1959, 1963). As discussed in chapter one, Foucault sees medicalisation as an extension of the power of the state, reshaping our subjectivity to create active, efficient neoliberal citizens (Foucault 2004, 2008). These themes continue to drive a lively academic literature. Critics of psychiatry often fear the worst, assuming that the discursive power of biomedicine is irresistible and that the adoption of medical terms and tropes signals the loss of alternate approaches. For example, psychologist Lucy Johnstone argues: 'it is no longer scientifically, professionally or ethically justifiable to insist on psychiatric diagnosis as the only way of describing people's distress and to deny people the opportunity to explore alternatives' (Johnstone 2019: 13).

Catriona's narrative challenges these theories in complex ways. She slides into mental illness. Somehow, homesickness and a perhaps praiseworthy moral engagement with the Chinese state ends up as anxiety and delusion. There is no clear dividing line between normal experience and symptoms, or between biomedical and other forms of knowledge. Medical vocabulary does not take over where homespun interpretation left off, and when medical terms are applied, they offer a very limited purchase on Catriona's distress. Neither Catriona nor the mental health professionals understand quite what is going on. As the years go by, Catriona uses multiple understandings simultaneously, combining terms that belong to diverging and ostensibly incommensurable worlds. She describes her distress as being a matter of both 'genes' and 'metaphysical forces' and presents her early experiences in both standard biomedical terms ('triggering illness') but also uses a more familiar vocabulary of being 'tired' and 'homesick.' She also reworks some medical terms, creating personalised hybrids that cease to correspond to medical dictionary definitions. And behind that, an awareness of the historical specificity of diagnostic thinking gives her a sense of caution and even scepticism towards otherwise authoritative ideas.

Catriona's agency is stressed throughout: she is an actor in her own recovery, observing and learning, taking advice, formulating and pursuing plans. The process of self-monitoring and taking additional PRN medication might be read as an instance of responsibilisation (Rose 2009). According to this view, Catriona has internalised the medical gaze and its ethical priorities to become a good, disciplined neoliberal subject. In a paper on mindfulness, Joanna Cook resists such an interpretation, arguing that viewed from a rich, ethnographic perspective it 'does not account for diversity in the motivations, experiences, and efforts of people practicing self-governance and the collaborative nature of the political processes by which it is promoted' (Cook 2016: 156). We make a similar argument here. Catriona is not being defined, contained or overpowered. She retains political commitments and an awareness of systemic injustice. Medical understandings influence her thinking, but do not expel or discredit other takes on distress. Instead they enter a fluid discursive world, subject to continued re-examination and re-interpretation. She is able, in Johnstone's terms, to explore alternatives, but without rejecting biomedicine.

One way of expressing the relationship between disparate discursive resources is through the figure of weaving. This is a way of capturing how divergent, even competing or contradictory knowledges may be brought together by agential individuals to become distinguishable but inseparable parts of a larger, functioning whole. In a memorable ethnography of a hectic psychiatric emergency ward in the United States discussed in chapter one, Lorna Rhodes vividly describes how clinicians deal with being placed in difficult, almost impossible positions by talking about care and making records of care using terms from a range of sources to create what she calls a 'patchwork quilt' (Rhodes 1995). 'The staff…were bricoleurs of psychiatric and social theory, using what was available according to whether it would fit a particular context…at any moment, and sometimes all in the same moment, a staff member might be a biological empiricist, a Freudian or a Laingian antipsychiatrist' (ibid.: 4). For Rhodes this mixing and switching is pragmatic, enabling staff to be conceptually nimble. It isn't always clear what they really believe, or if they really believe anything, but they know how to get the job done. In an elegant monograph on psychiatry in Iran, Behrouzan applies the figure of weaving to patients (Behrouzan 2016). She is critical of reductive notions of medicalisation noting that the 'psychiatrically medicalised individuals' she works with nonetheless exhibit autonomy and creativity as they weave together 'biomedical tenets with various discourses of Iranian affect: from mysticism to war-related feeling states, from stoicism to institutionalised codes of conduct, from poetic intricacies to globalising desires for happiness' (ibid.: 214). As with Rhodes' hard pressed doctors, this kind of pragmatic, inventive engagement cannot be inferred from biomedical logics and offers enlarged expressive range.

Both Catriona and her doctors appear to be weaving patchwork quilts. Catriona uses medical terms like 'psychosis' and 'euthymia' but also of her 'brain overheating' and of medication being 'like turning down the gas.' For her, thinking biomedically, rather than desocialising her distress, creates ties of relatedness, linking to family members who also suffer from mental illness, and to her mother's occupation as a GP. She finds that the link between madness and medicine is compassionate. The clinicians she describes also display a complex and qualified relationship with medical knowledge. They present the diagnostic categories of bipolar disorder and schizophrenia as fuzzy and as existing on a spectrum, and introduce medication as a blunt instrument, even a cosh, not a magic bullet. We might push the figure of weaving a little further. Weaving is productive, creating cloth that is designed and functional. And here, doctor and patient alike draw on biomedical and other sources, for clear and divergent purposes. Both types of meaning-making are explicitly oriented towards activity. For Catriona, that means making sense of her experiences and promoting better mental health. For the doctors, it is a way of responding to the affordances of their workplace.

Clinicians often explicitly teach patients medical terms and suggest that medical knowledge is helpful in bringing self-understanding and so establishing the preconditions for effective self-management. This is sometimes called psychoeducation, and framed in mental healthcare as an 'adjunct' therapy, to be delivered as a pedagogical intervention alongside medication. Our ethnography challenges the claim that specialist knowledge is superior to lay knowledge. In formal representations of knowledge, bipolar is framed by mental health professionals as a 'mood disorder.' Moods are said to be feelings felt in the moment that are either positive or negative, and more or less intense, and can be pathological if they last too long and interfere with 'function.' An excessive amount of low mood is depression. In a recent publication intended for medical students and junior doctors, it is stated: 'The main difference between normal sadness and a mood disorder is that normal sadness is usually a temporary state strongly relating to the person's current situation, whereas mood disorder is a more persistent pervasive change in mood which affects social and occupational functioning' (McKnight et al 2019: 259). The authors go on: 'Bipolar disorder... is, in essence, an intensification of the mood variability that we all experience, due to a relative lack of the homeostatic mechanisms that keep mood stable (ibid.: 276). In clinical care, moods are understood to include bodily experiences like sleep, appetite, and energy levels. They are quantified using questionnaires and rating scales. One such scale is the Quick Inventory of Depressive Symptoms-Self Report (QIDS-SR) scale, that measures depression (Rush et al 2003). The QIDS consists of 16 questions each of which is scored from 0–3. Questions concern sleep, appetite and weight, plus 'feeling sad,' 'view of self,' feelings of 'restlessness,' 'sense of self-worth,' 'energy level,' 'feeling slowed down' and 'thoughts of death or suicide'. For example, question 11 ('view of myself') offers the following options: 'I see myself as equally worthwhile and deserving as other people,' which scores 0; 'I am more self-blaming than usual', which scores 1; 'I largely believe I cause problems for others', which scores 2; and 'I think almost constantly about major and minor defects in myself,' which scores 3.

Catriona has appropriated and enriched, even customised, the notion of mood. The conceptual innovations she developed arose out of the experience of managing her mental health. Her five moods differ not in degree but in kind and combine to create complex personal 'moodscapes.' These moodscapes have a cognitive aspect, in that her thoughts may be faster or slower, and more or less metaphorical, but also a sensory and embodied aspect. They can't be quantified. Instead, they produce a richer sense of inner life than is possible on a simple continuum between low and high. These subtler categories appear to offer Catriona a more promising basis for self-monitoring and self-management than the ideas of McKnight et al or the QIDS scale. If she finds herself 'overheating' or 'accelerating' Catriona can take steps to reverse or mitigate the effects by tweaks in lifestyle and medication. And if she needs to talk with mental health professionals she knows how to translate these ideas into the simplistic medical up/down binary.

That repeatedly completing questionnaires like the QIDS can be irksome to service users is understandable. Patients and their families can be surprised to find that medical terms that can be used to deny a person their liberty are largely undefined, untheorized, and speculative. But it would be a mistake to see this as a problem that is arbitrary or unpredictable or forced by a lack of knowledge or resources. As discussed in chapter one, clinical categories enable clinicians to operate within particular institutional settings. In this sense, the intended audience is not Catriona or her family, but other clinicians, managers and regulators. The simplifications and reductions enable staff members to behave in legible, reproducible, defensible ways. Clinical knowledge is in Adams' terms, *actionable* (Adams 2013). If a person is said to have 'low mood,' that authorises a decision to give them antidepressants. If the mood gets worse, the dose can be increased. Using the same terms as the basis for psychoeducation is thus problematic. Clinical descriptions have a limited capacity to deepen a person's self-understanding and might not be well suited to service user efforts towards self-understanding or self-governance. There seems to be an inevitable payoff here. Catriona's personalised terms appear to be components of effective self-management but don't make her legible and don't help clinicians make decisions.

The epistemic orientation of understandings of mental healthcare can obscure relationality. For many patients, relationships with clinicians are central to their experiences of ill health. The information and advice offered by clinicians can be a means of establishing and enriching relationships. In the classic recovery narrative, a patient is reassured by diagnosis and able to turn biomedical knowledge into a transformative story (Woods et al 2022). Catriona remarks 'institutional relationships dominated my social space.' Her team share with her their uncertainty and doubt about both diagnosis and treatment. Catriona describes liking this 'because it suggested care was being taken.' She is reassured not by knowledge but by connection. When a psychiatrist recommended a film and a novel, Catriona didn't actually follow the advice. What was important – the 'magic' – was relational, being seen and cared for: an I-thou moment of attention and acceptance. The evolving arrangements for PRN medication enable a more flexible and responsive approach to medication, but the process also involves the building of mutual trust and cooperation. In her monograph on care, Stevenson describes how gestures of care are necessarily particular: 'In such moments, we recognise the uniqueness/specificity of the being in front of us (that he or she could not be otherwise) and a specific (and necessarily reductive) identity is not what, at that moment, is demanded' (Stevenson 2014: 166). Catriona is aware of moments when services are caring. Her time as a patient has involved emotional labour, seeking to elicit meaningful care from practitioners operating within an insensitive bureaucratized system.

This supportive sociality extends into an informal supportive network of people with bipolar. Paul Rabinow described how medical discourse generates a particular form of social life, which he called biosociality (Rabinow

1996). The benefits of biosociality, such as no longer feeling alone and recognising common experiences, turn harmful disorders into positive social connection. Emily Martin, herself diagnosed with bipolar, is sensitive to the inherent contradictions in mental health support groups: 'Even if the fabric is a taxonomy of *pathological* conditions, at least it lies within the realm of *vital* social relations' (Martin 2007: 147). Catriona suggests a disjunction between a pathological condition and vital social relations in her group by coining the term 'spotting' to capture how the group have their own skills in noticing each other's state of health and offering advice. Group members do not reproduce the medical gaze and its simple repertoire of calculations and decisions but have their own expertise based on personal experience of bipolar living in an overwhelmingly non-bipolar world. This is a chance to put hard-won wisdom to good use, to be valued and needed, to be able to enter sustaining relationships that are reciprocal and symmetrical.

Experiences of stigma are central to the ethnography of mental illness. Elizabeth Carpenter-Song describes how people who have recovered from the acute stages of schizophrenia in the US still find themselves 'saturated' by stigma (Carpenter-Song 2009). Stigma may outweigh the illness itself. It is a topic widely discussed by clinicians and service users as well as in the media and online. However, quite what stigma is remains a matter of contention. Goffman describes stigma as 'spoiled identity' and presents it as disadvantageous to a person in the competitive theatre of everyday life (Goffman 1963). Within biomedicine, accounts tend to be epistemically oriented, suggesting that stigma arises out of ignorance or false beliefs that might be remedied by education (Thornicroft 2006). Eli Clare makes a contrary argument, suggesting that biomedical ideas create stigma because they construct and valorise normality, and frame distress or disability as pathology that should be addressed or cured by medical intervention (Clare 2017: 15). According to Clare, even if a person dissents from what he calls the medical industrial complex, they struggle to evade the stigmatising implications of being understood as a sick person in need of a cure. All these approaches take the power of discourse very seriously. We might reflect that proximity to suffering is painful and challenging and stigma is a kind of defence, a means of defusing the affective and ethical challenge implicit in apprehending human suffering.

Catriona recognises her own capacity to stigmatise ('I had my own prejudices'). Her appraisal of stigma is less centred on reputational damage or competitive disadvantage than her capacity to contribute to the way she is represented. Catriona wants to 'handle conversations in her own way' and is prepared to spend £600/year to avoid using a bus pass that reveals her disability because using a disabled pass signals losing control of how she is understood. Although popular misrepresentations of mental illness, for example focussing on stalking, or as being in some sense unreal, are a particular source of concern, this take on stigma suggests that other kinds of externally dictated representation might also be stigmatising. This includes the reductions and simplifications of biomedical expediency but also non-coproduced ethnography.

Bipolar disorder is painful, frustrating and stigmatising, but Catriona also finds it fascinating and special. 'Just as nature throws up birds with astounding plumage, or people with a stronger ability to distinguish smells, or produce twins, … we have a quality of feeling, noticing, experiencing, minding.' Bipolar locates her within a population that possesses valuable qualities, such as an intense inner life and creativity. It is an opponent, but it is also beautiful, a rat in her pocket, a concealed intimate companion, potentially shocking but not unloved. It cannot simply be reduced to pathology and vulnerability. It is sometimes taken to be counterintuitive that people might want to be thought of as mentally unwell. For example, in '"I want to be bipolar"…a new phenomenon,' Chan and Sireling find it puzzling that patients express a desire to be diagnosed with bipolar and suggest that 'the implicit association of bipolar disorder with celebrity status and creativity' lead to people seeking out the diagnosis (Chan & Sireling 2010: 109). The phrase celebrity status carries a hint of condescension. It sounds like an unworthy, suspect and possibly pathological motive. We might wonder if a study by the same authors would consider an association with celebrity status as a motive for students to choose a career in medicine.

But it can be difficult for clinicians to know how to apprehend positive or desirable aspects of mental disorder. For Catriona, the relation between a bipolar diagnosis and creativity is not an 'implicit association' but part of the wider lived experience of feeling, noticing, experiencing and minding. It is painful. But, in her account, Catriona is not an inert container for painful and pathological feelings. The experiences are part of a gradually transformative process. Catriona has been changed by bipolar and these changes are part of her recovery. Medications and nursing have been important, necessary, perhaps, but not sufficient, in her journey. It is indicative of just how pliable medical descriptions can be that there seems to be no clear distinction between phenomena that might be understood as symptomatic of bipolar disorder and phenomena that might be understood as part of an effective strategy to recover from bipolar disorder. For Catriona the insights and self-knowledge generated by the experiences of bipolar have been part of her recovery.

Bipolar leads to social discontinuities that are a complex mix of painful and pleasant, wished for and involuntary. As a consequence of labelling but also the 'unique' and 'strange' lived experience of bipolar, Catriona finds herself othered. She is less recognisable and relatable, and her experiences can be hard to communicate. It may be that Catriona's rich personal understanding of bipolar, even as it enables self-understanding and promotes recovery, itself sometimes separates her from the world of consensual meaning. But this is a social process. Bridget Bradley describes how activism and support become bound together as bio-solidarity (Bradley 2021). As a member of a neglected and excluded minority whose struggles and achievements are neither acknowledged nor appreciated, Catriona is involved in advocacy efforts to change public perceptions of bipolar and in pursuit of this engages with biomedical and social scientific discourse. Working on this book is an instance of such efforts.

The game

There is a disparity between 'my' bipolar as it is represented in this chapter, how my doctors understand it, and how the DWP evaluates it. In the theatre, an actor playing the part of a mad person might hold their head in their hands. This isn't actually how mad people typically behave, but the gesture is a well-recognised shorthand, a way of conveying madness. The DLA claim forms set out their review of evidence with a similar kind of shorthand. The statements require me to 'hold my head'. They focus on a description of specific and external experiences as evidence of something unseen, ignoring the need for a context where the disclosure of unseen experiences feels safe. Examples of DLA theatricality are an over-emphasis on outbursts, suicidal ideation, panic attacks, hospital admissions, or talking to myself in public. These discussions are at the expense of internal manifestations of illness, such as bodily sensations, sensory changes, mental activity, 'unusual' beliefs, mood... a person's own values, the beliefs and losses they have accumulated during their psychiatric career, and their relationship with their own suffering. The forms also demand that I fully affirm these statements are 'true and complete,' forcing me into insincerity.

It took me 13 years after DLA was first introduced for me to apply for it... and then it was because my family believed it would have an increasing impact on future benefit claims I would need to make. This turned out to be prescient, as DLA has now become the default tool by which entitlement to access and support services is delivered, and it is not led by medical expertise. It took 18 months with professional benefits· advice, and multiple drafts, to complete the form - a damaging and highly unpalatable process. The distress forms cause is not discussed on the forms themselves, however. Dependency and vulnerability in the face of this struggle are a big part of the illness experience.

I dislike 'playing the game.' As a stance it doesn't fit with my personal ethics. I sought advice from an experienced benefits advisor of high professional standing, who carefully interview me, helping open out aspects of my life that we could 'use' for the claim. 'Tell me about your habits... Would you say that there are some places you never go...? Do you feel safe where you do go....? Would you say that when you go elsewhere that you feel less safe...? badly unsafe?' Any woman could answer this degree of exploration with a suggestion she uses 'safe routes.' And although it was factually true, I never normally look at my life that way. I was required to use concepts I

*don't usually use, and the form distorts what I perceive my experience to be.
I have to embrace these new concepts and work them into my truth telling
with as little jarring as possible. In this way I build up the picture, as I reply to
Question 36, that I do indeed 'need help when I am outdoors'.*

In August 2008 Catriona made a claim for Disability Living Allowance
(DLA). DLA was a benefit for people with a mental or physical disability who
had 'personal care needs' or 'mobility needs.' It was established by the Social
Security Contributions and Benefits Act 1992. In the 2000s, patients receiving
secondary mental healthcare from the NHS were often in receipt of multiple
benefits. Claimants could be in work or out of work to claim DLA. People out
of work might be eligible for Employment and Support Allowance. Council
Tax Benefit and Housing Benefit were administered by the council. DLA was
phased-out for the majority of claimants between 2013 and 2015 and
replaced by a new Personal Independence Payment. The form in use when
Catriona made her claim was the 'DLA 1 Adult April 2007.' It consisted of 47
pages divided into eleven sections. There were a total of 62 questions, some
of which were divided into multiple parts containing sub questions. There are
both tick boxes and free text. The form constructs mobility and personal care
as independent variables. Mobility needs may be assessed at a lower or higher
rate, whilst personal care could be assessed at lower, middle or higher rate.
The wording on the DLA form is straightforward and accessible, containing
some disarmingly informal phrases: 'keep an eye on you,' 'wandering off.' On
the back of the final page is an insignia 'Crystal Mark 14689 Clarity approved
by the Plain English Campaign.' We suggest that although the form uses
untechnical, everyday vocabulary and sentence construction, this is far from
plain English. The DLA form – and others like it – constitutes a subtle language
game with its own rules, conventions and grammar.

Section one, called 'About you' asked thirteen questions about nationality,
residence and contact details. The next section contained questions 14 to 24
'About your illnesses or disabilities and the treatment or help you receive.'
Questions relate to diagnosis, treatment and tests, and the details of a hospital doctor and GP. The phrasing of questions and the guidance in subsequent sections makes it explicit what to say. In Section three, 'Getting
around outdoors' (questions 25 to 37) the guidance indicated that claimants
unable to walk at all, or whose walking was 'severely restricted as a result of
physical disability' might get the mobility component of DLA at the higher
rate, whilst those who 'cannot walk outdoors in unfamiliar places without
guidance or supervision from another person most of the time due to a
mental-health problem or physical disability' may be entitled to the mobility
component at the lower rate. This makes the form transparent but it also
makes it discreetly coercive. Certain approved forms of words are
announced as legible, others are not.

A key concept on the form is a need for the presence of another person for
'help' or 'encouragement' or 'supervision.' Their presence is attached to

particular activities or locations and particular periods of the day and night. The form defines personal care as 'needing help or supervision…with everyday tasks like getting in or out of bed, dressing, washing, taking part in certain hobbies, interests or religious activities, or help with communication.' To be eligible for the highest level, a person may 'need help with personal care or need someone to keep an eye on you to prevent danger to yourself or others, during the day or night'. The threshold for the lower rate was described as 'you may not be able to plan or prepare a freshly cooked meal on a traditional cooker (in other words not using a microwave or convenience foods)…or have care needs for some time during the day.' The form states that this additional overseeing person may not actually be present. This gives the questions a hypothetical or counterfactual quality. The form asks claimants to imagine a different life, something richer, or safer, or fuller than they already experience, brought about by the presence of an enabling other. This begins to explain why Catriona uses the figure of theatrical gestures that convey meaning indirectly to convey the relationship between her understanding of bipolar and the way it is represented on the DLA form. From a philosophical point of view, it is a matter of debate as to whether counterfactual claims can have a truth value. In other words, it isn't clear whether it is possible for Catriona to answer truthfully because the form requires her to make statements describing states of affairs that did not exist. This affects some questions more than others. A claimant might find it easy to answer truthfully the tick box: 'I need help to use a shower' if she is able either to use a shower without problem, or if showering is out of the question without help. But question 41 is more challenging: 'I need encouraging or reminding about washing, bathing, showering or drying.' For a claimant living alone, the likely effects of an encouraging and reminding other might be a matter of pure speculation. Does needing help mean that the washing, bathing, showering or drying wouldn't ever be performed without that help? Or would it be performed less often? Perhaps it would be different in some other way, depending on the personal qualities of the other. An irritating other might generate stubbornness regarding washing, bathing, showering or drying. Similarly, statements like 'I am at risk of self neglect,' 'I am at risk of self harm,' 'I am at risk of wandering' have complex and uncertain logical properties.

Catriona ends up being as truthful as possible, but is conscious of being drawn into an uncomfortable complicity with the form. She is asked to confirm that her account is true and complete, yet we can see that in many respects no DLA form can be either. These effects can be illustrated by considering how Catriona responded to questions about mobility. The sections asks whether the claimant can walk, or if there are 'physical problems that restrict your walking' such as 'you walk with a heavy limp, a stiff leg or shuffle' or agree that 'I would injure myself without physical support.' Question 29 asked 'Please tick the box that best describes your walking speed' offering three alternatives: Normal or Moderate (about 51 metres or more a minute), Slow (about 40 to 50 metres a minute) and Very slow (less than 40 metres a minute). Of more relevance to mental health was question 34 'Do you need someone with you to guide or supervise you when walking outdoors in unfamiliar places?' Tick boxes include: 'I may get lost or wander off' and 'I have anxiety or panic attacks.' Question 36 included a half page of free text where the claimant was invited to respond to 'Is there anything else you want to tell us to help us understand the help you need with walking outdoors?'

Bipolar has been disabling. Not especially in regard to symptoms which come and go, but because of the impacts of illness. My access to educational opportunities has been impaired by bipolar. My enduring difficulties with concentration make reading difficult; going back to Uni or attending a formal course was unachievable, because I couldn't do the background reading. My disturbed education has affected my working life, and consequently my social presentation, even to the point where I felt I was living in a parallel universe relative to others of comparable age and ability. Where a degree was supposed to be evidence of a measure of intelligence, work ethic and social skill, in not completing mine, I couldn't produce this useful evidence. My intelligence, work ethic and skill remained the same, but instead these attributes weren't evidenced in the same way. Essentially, I became unrecognisable to mainstream life.

I won't deny I wrote my answers on the DLA application with an eye for my audience. My understanding is that someone, not medically qualified, who sees a huge pile of these forms and is working to a target, does the first screening. Not every form will get in front of an informed decision maker. So the intended impact was to seem as appalling as possible. Manic depression sounds much worse than bipolar. The greater the variety of drugs, the more serious the illness, surely, so I listed every PRN intervention, because the person checking your form won't know what those letters mean. I claimed when I did, because I'd recently been in hospital and that's often a good window for a claim, if you're going to make one at all. Why waste the opportunity when it comes?

Later, in preparation for a DWP 'assessment,' I began to keep notes in case I needed to use them in the interview. Then, I would stick the notes in the envelope, and hide it. It is not good in bipolar to behave like this - thoughts can build on thoughts, piranha-esque, so it's important not to set up cues that can trigger invasive and painful thoughts that would probably not arise otherwise. Even now, I can still hardly bear to open the envelope. The notes are still filed away where I won't come across them in the course of my everyday life - still hidden from my eyes and my mind. In demanding a 'complete' account, I think the DWP are over-stating their right of access to my medical history. Confidential medical treatment, in clinic time with my psychiatrist, doesn't, in my view, have to be shared with anyone unless I choose to share it. 'Crystal' clear language doesn't mean the request for information is reasonable.

I was deeply affected by the legal statement I had to sign at the end of the claim: 'I declare that the information I have given on this form is correct and complete as far as I know and believe. I understand that if I knowingly give false information, I may be liable to prosecution or other action.' Throughout the 17 months this form-filling took, it felt as if there was a strong emphasis on truth. Humiliating news accounts abounded of people who had been 'caught' making 'false claims.' Similarly, I had my own personal standards. I had personal pride and I didn't want to beg or say something that is demeaning in order to get this cash. I didn't want to compromise on my own moral standards, or set up a way of framing my experiences that would make them more painful and more dangerous. Everyone who completes a DLA claim knows the awfulness of the process...We just have to 'play the game' and try not to ponder it too deeply. 'Points mean prizes!' like a horrid, demeaning game show. But the alternative was the threat of destitution.

I was awarded DLA 'indefinitely.' Rightly and wrongly, it has been enabling, improving access to services in financial and bureaucratic ways. It was a means to an end. It is right that people whose lives have been shaped by illness, and excluded in many ways, should have support from a social welfare process that protects all. It's a shame that DLA was the solution we all ended up with.

A main argument of this book is that mental health problems that demand sensitivity, care and attention, bring people into contact with clinicians working within impersonal, algorithmic bureaucracies. Our interest here is not whether the bureaucratic instruments work well in determining who is eligible for benefits, but how the process impacts on Catriona. Contact with the DWP can be seen as revealing particularly uncomfortable, even disquieting features of the encounter between health and bureaucracy. At several points, Catriona expresses regret at the pain caused by the DLA form. She describes it as demeaning and compromising. The literature suggests several ways of understating this.

Ben Kafka draws on psychoanalysis and literary theory to investigate the extraordinary affective power of bureaucratic paperwork: 'I take it as a given that our encounters with paperwork and the people who handle it inevitably reactivates some of our earliest wishes, conflicts and fantasies about maternal provision, paternal authority, sibling rivalry or whichever familial division of labour happened to be in place in our childhoods' (Kafka 2012: 16). It is beyond the scope of this book to explore Catriona's familial division of labour, but we might be wise to retain a sense of the depths we are negotiating around. What Kafka calls 'the psychic life of paperwork' is likely to contribute to the kinds of deeper struggles that notions like moral injury gesture towards. One effect of bureaucratic encounters, according to Kafka, is that it makes us all feel powerless. We don't know if the unseen assessors of the form Catriona completed felt as powerless as she did, but, given the limited scope for discretion it offers them, it seems likely. The same language that Catriona uses on the form are also part of the required vocabulary of the clinic where they are used to discuss intimate, personal and highly painful experiences, to build trust and create moments of connection. But on the DLA form, these terms are used in absence of personal relationships to assess impairments and eligibility to payments in a context that is characterised by a lack of trust, even of suspiciousness.

In chapter one we discussed how the shortcomings of documentation are often seen in terms of 'epistemic degradation.' The 'real world' is too subtle and complex for simplified, standardised forms of knowledge, built out of replicable, schematic categories. We might see the DLA as an instance of a technology that makes the world legible and manipulable, but only at a price. The epistemic limitations of the form are striking. Organised around impairment rather than clinical decision making, or personal meaning making, the questions are narrow and, even for open text sections, the wording and guidance indicates only a small number of acceptable answers. It doesn't assess capacity to work, to fulfil caring roles, or to pursue a meaningful life. The form mentions physical pain and discomfort but does not refer to mental pain, other than anxiety and panic. There is no sense that a mental disorder might change a person's preferences.

In this strict discursive environment, Catriona's bipolar takes a distinctive, and, for Catriona, unwelcome, shape. DWP bipolar is located a considerable distance from Catriona's personal account described above. The acts of simplification, the need to consider how best to present her disability, the imaginative projection in response to counterfactuals embedded in the questions, all push her to the edge of dishonesty. It is a kind of moral injury. The notion of moral injury was developed independently by Shay and Bica and is used increasingly to understand the experiences of soldiers returning from war whose ongoing distress is not well captured by the notion of PTSD (Shay 1994; Bica1999). Where combat experiences contradict a person's moral beliefs, the dissonance between the two lead to guilt, blame and remorse, but also confusion and uncertainty, even disorientation (Molendijk 2018). Tellingly, the notion of moral injury diverges from PTSD because, rather than suggesting the distress arises out of cognitive distortions, the notion of moral injury takes ethical experiences seriously, as a painful but not disordered moral struggle. The DLA form contravene Catriona's personal ethics by forcing her to represent herself in ways that are, at best, theatrical gestures. The distress may be more intense because the process is impersonal. In her study of food documentation in Italy, Cavanaugh notes that sociability is essential to make good the representation shortcomings of paperwork (Cavanaugh 2016). The brusqueness of tick boxes can be leavened by warmth and good humour of personal interaction. In mental healthcare, rather than being the flexible means of getting things done, relationships are an effective part of care itself. But when a person applies for disability benefits, the performative power of documentation plays out without the benefits of sociability. Catriona found an intermediate sociality in the benefits advisor, but the impersonality of the exchanges with the DWP ultimately felt abrasive.

Although clinicians sometimes present themselves as advocates or champions on behalf of patients facing the might of the DWP, underlying institutional continuities challenge this stance. Biomedical terms are examples of what Bowker and Starr call 'boundary objects' in that they cross institutional frontiers and 'inhabit several communities of practice and satisfy the informational requirements of each of them' (Bowker & Starr 1999: 297)[Q4]. Psychiatry is not founded on a model of good or successful mental health, but relies on an imagined distinction between function and lack of function that is deemed to coincide with the distinction between health and pathology. Ill health is thus linked to impairment and disability. The DLA form that Catriona completed is as much the natural habitat of terms like bipolar disorder as is the clinic or the research labs of pharmaceutical companies. And when in conversation with a mental health professional, these other meanings and registers can never be entirely absent.

Entrepreneurship and decluttering: the self-built lifeboat

I have always found tidying my home to be immensely comforting and soothing. Initially, I wasn't aware how it was helping. What I was doing was reasserting my own personal space in the midst of an otherwise lively social environment, reinstating 'my' orderliness. It assists background reflection, while at the same time I wasn't really thinking of anything. I first called it 'picking things up and putting them down therapy,' but as time went on, this coping strategy became the seed of a business idea. Clear Space for Me, a decluttering service, was born. During this time, I was volunteering at a fair-trade cooperative, a highly ordered and systematised work environment. At the cooperative, there were established ways of working which I found led to productivity and – especially – harmony. My personal habit of good organisation was made even more intentional. I find good organisation conserves our interpersonal energies and eases stress in our emotional lives. We can have terrible cards in our hand but play them well, and organisational skills can compensate where talent or health is lacking.

Although decluttering isn't a treatment, it is a helping service – quite a lot is already formalised and known about good ways to help strangers, and I found completing a personal coaching training, and subsequent membership of a professional coaching organisation, was also a necessary conceptual structure to hang all these bits of learning into. Clients sometimes wanted reassurance that my clinical background was adequate. My own client experience was an important part of my approach. Client insights have been incredibly valuable, and guidance during my coaching training around reflective practice has been incredibly useful for me and crucial for clients with whom I sometimes had quite a long arc, sometimes over ten consecutive months. From time to time, my personal psychotherapy space did extend intentionally into sessions for the specific exploration of how I engaged with clients, paid for with business income. I learned a great deal – about life, and myself – during this self-employment phase. I met development needs that voluntary work hadn't been able to satisfy, and the recovery/ personal development/ professional development space began to resonate with the person I was capable of becoming, rather than the wounds of my past.

I did permitted work for a while in retail and came across a decluttering book that listed a lot of online resources related to decluttering (Sue Kay, No More Clutter). I came across the APDO website through it, and discovered that decluttering is actually 'a thing'. I thought: I love this, but this is something that other people do – I could never do this. I had a brilliant employment coach who helped me see myself as one of these people and envision a way into this unusual field of work. Previously our conversations had been about business admin which had always seemed so boring and didn't seem to be a world where a person like me would fit in all that well. It was obvious that I did need to at least give decluttering a go. I had no dependents and felt more free to take a business risk. I discovered that self-employment was acceptable in the long term as Supported Permitted Work on ESA, and from then on there was really nothing to stop me trying. The paperwork became increasingly complex, but the support and guidance I had from the MIND benefits team was outstanding.

Once I started my business, I found that the entrepreneurial demands placed on me, at a tempo of my own choosing, offered tremendous rehabilitation opportunities for me, aside from the service I offered my clients. In my own time, I could develop my fit. My first approach was to declutter friends' houses for free. They volunteered as 'guinea pigs', on the condition that they tell me everything that was good or bad, that I discreetly document the work in photographs and in my blog, and get a testimonial. I learned through practice, and from their feedback I was able to bring together a kind of decluttering bedside manner, cobbled from my own client experience and clumsy faux pas as a new kind of professional. My research and development phase lasted for two years. During this time I worked in a pro bono way for over 150hrs. I blogged about it regularly, as I had a sense that writing about my work as I went along helped me take my learning more seriously. Later, I had trainings from APDO, the Association of Professional Declutterers and Organisers (www.apdo.co.uk). The training was about business planning and communication as well as specific issues in decluttering, as there was a sense that declutters are born that way, not made. Their training helped me turn fuzzy instinct into something much more realistic and evidence-based. The peer relationships and accountability formed through APDO were also valuable in shaping the learning, and surviving the entrepreneurial highs and lows.

Everything was shaped by the DWP 'Permitted Work' mould. Work and illness co-existed - there were restrictions on earnings and the number of hours of work I was permitted to do, to allow for this incongruence. APDO also shaped the context – they insisted I had to charge clients if I were to remain part of their organisation, and also saw payment as part of an approach that valued me, my work, my learning, and the work clients and I do together. So thoroughness and professionalism wasn't a choice at all. Ultimately the administrative rigour required of me by the DWP, and the professionalism by APDO, brought about an experience I would definitely call 'therapeutic work.' The DWP concept of 'remunerative' work within self-employed permitted work framework was hard to grasp at first, and interpretations of this aspect of legis-lation were hard to come by even from very experienced benefits advisers. However, I eventually discovered that short training courses didn't count within the hours limit. I gained qualifications in book-keeping and personal coaching, undertook further study in writing for business, and trained briefly with a voice coach. Clear Space for Me had provided the developmental context I had needed – a genuine interface of the psychiatric world with everyday life, with my realistic learning needs at the heart.

My self-employment involved very carefully earning where I could (and sometimes turning clients away) and judiciously spending where I needed to, to be sure that I didn't make too much profit. I kept a time audit to measure how much time I spent on various activities, such as client contact time, finance, marketing, training, and APD -related accountability. In the end, a weird and stressful sequence of three identical proforma ques-tionnaires, inappropriate to my circumstances entirely, were sent to me. I wrote back to the DWP enclosing three consecutive months' profit and loss statements, explaining that the information they wanted was available to them from my tax return which they already had access to, and not from payslips which had never needed to be created by Clear Space For Me. I said I would be grateful if they 'could confirm that these documents were satisfactory', and they never wrote back. The message I took away was that if they could find the time they would be interested in finding grounds to challenge this and are keeping their options open. My suspicion seems justified in contacts with the DWP. Tax law and GDPR legislation require me to keep certain business documentation for a longer period of time, and obviously this material would be available to a DWP representative who wanted to explore what had happened. I don't think this fear will ever go away. Ultimately, permitted work conditions made it impossible for the business to succeed financially. However, I took the learning I gained from the experience to be my most advantageous outcome. With every word, every action of Clear Space for Me, I navigated this balance of sickness and health. I had a sense that I was building a canoe out of a tree, Robinson Crusoe-like, from an isolated island, and floating, extraordinarily, to a new shore, the becoming of a recognisable social entity. I now work in a part time role as assistant manager in someone else's business. Finally I had achieved what the DWP had wanted, and had simultaneously made impossible, for me to do. I 'came off the sick.'

Over a year later things still seem to be OK. It is a threshold in an important way, but it is not 'the end' of a need to self-manage, or my belief that bipolar can return to cause some of the problems I've had before. I increasingly value concepts of blurriness and messiness in how I describe my mental health. Holding solidarity with the bipolar world, by continuing to share my diagnosis with others, is a mark of gratitude for the help I had, some of which isn't available to current bipolar newbies and it is disrespectful to their struggle to pretend the help wasn't necessary. I have found that help in learning self-management in bipolar has segued to management of lots of things. I want to contribute to a wider public conversation where people who have lived with bipolar for a long time and who are not coping with new and frightening acute symptoms, can build a supportive cultural reservoir, a known perspective of a life with bipolar that is a life you'd actually want to be living.

5

LEARNING TO BE ILL, LEARNING TO BE WELL

Learning to be disenchanted

My career as a mental health patient started in the late 1990s and went on for about ten years. During this time, mental health professionals frequently asked me to tell them about myself. At first it was *Tell me about your childhood* or *How long have you felt like this?* Later on, once I become more known and more proficient, it was more *how are you feeling? How are things going?* The setting was sometimes a drab, anonymous clinic room, but sometimes I was at home. Just occasionally I was on a ward. I gradually learned the kind the story they were looking for. When they asked about my childhood, for example, I was unable to locate trauma or neglect in what were safe and secure early years, but I could tell them about an inner turbulence that started when I was young and was neither shared nor approved of by my immediate family. I had a sense that the volume of my inner world was set a little higher, or that the metaphysical challenges of existence pressed more heavily on me. Or, perhaps, that I was a little neurotic (even, self-indulgent). None of this was very pronounced. It might not even have been noticeable to others. Looking back, I wonder if my family's rather guarded emotional style magnified my awareness of these qualities and led me to promote them in my accounts of myself. One advantage of stressing these features was that it meant I had something to give the clinicians in answer to their questions. This was important. Clinical appointments are reciprocal. The professionals asked me a lot of questions, and, in return, I needed to have something to give back.

This quality that I'm calling 'inner turbulence' is ambiguous, without determinate shape or meaning. It could indicate psychopathology but might also be a thoughtful engagement with the mysteries of life. It might and might not be classed as unstable mood. Did I have profound metaphysical

DOI: 10.4324/9781003154235-5

sensibilities, or should we think more of failings of character? Perhaps I was just abnormally intense. Who can say? I am not suggesting that all narrative are valid. Some claims are false, others are true. I didn't experience neglect, for example, and any narrative about me that included neglect can be dismissed as untrue. But within the bounds of truth-telling, multiple accounts seem not just possible but necessary. Talk about distress has a slippery, multifarious quality. More or less everything I told my care team could be framed in multiple ways. My powerful inner states and odd experiences were all capable of multiple descriptions. This polyvalence appears inescapable. No single story ever seemed unquestionably and exclusively right.

The professionals clearly needed a certain kind of story. They navigated between alternatives produced by me to build a single, unitary story of their own. To do this they made editorial choices. As the years went on, I began to see that these choices were not just based on what I said. Rather, clinicians made decisions based on criteria that were external to me. They were typically on the lookout for mental disorders with quantifiable symptoms and scalable treatments. That is how they did their job. Mental health professionals listened in such a way that they could pick out familiar patterns and match them to things they can do. They were able to offer treatments for schizophrenia and bipolar, and so were on the lookout for stories that were suggestive of these disorders. When they wrote letters to my GP or in my medical notes, it sounded like they were just describing me, based on what they saw. But really the descriptions they produced were relational, based not just on what they saw and heard, but what they were listening out for, which itself was determined by things that they can and can't do. They never considered my personal response to life's metaphysical challenges but they did note unstable mood. I'll return to this theme later on. For now, it is worth noting that the informational needs and preferences of professionals determined my story as much as anything I said or did.

Here, in this chapter, my preferences and needs are different, and I tell a different story. It is a story of personal change, in which I become ill and then I get well. The changes are not caused by external agents. Neither mental disorders nor treatments for mental disorders figure all that much (although they are not erased altogether). Rather, I change myself. The way I tell my story here is that in my late teens and early twenties I learned to be disenchanted, which meant learning to live in the world in a certain way. Later, I learned to be mentally ill, and I developed a different way of living. And now I am well, I have moved on again, with a new life. To tell this story, and to bring out what I mean by *learning to live in a certain way*, I will draw on the anthropological concept of habitus. I suggest that thinking of my life in terms of habitus is in some cases preferable to the story produced by the mental health professionals. My claim is not to challenge or replace their story. My story would not fit their informational needs, at least not in the present institutional configuration of mental healthcare. But I believe my narrative offers a richer, more nuanced picture of a human life. In doing so, it highlights the costs of thinking like the medics, even, the possible iatrogenic harm that arises from the reliance of the professional's story. There is nothing inevitable or natural about the mental health narrative and we need to take care not to let it erase other narratives.

*

As an undergraduate in the late 1980s I found myself in a difficult position. I was a first-generation student from a comprehensive school who had somehow ended up at an unusually posh Oxford college. The discontinuities were stark. The unwritten rules of social interaction had completely changed. Or at least, they had completely changed for me and for the few others at my college from anything other than a highly privileged background. For the rest of my peers, college seemed familiar and unextraordinary, a smooth continuation of school. I had to learn fast, and to accept that in college, if not in the wider world, the values, styles and preferences of the social milieu I came from were inferior and slightly shameful. It created a demanding social world. I felt devalued and out of place. Although I did find friends and, after a few weeks, seldom felt isolated or alone, I never felt completely at home.

Something that added to my troubles was that in the months between the end of school and the beginning of university I had visited Bangladesh and become caught up in a major flood that was declared an international emergency. This left me with disturbing memories (of course, it left people in Bangladesh who were directly involved with far worse). Whilst surrounded by the beautiful built environment of Oxford, enjoying formal meals served by uniformed college servants (as they were known at the time and perhaps still are) I found myself revisiting traumatic scenes I had witnessed: queues of hungry people waiting, pleading for food parcels I myself helped pack and distribute; laughing kids swimming between corrugated iron roofs as fast-flowing water washed family possessions away. I was troubled by the larger meaning of the disaster, and its implications for notions like justice and fairness. What is the right way to live in a world like this? Should we even value justice if we are so powerless? Perhaps all lives are equally miserable anyway.

For the first time in my life, I found myself experiencing intense feelings of sadness, (or was it emptiness? Or despair?). Sometimes feelings arrived as affective visitations unwanted and unforeseen, like a thunderstorm. At other times they felt more like something that I deliberately developed and explored. Painful thoughts and feelings occupied my attention for hours and left me demotivated and lethargic. Compared with universities today, mental health had a much lower social profile, and depression was not very legible to the university bureaucracy (Crook 2020). There were few formal measures regarding student metal health, and no specific provision for support. Although informally I sometimes encountered kindness and leniency from individual academics, for example, regarding deadlines for work, there was no pressure to acquire medical documentation. Neither was 'depressive' a recognised social identity amongst students. I was aware of no social groups based on diagnostic categories and so no opportunities for connexion or activism, which anthropologists have called bio-sociality or bio-solidarity (Rabinow 1996; Bradley 2021). In some ways this might have been fortunate. I was under no pressure to subject my experiences to external definition. My distress was painful and disabling, but it was my own.

The way I have written this narrative suggests a causal connection between the social demands of Oxford, my experience of Bangladesh, and my depression or disillusionment. This connection might be understood in a variety of ways. Maybe Oxford and Bangladesh were 'triggers' that activated a pre-existing 'vulnerability.' A vulnerability sounds like an everyday sort of thing, blameless and human, but it brings with it the whiff of euphemism, as if we might say vulnerability but we really mean something much more damning. Perhaps more importantly, the notion of vulnerability doesn't really explain anything. What was it that made me vulnerable? How should we distinguish between invulnerability and psychopathy? Being undeflected by compassion is not always attractive. The notion of stress might appear to be a more substantial alternative. The language of stress is everywhere, a commonplace way of accounting for things going wrong, or problems occurring, located at some indeterminate point between metaphor and physicality, but without necessarily conferring pathology on the stressed person. We could class Oxford and Bangladesh as 'stressors.' But, despite the way the language of stress connects the biological and social sciences and thus promises increased explanatory power, it is not clear quite what it really means. As Rose and Fitzgerald suggest, 'everyone knows what stress is and no-one knows what stress is' (Rose & Fitzgerald 2022: 118). Doctors did sometimes talk of stress and vulnerability, but they took the view that I had a mental disorder and this occupied most of our talk. A story based on mental disorders gives clinicians something to do that matches their skill set and institutional role. Stress and vulnerability suggest I needed lifestyle advice, but a mental disorder demands medical intervention. And once you have a mental disorder, the antecedents begin to fade. What is important is the disorder, not how you got it.

From a more dispassionate standpoint, we might wonder if it is even a mistake to focus on Oxford and Bangladesh to the exclusion of other relevant factors. Perhaps they seem salient to me because I have picked up certain habits and norms regarding storytelling. We might speculate that stories about witnessing international emergencies or struggling with the tribulations of class are familiar because they meet other informational needs or preferences. For example, I found they helped me narrate my story in ways my friends could relate to and might even find entertaining. My impression is that other themes and ideas were inevitably submerged by these editorial decisions. For every story told, there are many that are supressed.

But, if I am to be true to my story, my room for narrative manoeuvre is not limitless. Bangladesh and Oxford need to figure somewhere. This is because, throughout this period I saw my experiences in these two places as being the keys to the story of my distress. They became built into the way I expressed my feelings. They were prominent whenever I thought about being sad, or told people about it, such that possible cause and possible effect merged. In terms suggested by William Reddy, my accounts of my feelings were 'emotives' that fed back into the experience they described.

> When one makes an emotion claim in the presence of another, one hears the words, one sees the reception of the claim, one feels one's face contracting in suggestive ways. These social and propriocentive 'inputs' create or alter activations, often in ways that confirm or enhance the state that is 'described'.
>
> *(Reddy 2001: 322)*

In his influential monograph, *The Politics of Storytelling*, Michael Jackson makes a similar case, arguing that narratives of distress cannot be separated from the distress itself: 'Storytelling can transform our experience, stir our emotions, and facilitate action.' (Jackson 2013: 14). Since Bangladesh and Oxford were key to how I narrated my story, the experience of telling my story that way might be expected to generate inputs that create or alter activations, or otherwise transform my experience of distress.

When I became a patient, I began to make the editorial decisions required to have a mental disorder. I began to think of myself as the doctors did, as having a dysfunction of the mind. Or was it a dysfunction of the brain? It might sound like an important distinction, but the professionals I met offered little clarity. Whether it was mind or brain, the disorder generated low mood and high mood. This way of representing feelings is also an emotive that produces inputs, a way of telling my story that transforms the experiences I am narrating. But that looping process was still years away. At this point, as a rather lost undergraduate, I saw myself as depressive, but I did not think of depression in medical terms. At this point, I was making my own editorial decisions. Depressiveness seemed to me to be more than just a flow of emotions through the mind, but to be joined to ideas and to ethics, neither wholly involuntary nor inherently good or bad. Depressiveness was a way of attending to the world around me, almost a form of description or mode of action. If there was dysfunction or disorder, it was in the world I was witnessing and responding to, not in my psyche. It makes sense to think of injustice as a kind of disorder, but it reframes my depressiveness in critical ways. I was depressive because I wanted to be ethical. I was depressive because I was disenchanted.

The phrase *mode of action* is not figurative. When I think back to my student days, I often visualise three or four of us sitting round a table, talking.

The table is crowded: cups, glasses, ashtrays, a coffee pot on a cork mat, cigarette lighters sitting atop packets of twenty, and, pushed over to one side, bottles of yesterday's wine. It could be at any time of day, because when we were students, time was large and flat and featureless, only gaining focus in the immediate run up to deadlines or unavoidable obligations. We're excited, but we're probably complaining about something. In-jokes and verbal games give a slightly ritualised quality to our conversation. What we say seems to us to be valuable, but without consequences to which we might be held accountable. Underneath all the undergraduate effervescence and foolishness, we're talking about disenchantment. We're thinking about what it means and how we might respond. It is serious, but also fun. We want to develop a shared philosophy of life and do end up formulating an explicit set of ideas, and even a few maxims to capture the essence of our approach. Feeling depressed was part of the answer to the question of the right way to live in a world like this, a world whose true nature had been revealed to be brutal and uncaring. This is the context in which my affective propensities took form. My melancholy was a part of a social endeavour. Even the messy table had a role. That might sound fanciful, but I don't think it is. In an essay about how spaces and objects can generate sadness, Navaro-Yashin remarks: 'Melancholia, then, is both interior and exterior. It refers to subjectivity and the world of objects at one and the same time' (Navaro-Yashin 2009: 17). In my case, I was aware of the aesthetics of happenstance, how objects haphazardly scattered on a disordered table might be beautiful and might open up the viability of a disenchanted life.

*

Years later, when doctors asked me about my life as an undergraduate, they concluded that I was depressed. It was all about low mood, the effects of low mood and, behind it all, the mental disorder, a shadowy presence that evades all efforts at detection, a kind of neurological haunting that can come to dominate a person's life. As you can see, that is not the only way of understanding these times. The mental health professionals didn't see, or didn't attend to, the ethics and aesthetics, the social context or the messy table. The doctors weren't wrong, but their editorial policy was highly structured, producing stories that enables them to do their job, sacrificing complexity for pragmatics. But there might be occasions when this sacrifice is less helpful, when other editorial policies might be preferred. Sometimes we are less interested in helping clinicians and more interested in telling a rich and complex story to promote self-understanding.

It is surprisingly difficult to tell your own story. Medical words and phrases keep cropping up. It is easy to end up framing personal experience as an instance of a medical category. I think this is revealing. Medical stories leave a kind of shadow which erases other expressive resources. This makes it harder to imagine alternative stories and harder to tell them. Finding the right words and concepts to tell my story has been challenging for this reason. It is as if medics don't have an editorial policy but just tell it like it is, as if their story is the only authoritative story. Another way of putting this is that the editorial policies that medics adopt to produce the narratives they need to do their job have become entrenched and naturalised outside healthcare settings. This has consequences. If we can't tell our stories otherwise then we can't tell our stories such that we can make sense of our lives. We become estranged from ourselves, cut off from critical life events.

Yet the idea that multiple stories are possible is so obvious and incontestable that it barely needs to be written. We know this. We know this when we talk with colleagues on a Monday morning about our weekend, and choose between telling a story of an unexpectedly enjoyable country walk and a story about feeling so enervated and exhausted by excessive work demands that we needed to destress in the countryside. Both are true, but choosing which one to tell the line manager making excessive work demands is clearly consequential. This is normal. Human lives are too complex for a single narrative. Yet in this book it feels radical to say the medical story is just one of many, and that other stories might have merits, and that they have become hard to tell because the medical story has become so dominant. Exploring my story – what is sometimes disparaged as my 'lay understanding' or 'subjective account' feels transgressive, even disobedient. But my aim here is not to topple the medical story. Medical stories have their place. That place is in the clinic, where the story serves the informational needs and preferences of highly institutionalised professionals. In this chapter my informational needs are rather different. I want to understand what was going on.

Because I am an anthropologist, I will use anthropological theory to try to envisage an alternative story of my undergraduate days, to tell a story not of depression but of disenchantment. To begin, I use the concept of habitus. Pierre Bourdieu developed the notion of habitus as a way of understanding how privilege in French society is transmitted across the generations despite legal and institutional efforts to erase it. He suggested that qualities such as an individual's tastes, preferences and personal style can be inherited and this 'habitus' can confer advantage or disadvantage. Success in competitive situations can often result from looking comfortable and knowing how to conduct oneself, rather than, say, excellence. That is habitus at work. He defined habitus as 'a structuring structure, which organizes practices and the perception of practices' (Bourdieu 1977: 170). Habitus is not having a plan, but having a sense of what a plan should be like, a plan about plans. It is open-ended and generative, and so involves the instincts and sensibilities we rely on to navigate new social situations, which Bourdieu calls 'feel for the game' (Bourdieu 1990: 66). A habitus may be recognisable, a set of shared, observable characteristics that are easier to sense than to define.

Bourdieu was primarily concerned with unconscious, embodied aspects of habitus, things picked up without reflection. But Saba Mahmood developed the concept further by drawing on its Aristotelian roots and focussing on habitus as a moral project (Mahmood 2012 [2005]). In a study of the women's Islamic piety movement in Cairo, she frames Qur'anic teaching, prayer, bodily style and clothing as techniques to remake the self according to a particular reading of Islamic theology. Religious activity is seen as a 'technology of self,' a means of personal change. Ritualised actions are not just symbols, but techniques, ways to become a certain, desired kind of person with particular tastes and preferences and motivations, which Mahmood calls 'pious dispositions' (ibid.: 128). Even if the ultimate goal is for the pious dispositions to become internalised and intuitive, it is pursued as an explicit personal goal, self-consciously taught, discussed and practiced.

I think that my disenchantment can be understood as a habitus. It started out with moral experience. I felt convinced that a society based on justice and fairness was impossible, and that other values were false or phony. There were no genuinely worthwhile goals to work towards. Effort was always disappointed. So I adopted a project of inaction. Doing nothing was an act in itself, a bit like going on strike to achieve better pay and conditions, or a policy of sanctions against country deemed to be unjust, or a boycott of an unethical business. I decided I would expend no effort whatsoever on formal work, not least the work I was expected to do as a student (although, ironically, I spent quite a bit of effort exploring why I shouldn't expend any effort). I would go through the motions, and learn how to camouflage myself so as not to be noticed, but I would really be pursuing my own agenda.

In place of conventional ambitions and life goals, or, failing that, obedience to rules and regulations that connect individuals to life goals, I developed my habitus, the lens through which I viewed those around me, and my guide as to how I should approach the business of living. My project was based on candour and integrity. I wanted to learn how to act in good faith and avoid the falseness that I felt came with the pursuit of status and empty conventionality. These were the dispositions I desired. I hoped that by conscious reflection and practice, I might acquire something like a direct and honest appraisal of the world. This was a pessimistic world view, in which few character traits could really be deemed virtues, but I think I hoped that a kind connoisseurship might be worthwhile, perhaps as an anti-virtue in the world without values. Religion played no role in this project, and I didn't draw on theological texts like the piety devotees. But, together with friends, I did engage with ideas found in books and films and discussed how this might help us to enact personal authenticity (often at exhaustive length). We explicitly cultivated new tastes, which meant, amongst other things, listening to a lot of jazz. Musicians such as Art Tatum and Sydney Bechet showed us how beauty could arise out of improvisation and flow, not conformity or mechanical reproduction.

We tried to learn to pay attention. We wanted to take the open, alert ear with which we listened to music and transfer it to our social life. The goal was to differentiate authenticity from facsimile, seriousness from bullshit, real values from realpolitik. At the time, the fall of the Berlin Wall and the first gulf war dominated the news. When chatting with friends and fellow students we were on the lookout for popular pieties about these huge events, instances where people tried to pass off empty speech or (what we now call) virtue signalling for real responses.

Because it was deliberately and self-consciously cultivated, my habitus of disenchantment enabled me to feel the deeper satisfactions of a coherent structuring structure tied to self-formation. But it also helped me navigate my uncomfortable social environment. I was able to create a successful social persona and finesse differences of class and cultural capital and problems with concentration because each of them blurred into my refusal to engage in worldly activity. As I developed my own feel for the game, my identity and positionality shifted. I was no longer a devalued other but a dissident, or a cynic, almost a conscious objector. My depressed feelings began to cohabit with their more attractive cousins, 'detached amusement' and 'chagrin', even a suggestion of 'wistfulness.' I may still be othered, but I am othering myself on my own terms. I think I hoped this would ultimately make me cool, blending sensitivity and attractiveness to turn myself into something like an intellectual goth. It didn't really turn out that way. It was not always a very kind way to live and at times, my habitus blurred into arrogance, as if my own self-regard could somehow solve the problems that beset me.

Looked at today, this could be read as a kind of youthful idealism, albeit of a rather pessimistic kind. As I write this, it is uncomfortable to find my younger self suspecting that my depressiveness marked me out as a deep soul, distinguished by being less distracted by the shiny and superficial. At very least, this is youthful folly, reflecting a slightly Holden Caulfield-like sensibility. I thought I was less deceived than other people, perhaps, even, a little bit of an existential hero. But it was also a way of gathering anything I could recover that was still of value after the shipwreck of Bangladesh. Depressiveness was not a matter of having feelings, it was how I understood the world, and of the kind of person I wanted to be in the light of that understanding of the world, coupled with methods to become that person. It was an instance of what Janis Jenkins calls 'struggle,' a vigorous attempt to deal with adverse experiences and environments (Jenkins 2015). The horrors I had witnessed, recalled from the glittering discomfort of Oxford, left me with limited resources and I did as best I could. My habitus demonstrated a genuine and committed engagement with life experience. You couldn't say that I was complacent.

An issue that Mahmood grapples with is that even if we might have questions about the moral project of the piety movement, we should take it seriously as an attempt to live a rich and meaningful life. Cross culturally and historically, efforts to change one's tastes and temperament in line with ethical intuitions about virtue and the good life are frequently associated with flourishing and wellbeing. My habitus might have been foolish, but it was also recognisably human, an attempt to find meaning and live well. I was trying to work through the difficult ethical implications of what I had experienced and what it might mean about ethics and the well lived life. Being liable to depression was just a part of my youthful attempt to make sense of the world.

There are reasons to value this habitus-based telling of my undergraduate story, and, depending on what we want the story for, we might prefer it to a medical narrative. Thinking in terms of habitus tells my story in a richer way, preserving my agency and recognising that feelings of sadness are just part of a larger attempt to make sense of life. If we want a story to illuminate a person's life, this story of depressiveness and habitus might be good. It highlights just how edited medical stories are. Stories based on mental disorders and symptoms seem extremely narrow and uninformative in comparison. The limited way that subjectivity is conceptualised, as individual cognitions and affect, all tied to potential treatment decisions, can feel tendentious, even unwarranted.

A second advantage of thinking in these terms is that it avoids easy assumptions about wellbeing or quality of life. As soon as the language of depression and low mood is used, it suggests that I was not having much fun as an undergraduate. The idea of mental disorder explicitly suggests that distress is disproportionate and causes impairment, that because of a disorder, a person is unable to do the things she needs to do. A reader might suspect that my quality of life was below average, and that I was perhaps in need of a mental health intervention. But I am not so sure about any of that. I don't think I was less happy than the average undergraduate, or that my overall enjoyment of life was diminished. Perhaps the reverse. I would see myself as having had a very rich and rewarding student life, full of social connection. There were certainly periods of distress, however, some of it intense and disabling. If, at this point, we were looking for pathology, it might be better to think of my habitus as being the (or a) problem, even that I was mildly disabled by my habitus.

As I left the protective bubble of college, the adaptive disadvantages of my habitus became clear. My life trajectory increasingly fell against the grain of those around me who were adapting and getting on. It was scary, disorientating, but also slightly exciting. Whatever my life was about, it wasn't about powering my way towards success, even if that now meant unsatisfying short-term jobs and travel. But I did not deviate from my trajectory. I was faithful to my project. So why didn't I change? How was it that I got stuck? I am not really sure, but I can see at least two reasons why this might have happened. The first is that my faithfulness was reinforced by the suicide of a close friend, the person with whom I had discussed disenchantment more than with anyone else. The disenchanted habitus was ours, not mine. Once he was gone, it seemed like an infidelity to abandon our commitments. A second reason goes back to the conceptual features of the concept of habitus, which was developed to explain continuities across time. Bourdieu's aim was to account for intergenerational privilege. Once acquired, a habitus is durable. Even if consciously acquired, and personally costly to maintain, a habitus tends to last. However we understand it, I was stuck.

Learning to be ill

Some years later, I started a PhD in anthropology. My research was about rural politics in India. I was back living in an Oxford college, but this time it was a friendly and progressive graduate college, and life was fun, at least at first. However, after a couple of years I ran into problems. My GP referred me to a psychiatrist and I ended up diagnosed with Bipolar 1. This led to ten years of appointments with psychiatrists, psychologists, occupational therapists, nurses and social workers, and I was prescribed and took around 30,000 pills. I was a diligent patient, but none of the treatments were very successful and overall I became worse, not better. Unable to work, I had to abandon my research and live on benefits. Life became gloomier, emptier, more effortful and less rewarding. Intensely painful feelings bleached my days into monochrome. I was told this was how it was going to be. I could do simple, voluntary work in charity shops, but I had an incurable brain disease. I shouldn't hope for too much.

But then, somehow, something changed. I had a breakthrough, a kind of epiphany. It was not as a result of treatments, or planning, or self-care. It was unlooked for, a surprise, even a kind of gift: slightly grand, a little bit melodramatic, possibly crazy. I'll say more about this later. Following the epiphany, I stopped all treatments and became well. I was discharged from care six months later. In the fifteen years since then I have been completely free of all mental healthcare and of the distress that prompts people to seek mental healthcare.

This narrative isn't a howl of rage about iatrogenic harm or structural incompetence, although it is tempting to write such a story. It isn't even a narrative about ineffective treatment. Those stories don't belong in this book. Also, I know that my case is unusual and relatively extreme. I am an outlier rather than typical. For the purposes of the book, these qualities are helpful. This is because the ineffectiveness of the treatments and my relatively unusual trajectory help highlight features that are present, but less conspicuous, when health trajectories are more familiar or when treatment is more successful. When my psychiatrist discharged me, he told me 'science can't explain this' and I take it he was right. My rather odd, or idiosyncratic, even slightly weird life is illuminating in part because conventional medicalised narratives have trouble explaining what happened. My journey foregrounds the expressive limitations of the medical genre. By pointing to the short-comings of medical stories, it opens up space for alternatives.

So what kind of story would we need to explain what happened? How might it look if our priority is getting a deeper or thicker sense of what was going on, rather than dealing with the informational needs of people working in an accountable healthcare bureaucracy? The concept of habitus is again useful in placing a human in their own story. In the above section I suggested that I cultivated a habitus of disenchantment, and that affective states played a role in this endeavour. These affective states draw clinical attention, but (as I hope the notion of habitus helped me show) they may also be understood as part of a wider moral project. I found myself to a degree disabled, unable to work productively and generally stuck. Clinicians tended to think that these problems arose out of affect. They said that I was too depressed to continue with my degree, for example. The habitus-based narrative suggests that cognition, ethics and social connections played a role. In this section, the process of becoming a bipolar patient can be framed as a transition between two habituses, from a disenchanted habitus to a mental patient habitus. Each habitus represents effort, values, learning, and is a way of trying to make sense of the world.

In this task, habitus works better than some alternatives. The term 'patient role' tends to privilege the clinician's point of view and is used in such a way as to suggest dependency or avoidance in the patient, as if the patient wants to be a child. It may be, of course, be true that a patient wants to remain a child just as it may be true that a clinician may want to parent. But habitus shows how personal efforts that might appear defensive or fearful in clinical settings, might have other qualities away from the clinical gaze. It also suggests something about chronicity and how people like me sometimes get stuck in the system.

Simon Sinclair used the notion of habitus to understand medical training (Sinclair 1997). According to Sinclair, student doctors at medical school pick up much more than just knowledge about health and illness or expertise in delivering interventions. Rather, they learn attitudes, values and tastes, including preferences around knowledge, decision making, cooperation and responsibility, as well as a certain way of conducting oneself when onstage in front of patients and backstage amongst fellow medics. This medical habitus is acquired as much from unconscious imitation as explicit pedagogy, from what he calls the 'hidden curriculum' and informal activities in the bar as much as from lectures or ward rounds.

Sinclair himself didn't extend this approach to the patient habitus, but if he had, he might have encountered a similar process. When mental health professionals brought me to the drab clinic rooms I mentioned at the start of this chapter, it was not purely a matter of gathering information or making and recording decisions. It was pedagogic exercise, almost an apprenticeship, in which there was both a formal curriculum and a hidden curriculum.

Some of the formal curriculum was straightforwardly didactic: doctors explaining to me what a mood disorder is, how medication might help, etc. They gave me leaflets, and I was able to read what they wrote about me in letters to my GP because they were cc-ed to me as well.

On wards and in day hospital and in home visits, I was explicitly taught to 'manage my condition.' Self-management is a set of ideas and practices oriented towards the control and reduction of symptoms of a mental disorder. Patients today might attend the local Recovery College, but when I was a patient, I 'received' psychosocial interventions badged in various ways – 'psychoeducation,' 'relapse prevention,' 'skills-based' techniques. They were all rather similar. They asked me to reimagine my life and to change my 'behaviours.' In particular, I was enjoined to do a lot of planning: to assess how I was doing, to mitigate risks, to build in protective factors. This might sound suspiciously bureaucratic. The goals of self-management do seem to resemble the goals of a good bureaucracy: evenness, predictability, standardisation, dispassionate decision making. It seemed as if managerialism was the answer to the human condition. Although I found some of the foundational assumptions of mental healthcare baffling, I did engage with self-management to the degree that I began to think that explicit routinisation is therapeutic and that a lack of order or planning was likely to lead to poor mental health.

Much of the instruction is more subtle than self-management training. Questions about my childhood and adolescence might be attempts by doctors to detect inherited 'risk factors' or 'precursors' of illness, but they were also opportunities for me to learn a new way of telling my story. Doctors were sometimes interested in whether I had relatives who had mental disorders, especially bipolar. It didn't really make a difference to treatments, but it gestured towards their expertise and hinted at my lack of expertise. Perhaps more importantly, talk of genes and heritability reified bipolar, presenting it as something that existed independently of their judgement, a heritable biomedical object, something demanding professional intervention.

Even less apparent was the hidden curriculum and informal activities that occupied my attention and shaped my learning, offhand remarks, tonal shifts, moments of interpersonal awkwardness. My psychiatrist appeared to take the effects of medication much more seriously than the effects of psychological therapies, which seemed to demand something more like lip service. He was attentive to my embodied state, and was sensitive to how low mood was manifest in bodily posture and motion as much as internal experience. Not taking medicine, or expressing concerns about the influence of big pharma on apparently objective science was uncool, a sign of a lack of sophistication. Certain doubts were approved, however, signs of a discerning mind. I found psychiatrists to be generally happy to rehearse doubts about what mental disorders were or how medication worked. They sometimes offered a kind of complicity. I was once told: 'we all know there is no such thing as the chemical imbalance,' which drew me into the magic circle of the truly well informed.

I didn't tell them about my habitus of disenchantment and how it seemed to be wrecking my life and yet be impossible to let go, because I wasn't able to frame my story that way yet. I did have a story about how a research degree required focus, productivity and planning and that my decades long project of critical inaction couldn't accommodate such demands. I had a clear sense that my past, many years of bluffing to cover my lack of productivity and finessing whatever it was that I had managed to produce, was, at last, catching up with me. However, the editorial policy of the mental health professionals I dealt with didn't really respond to a story like that. The asked a different kind of question: 'how has your mood been,' 'have you experienced racing thoughts,' 'how low is your mood on a scale of one to ten.' Questions were never directed towards my ethical commitments, or how my depressiveness worked in a social context, or how it was woven into a larger structure that contained elements of value.

It was difficult to respond to these questions at first. I wasn't sure I really had a mood, at least not in their sense. I thought I sometimes felt depressed, but that never seemed to be adequately captured by phrases like 'low mood.' Quantification seemed particularly irksome as it required me to treat differences of kind as differences of degree. In other words, what appeared to me to be distinct phenomena, such as feeling listless, finding the rugby boring and having doubts about the probity of the current Labour government, were all blurred together and considered to be a small amount of low mood. Likewise, distressing phenomena that were distinct, such as grief at the death of the loved one, despair at the absurdity of life, and fury directed towards myself, were all glossed as instances of a large amount of low mood. It was strange and unconvincing. It wasn't, however, up for negotiation. Was my post breakfast mood score a 3 or a 4? Was my irritability getting worse and turning into disappointment? It seemed silly, and I wondered how the professionals took it seriously.

There was nothing equal or democratic or symmetrical about my conversations with mental health professionals, in part because discursive resources were so unevenly distributed. The professionals had access to a crisp language of symptoms and interventions and treatment benefits. To take one example, in marketing materials as in medical notes, the drug olanzapine is said to counter psychosis. It is framed as a treatment for phenomena such as hallucinations, intrusive thoughts and delusions and is backed up by numbers derived from 'validated scales.' So a doctor may prescribe me Olanzapine and then, a fortnight later, tell this story: that my 'psychotic symptoms subsided on olanzapine', or my 'intrusive thoughts and odd perceptual experiences were less troublesome', or that my 'score on a measure of psychosis had fallen from 5/10 to 3/10'. Each of these might be interpreted as showing that taking olanzapine was effective or successful.

But, on the basis of my lived experience, we might read Olanzapine differently, as a 'cognitive muffler', or 'a dimmer switch' that makes the world a little less bright, or engaging or accessible. I found it hard to be committed to anything on Olanzapine. It was hard to care, hard even to act, as if the drug had added an additional force that resisted all effort and will, like psychic friction. These effects were just as real but were highly undesirable. The problem here is that it is difficult to find vocabulary to articulate these less desirable effects. Notice how unfamiliar and outlandish my wording is in the sentences above where I try to express something of what Olanzapine does. Even as I sit at home typing this chapter, it isn't easy to find ways to express these effects. Communicating them to a psychiatrist in a clinical appointment is much more difficult. If a patient tries to talk in this way, searching for ways to express how Olanzapine affects them, they may begin to sound incoherent, as if they need more Olanzapine. Perhaps no scale could ever be plausibly devised to measure existential stodginess or cognitive muffling. But this is consequential. The unequal distributions of accessible expressive resources authorises medical stories. It makes the health benefits of Olanzapine seem more real and undermines the reality of adverse effects. Comparing effects for which there are recognised vocabularies and measures against effects for which there aren't sounds like cooking the books, but is the norm in mental healthcare.

*

In his literary analysis of psychiatric notes, Petter Aaslestad warns us to look for silences: gaps and omissions that are passed over by the clinicians (Aaslestad 2009). In my case, some gaps are glaring. In over 800 pages of medical notes there is no trace of my framing my own sadness. My own understanding, so painstakingly developed over more than a decade, is either absent, or is treated as part of the disorder. But what is less obvious is the editorialising. In medical notes, everything seems calm and natural and inevitable. But this is just a rhetorical achievement. Even the 30,000 pills I consumed can be narrated in multiple ways. Medical anthropologists have suggested that pharmaceuticals are as slippery and polyphonic as anything else in mental healthcare. Such arguments are not intuitively obvious. For example, Hardon and Sanabria suggest that 'there is no pure (pharmaceutical) object that precedes socialisation and interpretation. We argue that molecules are not "discovered" but made and remade; they are fluid, ever evolving in relation to their context' (Hardon & Sanabria 2017: 118). Medication clearly has effects on both my body and mind, but those effects are not simply a matter a pharmacology, they are socialised and interpreted, never determinate, unambiguous or incontestable.

My medical notes revealed a world that was clever and sophisticated, yet mysteriously simple. When compared to my concept of a depressive habitus, (or, published memoirs of distress by others) this was a simplified, stripped-down world. It was like moving a small number of pieces around a board in narrowly circumscribed ways, the dullest ever board game. There was something appealing about it, but also constraining and unconvincing. It took effort to contain my scepticism, to hold back from voicing doubts. My impression was (and is) that it is a strain for staff as well. I was repeatedly told to focus on feelings felt in the moment. Despite my scepticism, clinicians insisted that such feelings could always be quantified, and located on a scale from high to low. I started to think in terms of 'mood' or 'functioning' or 'mental disorder.' What Jenkins calls my 'pharmaceutical self' had moods and anxiety and, occasionally, psychotic experiences, each occurring in greater or lesser quantities (Jenkins 2010). In my notes I am 'well,' or 'not doing so well.' Not doing so well has three forms. I might be 'depressed' or have 'low mood.' This is expressed both in medical terms and in everyday synonyms. So I might be described as 'slowed down' or exhibiting 'psycho-motor retardation' 'tearful' or 'labile.' A second way of not doing so well is to be 'accelerated', 'speedy', 'disinhibited' or 'manic.' A third is to have 'unusual ideas' 'psychotic experience' 'paranoid ideas' 'depersonalisation.' There is sometimes more detail at these times: 'believes people have been replaced by imposters' or 'appears to want to join a commune of bears, but am unsure if he is joking or not.'

The transition from well to not well is a relapse, a repeat of something that has already happened. The causes of relapse are related to 'stressors,' such as 'worries about accommodation' or 'concerns about whether he can finish his doctorate,' or 'lack of structure.' When not well, a decision is made whether or not to change medication, and whether more 'input' might be required. Input meant more contact from staff, admission to day hospital or admission to an acute ward. Improvements are linked to treatment: 'picked up on moclobemide' or 'the increase in olanzapine did the trick.'

In the notes we see mood going up and down and med doses increased and decreased or meds introduced and tapered out. There are graphs that map mood over time, based on the results of questionnaires. Mental health resembles the stock market. Using True Colours was like being turned into a computer game. The problem was: who was the player? Was it me? Or the researchers? I tried to experience myself being composed of measurable feelings felt in the moment, and to see this as being the target of mental healthcare, This never felt convincing to me. It felt odd and unlikely that my mood score reflected anything much. I tried to change my answers to record total scores that seemed more meaningful

It could seem as if the professionals thought that I had no valid ideas about my distress other than their ideas, or that their understanding of it was the only one that mattered: a unitary truth that made all others redundant. It is certainly the case that there is no room to agree to disagree in notes or in clinical encounters. Theirs was the only accepted way of framing my distress. In appointments it could sound as if clinical categories and clinical

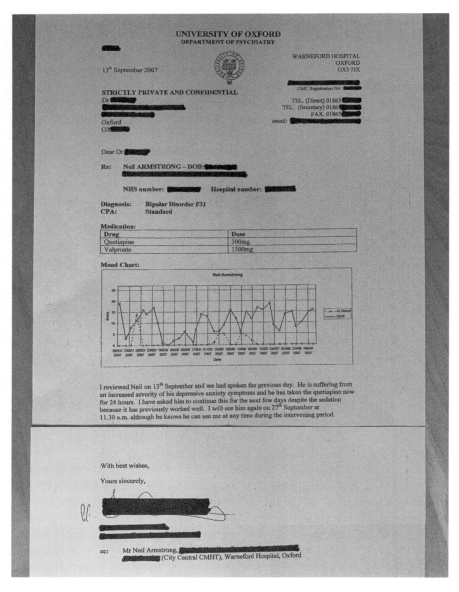

FIGURE 5.1

tropes mapped on to my subjective experiences and actions in a direct and unmediated way, as if there was a perfect fit between representation and reality, so that their version of events were the events. I knew that this was rhetorical, an effect of sealing off clinical appointments from wider debate about mental healthcare. I knew that the science was contested, that serious

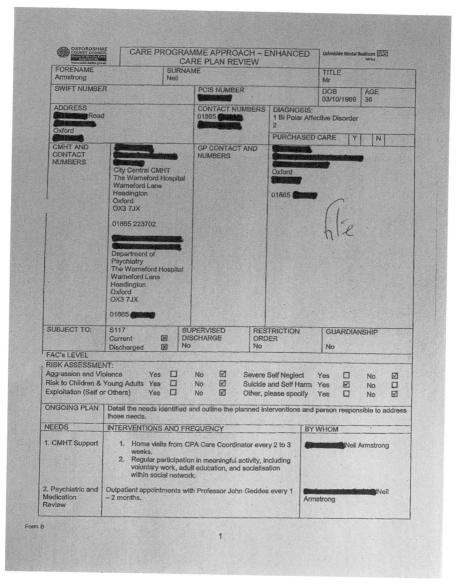

FIGURE 5.2

people from within mental healthcare and from the world outside queried or challenged the fundamentals of mental healthcare. In other words, I knew that the biomedical version was not the only credible or viable version of events, and that, even for the most ardent, there was no simple, direct correspondence between medical terms and human lives. But all this leaves

Medication: Instructions for service user
Moclobemide 1200 mg Epilim Chrono 1500 mg Aripiprazole 15 mg Lamotrigine 100mg Lorazepam RPN Zopiclone 1.75mg nocte

INVITED TO CPA (CIRCLE): (SERVICE USER) CARER (PSYCHIATRIST) CPN SOCIAL WORKER PSYCHOLOGIST (OCCUPATIONAL THERAPIST) SUPPORT WORKER WARD NURSE (GP) OTHER
ATTENDED CPA (CIRCLE): (SERVICE USER) CARER (PSYCHIATRIST) CPN SOCIAL WORKER PSYCHOLOGIST (OCCUPATIONAL THERAPIST) SUPPORT WORKER WARD NURSE GP OTHER
ETHINICITY AND INDIVIDUAL CULTURAL NEEDS (to include religion, dietary support, day care etc) None
UNMET NEED and comments None
CARERS AND OTHER SUPPORT (To include other services involved, eg student services, tertiary services) ████ Cohabiting partner. Good local social network of close friends and regular contact with family in Nottingham. Regular voluntary work with ████
SERVICE USERS VIEW ON CARE PLAN: Not yet discussed.

CARE COORDINATOR ████		DATE OF THIS REVIEW 11/5/2005	NEXT REVIEW TBA 3 months
SERVICE USER SIGNATURE	CARER SIGNATURE	CARE COORDINATOR SIGNATURE ████	
DATE	DATE	DATE: 11 5 2005	

2

FIGURE 5.2 (Cont.)

little trace in my notes. Psychiatrists who rehearse sceptical views about mental healthcare in seminars and research papers turned into true believers when writing notes. Categories and ideas that were widely deemed to be problematic and perhaps inadequate are treated in my notes as the only conceptual game in town.

There is a violence to this. It might be understood as an instance of epistemic injustice in a general sense. As we argued in chapter one, Miranda Fricker's thinking is helpful, without fitting my situation perfectly (Fricker 2007). Fricker introduced two versions of epistemic injustice: testimonial injustice and hermeneutical injustice. Testimonial injustice means disbelieving a person in an unwarranted fashion, for example on the grounds of their ethnicity. When mental healthcare professionals turned my habitus into their disorder, it isn't a clear case of being disbelieved. It would be more accurate to say that they were unable to listen. They needed a different kind of story from me, a story which enabled them to meet their informational needs. My framings didn't help with this at all. Highly personal, complex and not tied to treatment decision, they pulled clinicians away from the simplified legible world. They were ignored because they were not relevant or, most of the time, even perceptible.

We could, however, think of this as a process of creeping hermeneutical injustice. Fricker's central case of hermeneutical injustice is of a person experiencing sexual harassment but not having the language to articulate their predicament. A succession of unwanted and uncomfortable intrusions from male colleagues are hard to make sense of and complain about without the vocabulary of sexual harassment. What is needed is enlarged expressive resources to give people more insight into their lives, and as a means of political mobilisation. In my case, almost the reverse was occurring. The medical terms I was being told to use had a lesser capacity to make sense of my life. Even if I didn't think in terms of habitus, I still started out with a more sophisticated story about my distress, linking it to ethics and aesthetics. But the mental health professionals were trying to replace my language with theirs, leaving me estranged from my inner life and disempowered. It was as if I had made a complaint of sexual harassment but found the people dealing with the complaint didn't recognise the notion of harassment and instead wanted me to frame it otherwise, perhaps as something like: 'vulnerability to interpersonal discomfort.'

So why did I comply? What turned me from being a dissident, even a contrarian, into a collaborator? Was I somehow won over by the sophistication or glamour of technoscience or evidence-based treatment? Was I defenceless against the discursive power of psychiatry and psychology? None of that sounds quite right. Some of the appeal of medicalising my distress was that it offered the prospect of change. My disenchanted habitus had immobilised me. I was profoundly stuck. I was unable to move and yet found myself in an environment increasingly intolerant of not moving. So when I was told about how bipolar disorder was located in the brain, in mysterious substrates that made me vulnerable to 'mood instability' and 'mood episodes,' this suggested new directions, ethical and aesthetic departures from the closed circle of my life. Perhaps I could escape by becoming bipolar.

But my mental illness habitus turned out to be self-perpetuating just as much as my earlier efforts to be disillusioned. In this sense, bipolarity reproduced itself over time. Social scientists have been aware of this phenomenon for decades. Classic early works in sociology and anthropology noted that mental health labelling can incentivise or otherwise reinforce ill health. Goffman, following Parsons, noted 'secondary gains' for those who suffered the stigma of a mental health diagnosis (Goffman 1963; Parsons 1951). In a similar vein, Scheff argued that medical descriptions can reward mad behaviour and punish attempts to return to health (Scheff 1966: 84). In her pioneering ethnography of life as a mentally ill person, Estroff notes that: 'Problems arise when the benefits of sickness outweigh the obligation to get well. Further difficulties are generated when the constraints and symptoms of the illness outnumber and include not only a lack of capacity but a lack of desire to get well' (Estroff 1981: 240–241). For Estroff something about the social role of mental patient promotes weakness of the will and redirect a person's preferences and ambitions for themselves away from recovery and good health. These early accounts are not sympathetic to the plight of the patient. More importantly, they fail to really capture how care and patient become entwined. Healthcare runs much deeper than just a redirection of ambitions.

In a series of articles developing the concept of 'social defeat', Luhrmann gets closer to lived experience (Luhrmann 2006, 2007, 2008). She defines social defeat as the subjective consequence of repeated social encounters in which an individual finds themselves demeaned, humiliated, shamed or subordinated. Social defeat arises out of a range of social contexts, not least mental healthcare contexts (Luhrmann 2007: 151). Those who are socially defeated find their ability to make decisions and act on them to be impaired. This amounts to iatrogenic harm. For people diagnosed with schizophrenia in the US, she suggests, 'our standard model of care not only does not help but may even make the illness worse' (Luhrmann 2007: 136). Subsequent publications have suggested a more variegated pattern than Luhrmann proposes, suggesting that social defeat is less inevitable and less uniform that it might appear, without challenging the link between mental healthcare and chronicity (Whitley 2011; Wright 2012).

My autoethnography is consistent with Luhrman's work. Repeated experiences of bruising, asymmetrical social encounters impacted on my confidence, agency and sense of self-worth and left me deskilled, less able to deal with demands of sociality. My complicity with mental healthcare left me less confident and more fearful, less accustomed to responsibility, focussed more on my responses to the world than the world's responses to me. But there is another side to this. Once diagnosed, it became axiomatic for me that there was little or no relationship between the external world and my internal world. My bipolar self was socially differentiated, sealed off and self-generated, discontinuous with those around me. A diminution in social connection coincided with a diminution in ethical connection. Less could be expected of me because I was ill. I was less accountable, buffered by the ongoing mitigation of personal responsibility that comes with bipolar. There are advantages to such a status. Moral discontinuities helped me to negotiable areas of life I found difficult, to exit the games I didn't want to play, and only really engage in the areas of life that suited me. This meant that the responsibilities and experiences of ethical complexity that come from an engagement with the world were reduced. My sense is that this is a further source of harm. Ethical engagements are not just limits to conduct, or potential projects of personal change. They are essential to social lives. They help us grow as people. A reduction in ethical connection means a reduction in the kinds of social connection that a person needs to grow.

This might at first seem an implausible claim. Work on what philosophers sometimes call the second-person standpoint provides a way of filling in some of the intermediate steps. The literature is dense and full of controversies that are not relevant to my argument here. My purpose is just to use this model to articulate my experiences more clearly. The second-person standpoint is: 'the perspective you and I take up when we make and acknowledge claims on one another's conduct and will' (Darwall 2006: 3). Our lives are full of such moments, and there have been many examples already in this book. Darwall puts it like this:

> A second-personal reason is one whose validity depends on presupposed authority and accountability relations between persons and, therefore, on the possibility of the reason's being addressed person-to-person. Reasons addressed or presupposed in orders, requests, claims, reproaches, complaints, demands, promises, contracts, givings of consent, commands, and so on are all second-personal in this sense.
>
> *(ibid.: 8)*

The second person standpoint places ethical demands on a person that are not simply derived from moral codes or calculations. They are related to people. Relations of authority and accountability link humans together. Making a request means engaging another as a responsible agent. A customer can expect a barman to pour a pint. The barman might expect some degree of politeness from the customer. A barman who refuses to serve a customer without reason might be subject to justified reproaches and complaints. The same holds for an unruly customer. Darwall argues that the dignity and equality of persons arises out of relations like this. Moments where persons might expect something of each other, and might hold each other to account, are moments of mutual respect. The possibility of wronging someone, and the possibility of being found to be morally culpable are intimately linked to human relationality and dignity.

If moral accountability is diminished by illness (or by anything else) this diminishes a person's accountability to other people. It reduces a kind of social connection. Being bipolar could be seen to interfere with these second-personal reasons. I was less responsible for my actions because I was bipolar, and this limited the second-personal claims that could be made of me. People might be frustrated or angry at my misdeeds, but they weren't being wronged to the same degree because make claims of me like they could other people. I was shielded from Darwall's orders, requests, claims, reproaches, complaints, demands, promises, contracts and givings of consent. I was not fully accountable to the people around me and so excused from relationships that generate respect and dignity. This suggests an awkward payoff: by insulating me from moral demands that my distress quite genuinely impaired my capacity to honour, the bipolar label also insulated me from the moral pressures that enable personal growth and sustain the self-respect that is needed for personal agency.

There is a second aspect to this. As I began to inhabit the patient habitus, it began to have odd temporal effects. I was told that bipolar people's lives were made up of moods that went up and down cyclically like sine waves, or financial markets, or sports teams. In this vision, the future is just made up of past events reoccurring, as if time is cyclic. In the best-case scenario, one day was just like other good days. If things deteriorate, that is a relapse, a return of something already experienced. Nothing new can ever really happen. My job was to be on the lookout for patterns on the basis of what had happened before. I was supposed to be screening for stressors that might be planned for or unwelcome changes that might indicate relapse. Continuity, even sameness, was the goal. This is not without its appeal. Whilst I was a disenchanted student, it was hard to know what to do and which way to go. I had gone from promising doctoral student on a fully funded scholarship, at a prestigious university, conducting work that reflected deep and abiding interests, to a benefit claimant without hope of recovery, subsisting in an arid world of diminishing rewards. It is shameful to fail so badly and so publicly. Being bipolar had a redeeming feature: it took me out of time. I didn't need to do anything or go anywhere. But, again, it the cost of this was that it reduced my agency. How does a person move in a featureless landscape? How does one make progress if the future is a repeat of the past?

Learning to be well

Over the years, it became clear that neither the drugs nor the psychological interventions had worked. Whatever I needed to get better, it wasn't going to arise out of self-management or self-care either. I was at the mercy of a faulty brain and was told to expect the rest of my life to be like this. Bipolar became essential, an unwanted possession I couldn't bear to part with. Without it, my life was incomprehensible. With it, it was unbearable. What was I going to do? I knew that what I needed wasn't more care, or different care, or some glossy new intervention. Mental healthcare had become so entwined with the problem that it could never be disentangled.

Had I been a character in fiction, you might have thought I needed an epiphany. But, as Jenn Ashworth remarks in her beautiful and funny monograph on trauma: 'In real life, epiphanies don't arrive on time, like a train. They're a shock. They fall out of the sky like an apple or a rock or a shell and they hit you on the head and break a life wide open: ask St Paul' (Ashworth 2019: 22). Well, I did have an epiphany and it did break my life wide open. My epiphany did not occur on its own. A lot of good fortune lay behind it. I was able to see an NHS psychotherapist who listened as I described to him how strange, almost alien, my life had become, as if I was living on behalf of someone else. It was life-changing. A close friend who struggled under a similar diagnostic burden plotted with me to rebel against care to rediscover our self-worth and self-efficacy. Without him I don't think I could have recovered. A mental health professional gave me diary, a gentle nudge for me to rethink my attitude to time and activity. I realised that she could see me. Then, in an event that didn't at first seem lucky, I broke my leg and found myself taken out of my social world, coerced into uncomfortable self-reflection. But, still, when the epiphany came, it fell out of the sky.

My epiphany came about because I decided to kill myself. I had felt the attraction of suicide many times before. My closest friend from undergraduate days, my fellow theoriser of disillusionment, had killed himself. My 'suicidality' was one of the drivers of the escalation of my medication and other forms of input, including hospital admissions. However, really I had never felt equal to the task, and my suicidal explorations and gestures only revealed to me how difficult it would be. This time was different. I knew I could do it. I could end things at any moment. Death felt very proximate. It could be today, it could be tomorrow. I felt peaceful, as if the struggle was over. I could sleep again. This sense of time as limited, voluntary, malleable and shortly coming to an end brought with it a sense of transcendence. I started discreetly to say goodbye to friends and family.

For everything else that happens in this chapter, most of the difficulties in writing arose out of having to choose between multiple potential ways of interpreting events. This moment is different. It is hard to know what to say. I borrow the term epiphany from Jenn Ashworth to represent how something new, a new insight or new energy broke in from the outside. It doesn't feel wholly satisfactory, and there are probably disadvantages to using this term.

But it allows me to say this: one evening in November I sat in my chair and the next morning I got up and realised something had changed, that something like an apple or a rock or a shell had fallen on my head, and my life had been broken right open. Knowing that I could die made it possible to choose to live. If I was to live, I would have to change my life and myself. I felt a new confidence. Anything seemed possible. I secretly ended my meds, tapering down with what turned out to be excessive speed. This was an extremely painful experience. I woke several times an hour through the night. I also gave up smoking forty cigarettes a day. I was intensely agitated, so restless I was even admitted to hospital a couple of times. This physical ordeal began to seem like part of the healing process. Slowly, I began to feel calmer.

My notes reveal my psychiatrist as delighted, puzzled and aware that his expertise had very limited purchase on the situation. I mentioned earlier that he had commented that 'medical science can't explain this,' that turning point experiences are 'not supposed to happen.' It was clear that he needed much richer categories than 'mood' and 'stressor' to tell this story. The process was so personal, spontaneous, agential, risky, and painful that we might wonder how it might meet the demands of the editorial policy demanded by accountable healthcare institutions. It is certainly hard to envisage an institution that might 'deliver' a recovery that resembles mine. It is not that a group of people couldn't organise to curate such experiences, but if they did so, it would appear unprofessional, irresponsible and poorly evidenced. Those taking on supervisory or clinical roles would be opening themselves to reputational damage or worse. However, my psychiatrist trusted me. Five months later I was discharged from care.

The process that led to my recovery was not an instance of care, or cure, and was unlinked to self-management. Terms like self-efficacy; effort; will or willpower; responsibilisation don't have much purchase on the experience. I found that being ill was more effortful than being well. It is not easy to withstand the intense feelings and painful experiences, watching an imagined life and career slide away. My recovery marked a rupture with care, and a reversal of many of the habits suggested by healthcare professionals. My life was split open, but I didn't do the splitting. Recovery was more a process of letting go, of gaining self-respect, the overthrow of a certain kind of fearful, defensive self-governance. It was also of a surrender of distinctness, specialness. To be well I needed to be continuous with everyone else. What it required sound more like character traits, perhaps virtues, such as courage, hope, forgiveness and humility.

There is an additional layer of complication. I find myself unable to separate the epiphany itself from its interpretation. Part of its healing power lay in how I came to understand it. My struggle to make sense of the experience was part of the experience. This recalls my earlier discussion of emotives and feedback effects earlier in the chapter, but in this case the effects are not fixed. My interpretation was not clear or obvious and far from inevitable. In a sense, it was an epiphany because I made it so. I had met quite a few people on wards who told me they had experienced epiphanies. They felt sure about it, but I was not always convinced. So I knew it might not be an epiphany, that it might be a mistake, perhaps even a psychosis, but I nonetheless pursued the insights it suggested.

Moments of personal transformation have drawn anthropological attention. Jarrett Zigon introduced the notion of 'moral breakdown,' to describe a crisis in which what he calls 'unreflective moral dispositions' become subject to conscious personal scrutiny (Zigon 2007). My recovery certainly included a lot of questioning of my moral commitments. Scrutiny or re-eva-luation was a part of the process. It could be described as the disassembly of my habitus. But it doesn't quite address what was it about the moment of rupture that made recovery possible. My sense is that the event was less cognitive, involving my whole person. Two or three weeks into my post-epiphany life, I was walking home through the neighbourhood I had lived in for many years. A friend saw me and shouted after me: 'What has happened to you? What is going on?' I walked over to him. He was struck by some-thing about my manner or gait. 'You are walking like you are a different person. You are confident. It is amazing.' This friend knew nothing of the unfolding epiphany. He just perceived something new in me. Unexpectedly, perhaps, walking like a healthy person was a part of being a healthy person.

Andrew Irving discusses how, when HIV-positive people he worked with in New York approached the end of their life, and the insulation of imagined futures are stripped away, they are changed:

> often unseen transformations in knowledge and understanding that occur when living with existential uncertainty: transformations in self identity, and body image; transformations in everyday social roles and relations; transformations in the perception of time, existence and nature; and last but not least, transformations in the type of imaginative and emotional lifeworlds people inhabit when confronting death or attempting to negotiate a new life.
>
> *(Irving 2017: 2)*

This sounds much more familiar. Something about the possibility of death, a proximity that I could almost taste, enabled me to reimagine my future, radically change my roles and relations, and renegotiate my life. Somehow, another life seemed possible.

6

UNTETHERED

with Hugh Palmer

I should like to start at the beginning, but also the end. Because when I think of my child-hood daydreams, they were always about escape, about flight. Struwwelpeter was my favourite story book, and I always admired Flying Robert, the little boy whose DIY version of the Icarus myth (on the last page of the book!) appealed to me hugely.

All the other children in the book had their comeuppance, with frowning adults overseeing the appropriate punishments for failing to behave – death by starvation, thumbs severed, death by drowning, burning alive ('Pretty Stories, Funny Pictures' for Victorian children) ... But Robert got away - 'never seen again'! – that was supposed to be the cautionary punch-line, but for me Robert always had the last laugh: making good his escape, ending up running a bar, perhaps, somewhere in South America.

I think I also sympathised with his kinship with the natural world, his trust in the random forces of the weather rather than the confining grip of responsibility ('stay at home and mind your toys!'). The rebel 'flying Hugh' was in embryo back then, of course, or rather was in the form of a seed that started to grow inside a young human who outwardly con-formed to society's rules and expectations. That seed, that pattern of wishes, those drives, that potential, is how I define (with hindsight) my bipolar condition. Unless I had got ill, acutely ill, seven years ago, my knowledge of my full self might well have stuck at ground zero for all of my life. The impulse towards flight, as I now understand, was also my escape from the gravitational pull of depression and anxiety, both in plentiful supply at home.

I even looked forward to getting away to boarding school! But not long after I arrived there, I was dreaming of getting away... Books were a favourite

DOI: 10.4324/9781003154235-6

FIGURE 6.1

escape route, but throughout my time served, I remember looking through the window, longing to be on the out. The Sixties were firing away in swinging London... the Old Guard, with its regimental ties and tightly furled umbrellas, was losing its grip... the Answer Was Blowin' in The Wind. Meanwhile here was I, tied down by old-school rules (est. 1553) in a malodorous all-male boarding house, London a tantalising thirty miles out of reach.

Eventually the listings section of the New Musical Express proved too strong a draw, and I perfected the trick of conjuring myself up to Charing Cross station, where I checked my school uniform at the parcels office, donned my loon pants and three button t-shirt, and rattled out on the underground [subway] train to obscure venues in Catford or Walthamstow: freaking out shyly to my favourite bands before walking back through the sleeping capital to catch the 'milk train'. I can still feel the 'high' of those adventures… but from this remove I notice a strange aspect: I kept them secret! Why no co-conspirator? Why no confidant at the least? Maybe the story worked best inside my head, and to share it would have been to diminish its force: I wanted it to retain the uncertain boundaries and limitless potential of a dream – had it really happened? If corroborated, retold, it could have fallen flat.

The next archetype to get its hooks into me was 'The Photographer', unnamed hero of Antonioni's film Blow-Up, in which the ambiguities of Sixties London were lived out in the hedonistic adventures of a fashion photographer, crucial icon of the time. I reeled out of the cinema with my career path firmly set! This was my first X-film, and a severely repressed 16-year old schoolboy might also have been drawn in by the model-

FIGURE 6.2

straddling photographer-on-top imagery on the poster (much artistic licence), but in fact I was already a paid-up Antonioni junkie, and it was Blow-Up's mesmerising park sequences that grabbed me, took me back to see the film over and over again. I watched David Hemmings follow an impulse which magically untethers him from the world he knows. Up he goes, with Nikon (and twinkling white trousers) up the steps of the mysterious park, through the looking glass in effect, into a world where anything is possible, but nothing is substantial, nothing can be corroborated. He can't explain his experiences to others! They disbelieve him. All he has is the ambiguous 'proof' of his pictures. And eventually, he is lost into this oneiric world, he disappears, just like Robert.

Flight

Another, enduring fantasy had been set in motion... but my take-off was held in check while I served out my time at school. I brushed up my Ancient Greek and Latin ready for my University entrance exams, whiling away spare hours in the Photo Society darkroom, absorbed in the less glamorous aspects of my calling. As a reward for getting a place at Oxford, my parents sent me on a pre-university course in Venice. Needless to say, I fell in love for the first time as the train rattled south through France. The idea of the course, as with the classic Grand Tour, was that young British gentlemen (and gentlewomen) could acquire a veneer of European culture. But instead of adorning the exterior of my academic self, Venice invaded its core and blew it to bits. I was lost to beauty. For six long years my visual diet had been overcast skies, with the architecture of Victorian pretension and repression realised in grubby red brick – the retinal scarring was washed away in a welter of soaring marble and sparkling Adriatic light. Freedom! When the train rumbled off northwards to Victoria Station, I wasn't on it. Bewitched by the city and the promise of further romance I absconded from the return trip and busked my way through four more months of heaven, by which time textbooks and ink-stained desks were out of my system. But Oxford was worth coming back for. It was a Floating World in its own right by reason of its architectural beauty, the charmed life of its inhabitants – and by 1970 the laid back vibe of Haight-Ashbury was settling like a heat haze over the already dreaming spires. There was a solid coterie of us expensively educated horizontals who had been busily growing their hair since leaving school – they were quite easy to spot. While they spent their vertical hours in libraries and tutorials, I had found an alternative role for myself: The Photographer.

I 'came down' from Oxford with no letters after my name, but a portfolio full of pictures which won me a place at a photographic college in London. After my year there I answered an advert which said 'Photographer wanted'... the only time I have seen such an ad: did I dream it? Anyway I ended up truly floating, for two years, aboard cruise liners bound for the choicest of picturesque destinations, South Africa, the Caribbean... harder work than it sounds, with lots of hours splish-sploshing in the darkroom, but plenty of time off for twinkling my white trousers in the discotheque and gallivanting about under the palm trees, in the light of the silvery moon etc. etc.

Two years of that and I jumped ship again, literally this time, in New York, where photography was happening, where Richard Avedon, Irving Penn and the rest of my heroes still had their studios. I apprenticed myself to the masters, learnt to work my butt end off, powered by the non-stop night and day dynamo of the city, happy to drop my pose as The Photographer, instead proud to be a part of a team, giving my whole self towards the final two per cent that makes the perfect picture, in the centre of the photographic world. Learning to live off twenty bucks a week was also a good preparation for starting off as a freelancer... Back in London I had just turned thirty and I felt cut off from my confreres with their careers and families: but maybe that spurred me on. I specialised in photographing beautiful places where the lighting was gorgeous, New York studio-standard of gorgeous (the trick was to have insane reserves of patience while waiting for the magic to happen, then to work impossibly fast when it did).

For thirty years, I spent the fair weather months of the year surfing the high of 'being in the zone' for the duration of my commissions, which were typically intensive week-long location forays, following my own rules, un-grounded and perpetually in motion, making a religion of following each and every impulse, up the random steps, along the allées of the unknown... happy to be carried hither and thither by the currents of light and weather. The only responsibility was to bring back the rolls of film... and land with a bump into the home-bound labour of grinding out the text and editing down the pictures. Unfree at last! I remember feeling depressed through those winter months, though I would have viewed it as part of the creative cycle, as an actor might talk of 'resting' after the strenuous run of a stage show. So the haphazard and unstructured nature of a creative career successfully masked, for me at least, the extremes of my behaviour. Whether or not it was masked from the point of view of my long-suffering family is another question.... it was masked for me. What I would now call my condition was manifesting itself in other ways when I was on location: in haphazard sexual encounters, in risk-taking, in spending freely. At the time, I would have bundled all this into what I thought of as my creative nature, my 'heroic self '... I was unaware of the dangers of working creatively in isolation, driving myself too hard, relying on my reserves of manic energy, rarely moderated by the balancing restraint of co-workers or assistants.

It was when I stopped working and tried to navigate through the treacherous shoals of retirement, that things started to go wrong. In place of the rackety structure and seasonal rhythms of my photography/writing career, I had trained as a counsellor. I found I was able to use an untethered, ungrounded viewpoint, an open mind, to encourage curiosity: the position of a participant-observer, as some anthropologists like to see themselves. In the confines of my consulting room I felt oddly secure – a workplace that remained magically the same week after week! I was connected at last: professionally with my colleagues, my supervisor and with my clients, whose often turbulent inner life was patiently unpacked and mulled over.

At home, there was less connection, certainly less patience. My partner was trying to adjust to retirement from her own professional role, as a hard-pressed social worker, and had difficulty putting up with the 'projects' that I thought up, probably in place of the creative commissions of the past. Acrimony pushed me towards solipsism, aggression towards withdrawal. In 2011, wondering about a period of unusual excitability and patchy sleep, I asked my GP if I could see a psychiatrist. When I told my story, describing the seasonal variations in my self-esteem as photographer (from Master of the Universe out there in the summer, to cowering has-been at home every winter) her diagnosis was immediate: Bipolar II (later upgraded to Bipolar I). In response to 'what happens next?' she went straight into sommelier mode, proffering her menu of medications: the classic choice; this just in; showing promise; drinking up nicely &etc. etc. – I didn't fancy any of them.

Reflecting back, I was heading towards a crisis, through my grandiose upward progress. I wonder now, what would have happened if I'd got myself on a mood stabilising medication earlier. I might have kept my breakdown at a distance, kicking it down the road perhaps for ever. But I needed to reboot! Grandiosity, flights of fancy, an idiosyncratic and unpopular shed built in the garden (a.k.a. the Hughgenheim), and a further, challenging counselling role where I was in charge, working alone, with insufficient supervision, as it turned out.

I felt excited, super-fortunate and in the right place at last. I made good connections and felt trusted. Feeling high, without the loneliness of flight? But I found the benefits of an untethered overview were lost when I started to soar upwards vertically, far enough that I found I had no navigational beacons visible, left floating in space like Major Tom in his tin can. I wasn't making sense to anyone else either, and it's scary how quickly without connection one can lose a sense of self.

I was invited to take sick leave then waited in suspense – would 'my' place still be there for me? Not long after I received the inevitable negative, I headed off on a secretive 'mission' that involved sleeping rough and randomly testing the limits of my old person's bus pass – part 'Winterreise' (it was March), part 'Down and Out in Paris and London'. There was a longing, I suppose, to experience Robert's flight, his freedom of choice, reliving my teenage escape into the anonymous streets of the city. By this time I was getting nearer to the other extreme of my life – was I seeking the Sadhu's simplified life and spiritual goal? To the outside world I was displaying the grubby aimlessness of a tramp, but by this time the mania had taken over:

the myth was occluding the reality. Only recently I had been feeling that I had reached home base: my dream job, my longed-for destination …now I was driven to play-act the homeless outcast, stress-testing my solo survival resources to the maximum. My social connections had dwindled to base level: risk-laden 'challenging' interactions with drunken strangers in pubs; leaving cash and chocolate bars in secret crevices by bus stops, where future itinerants would magically find them. Luckily for me, one friend whom I still trusted gave me shelter, weathered the experience of seeing me hallucinating and unhinged, and drove me to Oxford in time for an existing outpatient appointment at the Warneford Hospital. Home at last! Landed at least. I ran out of the appointment and gambolled chaotically in the grounds until expert hands restrained me and I was taken in.

Behind two sets of locked doors, I was safe at last.

Landing

My mythic self evaporated as the in-house medications kicked in, and any 'meaning' in my episode remained lost until the archaeological piecing toge-ther began during my analysis. The psychiatric staff, after all, were constrained by a bureaucratic system of care: bureaucracy and curiosity don't mix.

The medical notes, marvellously dispassionate and non-judgmental, tell of a very unheroic Fall of Icarus, not into an azure Aegean Sea, but splatted onto a buff NHS proForma.

…this 62 year old gentleman…presented as floridly manic, with disordered, pressured speech, chaotic behaviour and hostility. He could not be engaged and ran out of the assessment. MHAA was arranged and he was detained under section 2.

Caucasian 62-year-old man. Casually dressed. Completely disinhibited. Unable to engage in conversation. Pressured speech. Hostile body language. Evidence of grandiosity 'I am President Obama' and paranoia 'I will not drink the water'. Shouting, running and dancing around the room. Threw a glass of water over his own face. Cognition needs formal assessment. No insight. Refused oral medication.

He has been evident in social areas of the ward throughout the shift. He was initially nursed on level two observations but was observed to become increasingly chaotic in presentation attempting to kick out the window in the Quad area, stamping on the table tennis balls, tipping the bin upside down and pouring water on the floor. He did respond to verbal prompts from staff to stop although he could not give rationale for his behaviour and stated that he felt confused.

It was felt that he required more support and therefore observation levels were increased to level three. He was given 2 mg of Lorazepam and encouraged to spend time in a lower stimulating area of the ward. He spent time discussing with the nurse about life experiences and past admissions, self-occupying reading the paper and playing table tennis. After two hours of settled and calm presentation he stated that he felt tired and requested to go to his bedroom. He was observed to remove most of his clothes prior to going to sleep, when it was also noted that he was observed to be wearing more than five layers of clothing. After this he went to bed to sleep.

I can remember 'Level Three observation' vividly! Two nurses sat at my door all night watching me in bed (one might have fallen asleep?), while I struggled to stay awake, convinced that they were under orders to do away with me, the minute I closed my eyes...

Grounded

The agitation and confusion began to clear after a week or so, and I was allowed to leave after a month. I chafed at the confinement (plenty more gazing out of windows) but remember enjoying the safety of being inside, with a predictable routine imposed on me. I felt vulnerable, like a hermit crab without a shell. When I emerged blinking into the light, I found I had disappeared from myself. Lost, like Robert. My Best Man Alex was

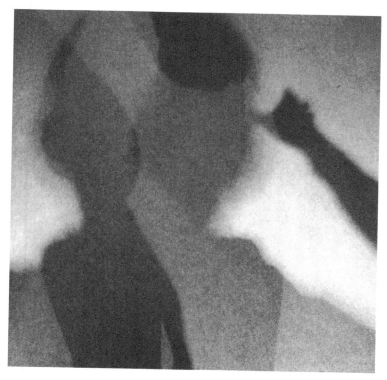

FIGURE 6.3

there for me again, taking me in and giving me shelter, calm and care for the first months. My hard drive had been effectively wiped clean by a month of heavy drugs. I didn't have an idea of what I wanted to do, what I could do. By a happy chance I was in the charge of a Buddhist psychiatrist. 'You should try doing nothing' was his prescription. 'You might find it an interesting experience'.

So I lived on my own, confining myself to a hermit's existence, which ironically is what I had dreamed of, as one of my fantasies, before I got ill. The reality wasn't as much fun as I had imagined. A lifeline came from a chance connection with Phil – my mystic pal. We met at a Mind event where he was my Minder, and after that we met up for the occasional discursive beer, and between times kept in contact by text: a comforting, constant stream of phenomenological badinage. In neither context did he try to 'bring me down to earth' by steering our conversation towards the mundane. his well-travelled psyche was comfortable drifting alongside my flights of unconscious fancy. I also tried taking pictures again, with a phone, not a camera. Just recording my daily moods. And after nine months I managed to be reconciled with my partner – my most important connection.

FIGURE 6.4

FIGURE 6.5

Shortly before then I found a useful helpmate in the form of a Jungian psychoanalyst. I re- member specifying that I didn't want him to help me to 'return to normal', defining my breakdown as an aberration that I wanted to leave behind me. I very much wanted to be able to understand my condition, thinking of it not as an illness, but as a part of my character, exploring the ways in which it manifested itself in my illness, and continues to do so in my life. As an example, I now relate to flight, and the feeling of being tethered, in a more multidimensional, dynamic way, using the stories, the fantasies imagined and acted out, as a way of exploring my emotional self, which is now becoming accessible to me. The idea of 'tethered' I see now not merely representing the feeling of being constrained, but also being connected. I see 'flight' as having richer possibilities – maybe by means of a kite, in collaboration with others. not just a solo one-way trip at the mercy of the elements. If I hadn't had the acute episode, what would I use for material? It would be like the fable of the boy who couldn't dream... The experience of my condition had to be looked at, reflected upon, for it to become integrated. I'm aware from years spent helping to run a local bipolar support group, that there are opportunities to unravel and reweave myth and story, to review our expectations of life, that are missing in the psychiatric response. Medication-heavy treatment, targeted at the acutely ill, certainly works in the short term, and can keep people safe. But when I listen to the stories of those who have managed to struggle through decades stuck on heavy anti-psychotics, I feel that it is often the medical treatment, rather than their bipolar condition, that has robbed them of their life. Perhaps I'm just lucky, lucky with timing and lucky with the love and support from those around me.

Hugh opens his story by saying he would like to start at the beginning, but also at the end. If the beginning of a story is also its end, an unsuspecting reader might assume that little changes. This might be one of those stories in which the characters learn nothing but instead arc back on themselves. Stories like this can be funny, portraying worlds populated by helpless, hopeless people who keep on repeating themselves. Or they can be tragic, featuring individuals who find themselves powerless, frustrated and doomed. But as the reader progresses, it becomes clear that Hugh's narrative is nothing like that. In this narrative, everything changes, not least Hugh himself. This is a narrative of both continuity and discontinuity. Various types of discontinuity are encountered, some substantial and real, others misleading and false. Hugh himself changes in important ways. Hugh as he is at the end of

FIGURE 6.6

the narrative is discontinuous from Hugh at the start. This personal change is enabled by social, cognitive and narrative discontinuity. Coproduced with an analyst as well as an anthropologist, this is also a narrative about narrative, in that Hugh revisits his formative narratives, encompassing them in a new, larger story that reinterprets the old. Hugh changes in such a way that interpretative change coincides with personal change. Narrative emerges both as part of the problem and as part of the solution to that problem.

Hugh broke out of his boarding school in search of London, music and nightclubs. It was the sixties. He was in rebellion against the Old Guard and their tightly furled, increasingly superseded, umbrellas. This was a generational rebellion, but also very personal. In a telling phrase, he says 'I perfected the trick of conjuring myself up to Charing Cross station.' In his spartan, repressive school, Hugh was a magician. He was without assistant or familiar, and he performed in secret, away from the eyes of a possible audience. Nonetheless, he was able to magically free himself. It was a role that, I imagine, required premeditation and a cool (or maybe *cold)* nerve, as well as a change of clothes. And if achievements are really tricks or illusions, it indicated a close connection between personal agency, creativity and concealment, even deception. Perhaps the concealment of the premeditation and cold nerve is an (invisible) part of the trick. In any case, Hugh's narrative is funny, transgressive, creative, unconventional, and knowing. The qualities of the text are also qualities of the person. We might almost say the chapter conjures Hugh, just as much as he conjured himself to helpfully located railway stations. In both form and content, in style and tone and visual images as much as in factual detail, Hugh manifests himself in the narrative.

The idea of being tethered is central to Hugh's story, to his archetypes and his agency. In his formative myth, Flying Robert opens his umbrella to be carried away by the wind into the sky, and, in Hugh's version at least, away from the punitive, petty world beneath him. A mix of magic, spontaneity and rebellion untethers The Photographer, and releases him 'into a world where anything is possible, but nothing is substantial, nothing can be corroborated.' Being tethered meant being opposed to beauty. Becoming untethered meant being alive to the flow of history and open to the sensory world. At least until his breakdown, Hugh's goal is to avoid being tethered. He just doesn't want to be tied down and exposed to the painful feelings that this entails. It started with breaking out of school. But it continued, and came to be Hugh's modus operandi, his calling card, his habitus. It made it possible for Hugh to be responsive to the beauty of southern Europe and to appreciate, from a horizontal aspect, the floating world of Oxford University. Working as a photographer on a (mostly unmoored) cruise ship sounds about as untethered as a person can be.

At this formative stage, tethering is restraint, a curtailment of freedom that coincides with a curtailment of fulfilment. Becoming untethered is thus liberation. It means being free, autonomous, independent, saved from the cognitive deadweight of intersubjectivity. An untethered person can shake off outmoded ethical demands, indeed all unwanted ethical demands, and really live, unencumbered by responsibilities, unconstrained by others. It sounds appealing. It answers a wish to live in the moment, be spontaneous, commune with nature, find enjoyment. Who doesn't want to wear twinkling white trousers, at least some of the time? Being untethered allows Hugh to focus on internal states and develop a kind of connoisseurship of his positionality. He is always on the periphery, an observer as much as a participant, a role that might at the time have seemed something like a dissident, or a spy, maybe, even, an anthropologist. Now, with an awareness of the costs to those around him, Hugh might re-evaluate this. By developing his own archetypes and by appropriating and adapting clinical categories, Hugh comes across as agential and empowered. His creativity is suggestive of confidence, vitality and health. Being an outsider looking in helped his creative process as a photographer and gave him an open-mindedness that became an asset when he started to practice as a counsellor.

Anthropologists have shown enthusiasm for illness narratives. Byron Good described such stories as 'an especially fine mesh' to catch the 'grand ideas that seem to elude life and defy rational description' (Good 1994: 165). Flying Robert and The Photographer seem to fit the bill, capturing grand but elusive ideas through the fine mesh of archetype and narrative. The potential benefits of certain kinds of narrative has been a theme in medical anthropology. 'Therapeutic emplotment' can help people come to terms with pain, disability and distress, rediscover their agency, negotiate a new role in life and perhaps a better future (eg. Rita Charon 2006).This can be seen as critical, even though it might not always coincide with clinical goals and may not be well understood by clinicians. Mattingley notes that

> The practice of hope...is often deeply connected to notions of personal transformation and to the idea of life as a kind of journey that demands self-transformation. Hope, in this genre, can in no way be reduced to 'success' or 'cure'.
>
> *(Mattingley 2010: 73–74)*

At first glance, Flying Robert and The Photographer look like they might be deeply connected to notions of personal transformation, as if they are liberating counternarratives. Hugh appears to be discovering his agency in opposition to old school values and unfeeling, bourgeois mediocrity. It is as if untethering enables journeys to be made. Thinking in terms of untethering places a value on freedom conceived of as personal liberty and calls attention to how freedom might be pursued. If life is framed as a series of escapes and escapades, there is always reason for optimism. But can Flying Robert and The Photographer really inspire Hugh and enable a renegotiation of life role?

Hugh's ethnography certainly enables the reader to share in the excitement. He is a dreamer in the waking world, a fairy story character gallivanting under the silvery moon in a world of mundane consequences, dreary repercussions. But it suggests a note of caution. Hugh seems unreachable, an actor who denies his own agency. From the vantage point of the present, the archetypes have a kind of pathos. This is a book about mental healthcare, about distress and recovery, and we know where Hugh is headed. We know that flying Hugh's days are numbered. We know which way the wind is blowing Robert, and whether the Photographer can really get by on charisma alone. The hope they symbolised appears to be less salutary than the hope Mattingley has in mind. Untethered Hugh turns his back on human connection. Escape through separation begins to look like isolation. This can be seen in both the archetypes. The wind that keeps Robert aloft and apart from undesirable sociality also separates him from forces that might change him. The Photographer's dreamy non-attachment insulates him from intimacy. At its heart, untethering is a negation of relationality, a rejection of community. At times it seems solipsistic. Once untethered, the external world feels slightly less pressing, less important, less real. It is as if all the air has been removed, leaving an impersonal vacuum where movement is frictionless, almost effortless. If anything is possible because nothing is substantial or corroborated, we might wonder if anything is worthwhile. Narratives are not always liberating. This, sadly, is likely to be true even when they are coproduced with anthropologists. Narrative autonomy and vitality can be ways of glamorising being stuck, of feeling good about feeling bad. Hugh's formative archetypes support and even justify stasis. The narratives they belong to are narratives of non-transformation, of continuity.

The next thirty years Hugh's life alternate between being tethered and untethered, being free and unfree, being Master of the Universe and a cowering has-been. It looks cyclical, a repeating pattern not going anywhere. Biomedical terms and biomedical reasoning begins to push through at this point. In the summers, away working, intense and focussed, Hugh describes himself as fuelled by a 'manic energy.' He notes that this led to haphazard sexual encounters, risk taking and free spending, all of which are diagnostic of mania. He says he was manic, but also that this is his heroic self. And in winter he was 'unfree,' 'like a resting actor,' but also 'depressed.' It is no surprise that a psychiatrist diagnoses bipolar.

When Hugh says 'What I would now call my condition was manifesting itself' it is noticeable that this framing suggests a distinction between Hugh and his condition. If a condition can manifest itself, it has a degree of agency independent of Hugh himself. This, of course, is said to be the logic of medicalisation. It is probably what the psychiatrist had in mind. But earlier Hugh mentioned that 'The Photographer was the next archetype to get its hooks into me' which sounds rather the same, but in this case it is the archetype that is separate and agential, rather than a disease. Identifying agency outside the self as a cause of subjective states, or framing the self as subject to external forces, is not unique to Biomedical thinking.

Hugh describes being bipolar as 'a pattern of wishes...drives...potential' and, later, 'a condition...a part of my character.' But wishes, drives and potential do not figure much in diagnostic manuals. Indeed, in principle, mental disorders are conceptualised as independent of personality, existing on a different 'axis,' in what are sometimes called 'substrates.' Quite what these substrates are is unclear and the subject of controversy. And, anyway, Hugh adds that he doesn't think of bipolar as an illness. What is important here is that discrepancies between source material and archetype are not a problem. A GP might query this way of uses the term Bipolar. They might conclude that Hugh doesn't understand the category or is misusing it. But in this context, when Hugh uses the term bipolar it is not so much a diagnosis as something mythic, another archetype, to join existential escapee Flying Robert and the inspired hedonist Photographer. Each of these archetypes is the product of a creative engagement with wider cultural resources. They are complex and highly personal. Michelangelo Antonioni, director of Blow Up, could dispute Hugh's reading of the Photographer, just as much as the GP could dispute his vision of bipolar as a part of character. But it would be beside the point. Hugh is not trying to challenge Antonioni or rewrite Blow Up any more than he is trying to rewrite the DSM. Discrepancies are not corrections. Rather, they are something like creative elaborations that might make the archetype fit better, be more illuminating, or in some other way be of use to Hugh as he tries to make sense of his life. These elaborations come at a cost. They are likely to demand more time and attention than diagnoses and be less pliable, less amenable to the constraints of bureaucratic working. In chapter one we suggested that psychiatry was like a gas that expands to fit any institutional space in which it is placed. Hugh's archetypes seem very different, to be like solids rather than gases. They not only occupy more space, but they are not flexible. If they are to be housed institutionally, the institution needs to be built around the archetypes and not the other way round.

Hugh rejected the psychiatrist's range of medication, and his life continued. He is excited, feels super-fortunate. He is in the right place at last, but also he is making good social connections and is trusted. At least for a while, it appeared that Hugh might have solved the paradox at the heart of untethering. He appeared to have found a way to escape without becoming isolated, to create distance without loneliness, to achieve freedom without solipsism. It looks like an epiphany: he is both disconnected and connected. It couldn't last. Perhaps it never really started. Perhaps things had never been as they appeared. Hugh describes how he made 'upward progress,' which he glosses as grandiosity, flights of fancy, idiosyncrasy. It wasn't entirely new. Rather it was a kind of escalation of qualities that had been there all along. There might be a lot of ways of capturing this process within Hugh's narrative world. Perhaps the winds were getting stronger. Or was The Photographer going on missions further and further from home? It could also be that the symptoms of a disorder began to emerge and become stronger of their own accord. Whatever view we take of how to understand the pathway itself, we know the direction of travel. Hugh was progressing towards a breakdown.

*

Psychosis can look like performance art. To both participant and onlooker, it can seem like an exercise in symbolism, an effort to negotiate the world via otherworldly creativity. Equally, it can have the feel of an art project that has got seriously out of hand. Hugh became a kind of mendicant. Like a holy man, he renounced property in favour of simplicity and intense, drink-fuelled encounters. It was play-acting, and also stress-testing, performative and experimental. He understands it now as a reboot, that familiar cessation of computer functionality in order to update software and eliminate problems. However painful for Hugh and for those around him, this experience was critical and valuable: 'If I hadn't got ill, acutely ill...my knowledge of my full self might have been stuck at ground zero.' But that is not what it looks like in his medical notes. In the notes, everything is wrong, disordered, pathological. Exteriorised and drained of context and meaning, no room is left for symbols, or archetypes or personal narratives. There is nothing helpful or educative in Hugh's distress. It isn't really a comprehensible human experience. The admission notes are particularly heart-breaking. Spare, matter of fact terms disenchant a world overflowing with meaning. Hugh has fallen out of reach, a subject of compassion, perhaps, but not empathy. Hugh is out of his mind.

Hugh couldn't, or wouldn't, talk to the doctors. As is common in mental health notes, a lack of cooperation is read as pathology. But it isn't clear who wasn't listening to whom. On day one, a lot of the description is generic. Defenders of biomedical approaches to distress present biomedical knowledge as morally neutral, appealingly, helpfully non-judgemental and non-censorious. Here, these qualities appear in a different light, as a genre made more poignant because of its insistence on the external and superficial, resulting in a particular kind of woodenness and formality: 'chaotic in presentation,' 'responds to verbal prompts,' 'could not give rationale' 'said he felt confused.' The notes suggest Hugh mentioned previous admissions, which is possible, but since this was his first admission, it might also be a mistake (see chapter seven for a discussion of the unreliability of ward notes).

The two direct quotes reproduced 'I am President Obama' and 'I will not drink the water' are tied to diagnostic terms 'grandiosity' and 'paranoia.' And Hugh is said to have been 'shouting, running and dancing.' These details are personal and specific but they don't humanise Hugh. Rather, the reverse. Their selection and framing make everything look involuntary and meaningless. Hugh is othered, depersonalised, even exoticised, as if he is under the grip of occult forces. This isn't a mistake or lack of insight on the part of the clinicians writing the notes. Neither it is an instance of documentary failure. These are high quality medical notes. It is just that the aim of medical notes isn't to make patients easier to understand, or to contextualise distress. The doctors objectify Hugh to discredit him, to justify the coercive treatment and mental health act assessment he needs.

What the clinicians see owes as much to the agency of the institution as anything they see in Hugh. The medical notes are based on simple observables, described using a small palette of terms: legible, actionable units that can be tied to bodies of evidence and thus enable clinicians to address the needs of the institution. So he was 'floridly manic' and 'completely disinhibited.' In his ethnography, Hugh says that there were no navigational beacons visible and that he was left floating in space in his tin can like Major Tom. This elegant formulation might say a lot about Hugh, but it doesn't really help the doctors. As Hugh's narrative develops and we see how clinicians described Hugh in his medical notes, we are not surprised to see no reference to Flying Robert or The Photographer. Medical notes and the reasoning and decision making they represent can't be understood apart from the agency of the institution in which they are written. The purpose is to make and record defensible decisions, according to a particular set of documentary practices. This enables medical notes as a sequence of calm, predictable, almost inevitable, care decisions. What the clinicians need to know is not what service users need to know. The sophisticated descriptions provided by Flying Robert, The Photographer, and bipolar each refer uniquely to Hugh. Even if aspects of The Photographer might feel unsettlingly familiar, as represented in this ethnography it applies solely to Hugh. The same logic applies to Hugh's version of bipolarity. Only Hugh is bipolar in this sense. Understanding Hugh in this way conflicts with clinical responsibility in that it diminishes the expressive resources available to clinicians to produce defensible, recordable decisions. The greater descriptive reach of these archetypes and narratives comes at the cost of generalisability. In its uniqueness and allusiness, its nuance and tonal complexity, it pulls away from the contextual needs of clinicians, acting in a highly bureaucratised environment.

We might understand the temptation clinicians felt not to listen to Hugh and his narratives, to dismiss Flying Robert, perhaps by classing it as 'disordered thinking,' or 'overvalued ideas.' It is not that clinicians are necessarily taking the view that Hugh is mistaken, or that his views are false, but that this is simply the wrong kind of knowledge. Understanding Hugh in this way doesn't help a clinician do their job. These two forms of knowledge diverge because they reflect different needs, uses and contexts. Bipolar disorder is a useful term for clinicians. Its thinness is a way of containing complexity that would be troublesome for clinicians working in a contemporary healthcare environment. In contrast, Hugh's version of bipolar is useful because it can contribute to the kind of rich description that is needed to re-evaluate a life and establish a change of direction.

But there might nonetheless be a concerning underlying continuity between Hugh's personal archetypes and the clinical imaginary in that they appear to share notions of personhood. There is a rich anthropological literature suggesting cross-cultural variation in how we conceive of persons, and, thus, how we experience ourselves as persons. A major focus of interest has been on boundaries. There is an opposition between more and less boundaried ways of being a person. Some understandings of personhood suggest a dense, impermeable boundary between the person and the world, whilst in others the self is more open, constituted not so much by what goes on inside, but the relationships and flows between inside and outside. In a hugely influential essay, Marcel Mauss argued that a Western Christian category of person evolved over centuries, culminating in certain common-sense assumptions: that people are separate, and highly individuated, with distinct and personal interior lives (Mauss 1985 [1932]). In contrast, generations of anthropologists have found selfhood in other societies to be so different that they introduce new terms: partible selfhood, dividuals, fluids selves and more (Mosko 2010). The philosopher Charles Taylor sees the disengaged, disciplined 'buffered' self to be a critical part of secularism, contrasted with religious selfhood that is porous, and collective, embedded in an enchanted world (Taylor 2007).

These different formulations are not equivalent and important differences are to be found. But we can note resemblance between how Hugh understood himself prior to his breakdown and the notion of individuated or buffered personhood. A person that can be tethered or untethered is necessarily distinguishable from their environment. Robert is able to see the world from on high because he allows meteorology to divide him from other people. In this fairy tale of moral personhood, Robert's evasion of what Hugh calls 'the confining grip of responsibility' creates a detachment, an imperviousness. His goals and strategies, values and habits become the habitus of the lone magician. The Photographer is an itinerant, unlinked to people or place, whose camera lens is itself a barrier, enabling him to create his own highly individuating, non-intersubjective representation of the world.

This highly individuated personhood reappears in medical notes. The psychiatric imagination individuates distress. Hugh's distress bubbles up from within. It is incomprehensible and unlinked to his life or his relationships. It is as if the doctors imagine Hugh as a lone magician too. The medics might be said to discursively untether Hugh, focussing on his interior states – the 'highs' and lows of his private adventures – but not his character or relationships or social world. Flying Robert may be the stuff of myth, but he is also a perfect psychiatric subject. If clinicians are to make defensible decisions they need to contain the problem, isolate such that they can act. If Hugh's distress were relational, or contextual in any way, it erodes the capacity of clinicians to act accountably. Hugh already understands himself this way. He sees himself and experiences himself as a detached individual whose moods felt in the moment are central to his life.

This prompts an unsettling thought. If Hugh started out as a buffered person, and if his recovery consisted in becoming more porous, then it might suggest that buffered personhood is linked to his poor mental health, to the oscillations of high and low and his breakdown. This is unsettling because bureaucratised mental healthcare also seems to promote buffered selfhood. When Hugh describes his journey to health, it involves not just a reduction in mood problems and the cessation of unusual cognitive experiences, but a richer sense of personhood, a deeper sense than is found both in his early personal myths and in clinical myth-making. In recovery, Hugh discovers a more relational way of being. For him at least, personhood appears to have been part of the problem, constitutive, even, of his disorder. And the transition to better health includes a change in his sense of personhood. By his own account, had he continued to believe in, and rely upon, his heroic self, he would not have recovered. The anthropological literature provides some support for this. For example, Parish suggests that personhood shapes our experiences in ways that are ethically consequential (Parish 2014). Less sealed selves create an awareness of, even concern for, others: 'Concepts of the person afford and shape such "affective" experience; they also link moral conceptions' (ibid.: 34). If this is right, then certain kinds of personhood, such as Hugh's heroic self, but also the kind of personhood implied by clinical records and discourse, is ethically impactful in clinically relevant ways. At very least, just as we might be cautious about promoting heroic selfhood, we should be cautious about promoting other kinds of buffered self, including clinical selfhood. However, as our ethnography in this book shows, learning clinical personhood is actively disseminated in self-management advice, in formal psychoeducation, and in instruments such as outcome measures. All promote concepts of personhood that might be a source of iatrogenic harm.

*

Social scientists often worry about the unseen harms of mental healthcare. Ethnographic accounts of healthcare experiences can reveal features that are disturbing and yet invisible to RCTs. But Hugh's ethnography suggests something different: that there may be aspects of care that seem undesirable at first glance, but can be therapeutic, and that these therapeutic effects are not accessible to biomedical research. Hugh's experience of mental healthcare is deeply ambivalent. Some aspects of his care were welcome and helpful, others less so. Hugh does not engage particularly with medical accounts of bipolar. He benefitted from being admitted, but the benefits don't seem to arise out of interventions that successfully treat an illness. The positive effects of medicalisation did not lie in expertise, or targeted treatments, or diagnostic know-how. Instead, unanticipated links between admission, meaning and moral emotions that in the social science literature might be seen as burdensome, here appear to be part of the healing process. Hugh says that admission made him safe. In some sense he was home, no longer suspended in the skies but securely located on the ground and cared for by expert hands. Perhaps the parallels between school and ward shaped the experience. But we don't normally think of psychiatric wards as settings in which patients learn to do without their heroic self. Pharmaceuticals purport to address mental disorders, not qualities of character. How was it that admission was a part of Hugh's recovery? Does Hugh's ethnography permit an alternative way of thinking about treatment efficacy?

As Jenkins and Csordas point out, whatever has been going on in the person's life, admission to a psychiatric world is always a kind of rupture (Jenkins & Csordas 2020: 45). The notion of rupture is helpful here, hinting at a therapeutic pathway. Admission took Hugh out of the world. For him, the ward is liminal, a place apart, suspended, unconnected to the demands of ordinary social life. Anthropologists have long been interested in liminality. Work has often focussed on the scope for bonding and the creation of human connection (Turner 1969; Whitehouse 2021). But here the role seems to recall very early themes, where liminality in life cycle rituals enables a change of status, a process which Arnold van Gennep famously called 'rites of passage'(1960 [1908]). Rites of passage are moments of discontinuity in a life trajectory that enable a person to leave one group and join another. In a rite of passage, a person is taken out of the everyday world, located for a while betwixt and between, and then returned to the world with a new identity. Liminal moments are often disorientating. They can involve uncomfortable or painful ordeals, and humiliating activities that include a denial of personal sovereignty and the imposition of radical equality. This is how rites of passage turn children into adults, makes a partner into a spouse, a medical student into a doctor.

What helped about medicalisation is the way that it introduced discontinuity. Medicalisation transforms Hugh's narratives of twinkling trousers and picaresque adventures into something problematic. Medicalisation suggests that Hugh wasn't a hero. Rather, he was disordered. His narrative is undermined and so the repeating cycle of summer energy and winter lows is challenged. This change created the conditions for him to rethink his life and redirect his path. Thinking of Hugh's hospital stay as a rite of passage unpicks medical readings and suggests an alternative perspective on what are otherwise familiar medical processes and technologies. This has a number of aspects. Admission put a stop to Hugh's madness by extracting him from the social world. In this sense, a mental health act assessment is a ritual of separation, enabling Hugh to be held against his will in the company of others who have taken leave of their senses. On a ward he could no longer continue with his adventures or his dreams. He couldn't even leave. No longer a saddhu, he was unable to write his own script or tell his own story. It was a kind of violence, but it created a liminal space and that appeared to be what Hugh needed. It enabled a change of direction, a gradual, iterative, self-transformation.

The built environment of the ward, with its locked doors and intensely observed spaces add to the liminal experience. Life is contained, perhaps dominated, not just by bars on the windows but by rules and routines. Interaction between staff members and patient is routinised, asymmetrical and non-negotiable. Patients are cared for but disempowered. The result is a social world that is typical of the harsh and sometimes humbling liminal stage. In this reading, the limitations of psychiatric knowledge contribute to the production of liminality. We see how Hugh is represented in his notes in a distanced, objectifying way. He doesn't even read a newspaper he 'self occupies.' The standardised, impersonal, selective gaze of clinicians lifts patients out the world of everyday representation, creating a discursive liminality in which experiences are reframed in unfamiliar and obscure ways that conceal, or diminish personal agency.

The blunting effects of medication might also be seen to contribute to liminality. At first this might sound counterintuitive. We typically differentiate the specific effects of treatments from placebo effects. The former are the real thing, the source of healing efficacy, whilst the latter are inevitable but slightly unrespectable, a distraction from the focus of treatment, and impurity to be removed from treatment trials. Anthropologists have critiqued these intuitions. Indeed, Wahlberg argues that medical anthropology has been influential in rethinking the role of meaning responses (Wahlberg 2008). Moerman prefers to call placebo effects 'meaning effects'(Moerman 2002). He argues that meaning effects are interwoven with pharmaceutical effects in biomedical care, even if the deliverers of that care tend to focus on biological effects. Hugh's account of being on a ward suggests that the subjective effects of the medication he received might be understood as having meaning effects. He described how his 'hard drive had been effectively wiped clean' by the 'months of heavy drugs.' Antipsychotic medications diminish focus, and create a sense of distance, even unreality. As Jenkins puts it, pharmaceutical selves are slow and sluggish. Our claim is that medication can be understood as producing and interiorising a kind of pharmaceutical liminality.

This suggests a continuity with the radical psychiatrist Joanna Moncrieff, who argues for a reconceptualisation of psychiatric medication (Moncrieff 2008). Rather than calling antidepressants or antipsychotics, we should accept that these pharmaceuticals are not cures and do not counter illness mechanisms. Rather they have lots of effects that might sometimes be helpful and sometimes not. This seems closer to Hugh's account, where the medication creates a kind of erasure. The medication effects are very broad – it wipes his memory, rather than treating an illness. The cognitive effects of the pharmaceuticals created discontinuity and rupture characteristic of liminality and thus created the conditions for a status-changing, we might even say life-changing, rite of passage.

This rite of passage, comprising of multiple forms of liminality, enabled Hugh to change. The breakdown itself, admission and containment on the ward, the administering of powerful psychoactive drugs gave Hugh an opportunity to re-examine his life and redirect his trajectory. When he was discharged, Hugh describes himself as having 'disappeared from myself.' He couldn't just take up where he left off. The cycle of high and lows, tetherings and untetherings, just couldn't continue. Discontinuity with the past meant everything had to be renegotiated. It was like starting again. He didn't know what he should do, even what he could do. He had become estranged from his partner. His psychiatrist, a Buddhist, suggested: 'you should try doing nothing…you might find it an interesting experience.' So, he lived on his own as a hermit. This was a fulfilment of one of his fantasies when he was ill. But it wasn't much fun. This was radical change, but it perhaps took a form Hugh wasn't expecting. Part of that value came afterwards, from reflecting on the experiences.

Clinical accounts of psychosis see it as an aberration: faulty cognitions leading to confused people with bizarre and often disturbing beliefs. Clinicians who talk in these terms would inevitably find it difficult to engage with Hugh. There is an emerging philosophical literature on psychosis that tries to broaden the category, so that it might accommodate affect, bodily sensation, and what Ratcliffe calls 'existential feeling' (Ratcliffe 2008) We don't want to engage in debates about the nature of psychosis per se. Rather we want to think through what this instance of psychosis might look like if we apprehend it not through the lens of a clinician working for the NHS, but if we want to produce knowledge that might help Hugh understand and get the most out of the experience. Hugh's breakdown was clearly very painful. Our contention is that it was also valuable, and that part of that value lay in its pain. Negative emotions and disordered thinking helped Hugh change. It is striking that after the breakdown, Hugh didn't want to return to normal. In a sense, Hugh's recovery wasn't recovery at all, not a regaining of his former health. For Hugh, psychosis led to new perspectives on the self, breaking down old cognitive habits and barriers, leading to new moral projects. Hugh's restlessness was a kind of defence. A career that, by its nature was haphazard and unstructured 'it masked, for me at least, the extremes of my behaviour.' But he didn't see himself as ill or abnormal. Rather, he thought of this as his creative nature, his 'heroic self.' Now he sees things differently. His flights were journeys away from responsibility. His escapes were from 'the gravitational pull of depression.' And he is conscious that this impacted on others. He sees his lack of awareness at the time as part of the problem.

A new future arose out of a new relationality. Connection with people started to be more than constraining or limiting: it was enriching. It sounds like Phil really listened to Hugh. He wasn't on the lookout for evidence of symptom severity, or risk, and he did not reject or dismiss Hugh's preoccupations. This connection was not tethering but a lifeline. After nine months he reconciled with his partner and began work with 'a useful help-meet' a Jungian psychoanalyst. This is no longer Hugh as a participant-observer, or a buffered self. Indeed, his work helping to run a local support group is suggestive of a wider moral vision, making a link between moral transformation and recovery.

Hugh's ethnography offers an alternative reading of the benefits of psychosis, diagnosis, admission and medication. We do not suggest that Hugh's case is typical. The imposition of biomedical expertise and the heavy psychiatric medication that goes with it can be linked to chronicity and helplessness, not liminality and change. Treating distress medically was helpful to Hugh but not necessarily for reasons that are apprehensible to the medical mind. Terms like 'delusion' or 'hallucination' help clinicians respond to the needs of the institutions they work for, but do little to help make sense of the lived experience of psychosis as something positive and illuminating. Nonetheless, Hugh personally benefitted because the imposition of the language of bipolar interrupted and undermined his narrative defences. Admission enforced discontinuity. The intrusive, paralysing effects of antipsychotic medication, alongside the discipline, scrutiny and equality of the ward created a liminal space, setting off a trajectory in which Hugh might remake himself. They made change possible. Part of that change comes from reflecting on illness experiences, being able to break free of purely medical readings of his distress. This is therefore an argument for the necessity of polyphony in mental healthcare.

7

US AND THEM: WHY NOBODY WINS

with Rowan Jones

Self, positioning and context

As a teenager I wanted to help people. To make the world a happier place. I studied psychology and worked in mental health, in psychiatric hospitals and community charities. I still work in mental health services, but I do not expect to help people. After thirteen years I expect to complete administrative tasks to hit Key Performance Indicators (KPIs) in order to maintain my organisation's funding and my salary. I steal what therapeutic moments I can, but they are few and far between.

Eleven years ago I received a diagnosis of Bipolar 1 disorder. Seven years ago I was sectioned for the first time of many. I have been treated by former colleagues in wards I have worked on. I worked in a day hospital service where I have previously been treated. Former patients have become comrades, our friendship forged under detainment. Respected colleagues have become hated foes, their incompetence only discovered through treatment.

As a patient I have seen the external face presented by staff, while fully knowing what is going on behind the scenes. As a staff member I can see the contrast between how patients are seen, and the concealed reality that is hidden from professionals. I see how patients are deceived about the mechanisms of the mental health system, and the lack of insight professionals have into the lives of their patients. Neither side knows how much they are missing of the complete picture. Over a decade of professional work, and more than a year cumulatively spent as a patient in psychiatric wards, have given me a set of experiences and contrasts that enable a more complete understanding than somebody who has only been inducted to one side of 'them' and 'us'.

DOI: 10.4324/9781003154235-7

A central paradox in my life is that as a professional I like and respect my colleagues, while as a patient I end up hating most mental health professionals. Both perspectives evolve from rational thought and observation – but initially appear contradictory. This happens because as a professional one rarely sees colleagues give care. Support is given one to one, and that fundamental act of care is almost entirely secret. Reports back to the team are seen, and notes can be read. Therefore if the staff member knows what to say and write they appear competent to fellow team members, even if to their patients their incompetence is clear.

Accountable bureaucracy

Bureaucracy has replaced good quality care as the core of my daily work. Senior managers do not talk about how we can better help service users, instead they brief us on how to hit Key Performance Indicators (KPIs) and the latest paperwork we need to fill in. In every paid role the sign of being an experienced and valued team member is spending less time interacting with patients, and more time navigating the surrounding bureaucracy required by the organisation.

My first paid role after university was as a health care assistant in acute and intensive care psychiatric wards. We received ten days of training. One hour of the training was about mental health, five days on restraint, with much of the other time spent on how to navigate bureaucracies such as record keeping and data protection. I had assumed the main component of my work would be interacting with patients and talking to them therapeutically. This was not the case, because patient interaction was not a priority.

Three main institutional factors shaped the behaviour of the nursing team away from speaking to patients. Firstly there were other 'allocations' which had to be completed each shift (e.g. checking smoke alarms, that no keys were missing and that certain documents were printed for the next shift). Secondly all therapeutic contact with patients was meant to be documented. Therefore if a conversation with a patient went beyond trivial pleasantries – becoming a 'one-to-one' – it was meant to be written up in notes. During a busy shift, and with limited access to NHS computers, this could be hard to do. Sometimes one would be in the uncomfortable position of having had a beneficial conversation with a patient, but not having had a chance to write it up. This would be seen as actively poor performance, when otherwise if one had not spoken to patients and completed allocated tasks, one would be seen as having performed well. Finally a ward culture emerged where doing unpleasant bureaucratic tasks was seen as the real work, and a source of virtue, while speaking to patients was almost a fun luxury.

Each shift every member of the nursing team was allocated a number of patients to write notes about. Speaking to that patient was optional – aspirational, but not required. The accuracy of the notes was never checked and was of less import than the length and existence of the notes. I commonly observed colleagues trying to find out more about their allocated patients via staff discussion in the office – often leading to confabulation when there was a lack of knowledge. Relatively unimportant facts, such as whether a patient had used leave or not and whether they attended meals, gained a currency due to their ability to increase the length of notes. Similarly vague statements such as 'engaged with staff and peers' or 'spent time in communal areas', were often used when a staff member had been unable to talk to a patient. This was to increase the appearance of thorough record keeping.

In one case a patient wanted a cup of tea, and I had to ignore his shouting and banging on the office door until my notes were finished. My colleagues teased me about staying five minutes over time to get him his tea when the start of shift admin would have prevented him getting his tea for at least another thirty to forty-five minutes.

As a patient I have experienced this ward culture focussed on documentation and found it deeply frustrating. The notes appear to be of little benefit to me, are often inaccurate, and rarely seem to impact outcomes beneficially. I have also found it frustrating when notes are believed instead of me. For example during an admission, whilst still very unwell, I washed my hair one weekend after being prompted by staff when I had not done so for many weeks. This was put in my notes alongside a statement that I had significantly improved; despite the staff not speaking to me otherwise. This led to discharge being suggested at the beginning of a ward round, a plan being made despite my wife's protests – as the notes said I had been better – until a week later it was clear I was not ready for discharge. This uncertainty and confusion caused me unnecessary distress.

However as a staff member I understand why notes have to be believed. Some patients are unreliable narrators, or struggle to communicate. A service runs far more inefficiently if you cannot trust your colleagues and what they say. Particularly as some individuals can lack insight into their condition. However at times I'm acutely aware of notes kept by colleagues being inaccurate, due to my own interactions with a patient or due to my witnessing an incident. Levels of uncertainty around notes are never considered during staff discussions I have been part of, and there is a discomfort when professionals disagree.

After working in inpatient settings I worked for mental health 'Charity A' providing NHS commissioned community services and the equivalent of a day-centre drop-in. My record keeping for Charity A served a different purpose. The information collected was recorded to demonstrate meeting KPIs or to defensively record an appropriate response to risk in order to avoid potential criticism (e.g. if a patient committed suicide after disclosing their intent to us).

The most visible KPIs we had to hit related to initial assessments of potential service users. This meant each assessment began with an awkward five to ten minutes of data collection that would not affect the care of my patient, but had to be completed in order for the assessment to count towards the KPI. This was not beneficial to the client, particularly when done over the phone, as the data collection delayed the formation of a therapeutic bond. Logically this data could have been collected at the end of an assessment, but this was not our policy due to clients sometimes leaving when the assessment was complete or staff members forgetting to complete the paperwork after a cathartic (for the patient) therapeutic interaction. As a patient being treated by a home treatment team I have seen how irritating a focus on form-filling before care is, particularly when it must be completed before any therapeutic conversation can happen.

Assessments were meant to be done on individuals who had not used our services previously. However some weeks we would not have sufficient new patients attending, either due to a lack of interest or people not attending appointments. When this happened we would assess an existing patient who had been using our services for long enough they pre-dated our having initial assessments. Therefore they were not on our computer system in a way that would prevent their assessment being counted towards a KPI.

Occasionally we would be particularly in need of a specific demographic for our assessments to hit KPIs, e.g. older adults. In this case we could select an existing member who belonged to that demographic. Typically we already knew these patients well, and so they would not gain a lot from the assessment. In some cases we even asked them to do it as a favour to us.

During the initial assessment patients complete a Warwick and Edinburgh Mental Wellbeing Scale (WEMWBS). KPIs require a follow-up phone call several months later to see if an individual has improved their score on the WEMWBS. This is regardless of whether they have accessed any of our interventions. These phone calls have minimal time allocated to them, and the main thing that affects the KPIs is the WEMWBS. Therefore this follow-up phone call is described to patients as a therapeutic and supportive follow-up, but in reality must be a brief piece of data collection.

Some of our targets are linked to a concept called 'mental health care clusters'. This is a new way of categorising people according to their symptoms and severity of illness. They operate in parallel to conventional diagnoses and formulations of difficulty. Senior managers expect us to cluster patients, even though we do not feel able to due to never using them as a concept in our clinical work and training. If we do not try to cluster our patients, a member of admin staff with no frontline experience of mental health will pick a cluster grouping for us based on our notes. It was emphasised that accuracy was not essential if we did our best, and it was suggested that if we were uncertain we should cluster our patients in whatever way was most useful for achieving our KPIs.

Year on year our KPIs require us to do more assessments. However our treatment services do not contribute to KPIs, and therefore have been cut by approximately fifty per cent in order to create more time for assessments.

This often means that after we assess an individual, there is little we can offer them as a service. In theory the intention is we could signpost them on to other services. In practice these services have often been cut and/or the patient we are assessing has been referred from those services. It is very common that we assess a patient as needing services from IAPT, but IAPT have referred them to us for reasons we consider flimsy. Anecdotally it seems clear that this is because IAPT is also struggling to meet the level of need. The same is true for the adult mental health team.

Therapeutic engagement and constructive work within a therapeutic relationship can feel as if you are achieving little for your time. For example listening to a patient talk about their pets or other minutiae of their life can feel like non-work; even if it is also the foundation of building a relationship with an individual who struggles to engage with mental healthcare. Paperwork can feel like real work, while spending time with patients can be dismissed as non-work unless core therapeutic topics come up.

Limits of bureaucracy/accountability

As a worker I constantly feel held to account. If paperwork is not completed, I will get in trouble. If a patient discloses risk, and we do not document an appropriate response, I will get in trouble if that risk actualises. However – as a patient – I have seen that most care given is of poor quality, and that staff face no repercussions for inappropriate behaviour. Polite indifference and a casual lack of competence is the norm. A significant proportion of home visits have lasted between two and five minutes. Cruelty is rare, but hateful comments about my LGBT status are semi-regular. Occasionally I will be told prayer is the answer and I simply have to embrace God. Nurses, social workers, occupational therapists and consultant psychiatrists have all behaved in ways that meet the definition of abuse I learned in my training. However, the protocols around abuse are never enacted.

In theory patients could complain. However, as a staff member I have never seen a complaint be successful. Instead the patient is labelled as difficult or unreasonable. This is understandable. Every worker – good and bad – receives unreasonable complaints. In some cases they are spurious, and in some cases because difficult situations are inevitable in mental health. To take all of these complaints seriously would eat up an unsustainable amount of time and be stressful for all staff members. We have each other's backs. Unfortunately this also buries reasonable complaints, particularly if the staff member appears capable by reporting to the team effectively.

Occasionally one will see a fellow staff member at work, and over years may build up enough data to have a sense of that staff member's quality. Sometimes an entire team may realise one member is incompetent. This appears to have no consequences for the staff member. Provided they continue to produce appropriate notes and reports to the team there are no consequences for giving poor care.

As a patient I have witnessed how some institutions have formalised this suppression. When a complaint is made to front-line nursing staff, the response is to 'bring it up in the "have your say" weekly meeting'. When it is brought up in the meeting, a note is made but there is no follow-up. If the complaint is persistent, it becomes labelled as an individual complaint and therefore not appropriate for the meeting. Alternatively the low-level staff member holding the meeting explains they can bring it up with management but they do not have control to institute the change. This traps complaints between staff members and the meeting, with a constant diversion of responsibility and obfuscation to avoid change.

As a worker I have made use of this gap in accountability. At times patients have come to me with ideas that are reasonable and good but I have no power to action – the institution will not allow me to make those changes. Neither will the institution allow me to explain that I do not have the power to enact them – in fact the institutional message is that patients should come to me with these ideas and I should enact them; despite the bureaucracy making it impossible. Therefore I suggest they bring it up in the weekly community meeting, claiming that is the forum for new ideas. However the weekly community meeting runs in a way that makes real change unlikely to occur. Instead of saying no, I allow these patient suggestions to quietly die in a black hole of bureaucratic inactivity. I know what I am doing, and I do not find it an acceptable way of behaving, but I have no alternative – I would be disciplined for inappropriate behaviour and an unwillingness to promote service-user inclusion if I explained the reality of the situation.

Safeguarding

'Safeguarding is everybody's business' – one of the most repeated mantras in any organisation trying to help people. In the context of child protection, perhaps it works as intended. However adult safeguarding is a grand folly. An endeavour of copious paperwork, hours of staff time and no discernible benefit.

Everybody wants to help vulnerable people – it is the core of our work – but that work is divorced from the processes labelled 'safeguarding'. We do what we can to help our patients, then spend hours filling in paperwork, phoning ignorant senior managers who have never worked frontline roles ('safeguarding leads'), and phoning multi-agency safeguarding hubs. Invariably the conclusion is to offer mental health support and contact the adult mental health team (which we have always already done). The only benefit is that we have followed established procedure, spread the accountability between multiple organisations, and created a web of societally sanctioned inaction that protects individuals and organisations from blame.

In the same way our core work no longer aims to care, safeguarding does not aim to help people – it is layers of artifice for no reason save to create a gap in accountability for organisations to exploit. Safeguarding did not help my severely manic patient at risk of bankruptcy and homelessness due to financial exploitation by an acquaintance. There was no intervention for an imminent threat of arson. It has changed nothing about how we try to help victims of domestic abuse, controlling behaviour, or any other form of human cruelty that so often is experienced by the people we support day to day. It simply means we waste hours documenting it.

Many of my colleagues share my scepticism around safeguarding proce-dures; however all of us feel required to follow them. There is a nebulous fear of the consequences if we do not. Some of my colleagues find solace in safeguarding procedures as a concrete act they can take in response to risk information. It does not appear to matter if it leads to an improved situation for the patient, but it makes them feel as if they have done something. Mental health work is stressful. Holding risk is anxiety provoking. An inability to help is uncomfortable. It is entirely understandable that taking several hours to do something relieves this discomfort and displaces the anxiety. They equate acting with helping, and I do not know if they are wilfully una-ware of its inefficacious nature.

*

In earlier chapters we explored how the institutional setting of mental healthcare shaped how clinicians describe patients. Our emphasis was on polyphony, recognising that forms of knowledge are partial and incomplete, and organised around need. Ethnographic accounts, we suggested, should not be placed in competition with clinical narratives, because each is produced for different purposes and each has a role to play. Here, things take a turn for the worse. Nobody reading Rowan's ethnography could feel that this is good mental healthcare. There seems to be a contradiction between the clinical set-ting and Rowan's desire to help, between KPIs and care. Home visits only start with paperwork because the organisation needs to gather data required to compete for tenders, not because there is any therapeutic rationale. Patients on the acute ward are isolated and lonely because staff members find being sup-portive bureaucratically cumbersome and therapeutic progress is hard to record. If you need mental healthcare, you might want to look elsewhere. Staff members like Rowan sincerely want to help, but the care they give can at times seem brutal. The institutional setting impacts on clinical relationships, and the capacity of staff members to really engage with their patients. The result is care that is superficial, disingenuous, rigid and calculating. The way that care is institutionally organised seems to be inimical to what we might otherwise think are essential elements of actually caring. The needs and interests of the institu-tion do not appear to coincide with the needs and interests of service users it is supposed to be caring for. Somehow, the cart has ended up pulling the horse.

So why is it happening? What is it about the institutional setting that forces Rowan to steal therapeutic moments, rather than base her day around therapeutic working? And what might a solution look like? There is a large social science literature that tries to account for the shortcomings of bureaucracy and what are sometimes called 'audit cultures.' In chapter one we tried to review this literature. Many of the contributors argue that something about how bureaucracies work – their machine-like reliance on records and procedures and routines makes them inevitably reductive. In particular, bureaucracies have to use simplistic categories of thought, and encounter problems when these categories are used to represent complex real world events. James Scott, for example, famously showed how bureaucratic categories of knowledge are crude and reductive, and this leads to sometimes catastrophic failures of state planning (Scott 1998). Marilyn Strathern queried the wider effects of taking technologies and rationalities from accounting and transferring them to other areas of activity (Strathern 2000a). According to David Graeber, it leads to 'structural stupidity' and 'dead zones of the imagination' (Graeber 2015). Jerry Muller describes 'flaws' and even 'epistemic degradation' arising out of a 'metric fixation' that 'has elements of a cult' (Muller 2018: 20). The broader suggestion is that the problems of bureaucracy are not intended, or wanted or, even, anticipated. Rather, they are side effects or collateral damage caused by systems that are being asked to do too much.

So are the problems that Rowan describes examples of audit cultures, of bureaucratic technologies and rationalities being taken out of their natural domain and being placed in a setting where they function less well? Is Rowan describing instances of structural stupidity or epistemic degradation? Should we perhaps view the NHS as having elements of a cult? There appears to be something to be said for this kind of interpretation. The categories and rationalities Rowan describes seem more suited to managerial tasks than the task of representing suffering. The care that Rowan describes seems crude and rigid and not at all suited to the complex, shifting, mysterious nature of human distress. But our sense is that this kind of account only takes us so far. To investigate this, we need to decentre clinical knowledge and start to take the agency of institutions more seriously.

As we discussed in chapter one, psychiatry can be presented as an encounter between dominating knowledge and a hapless individual. Knowledge can seem to be the primary agent shaping mental healthcare and so it becomes the primary object of analysis. Looked at this way, understanding psychiatry can almost be equated with understanding psychiatric knowledge, not least in the form of the DSM. Medical staff are like vectors, bringing knowledge, and thus, implicitly, the networks of commercial and professional interests that make up the assemblages of global technoscience, into contact with distressed people. None of the ethnography in this book sits comfortably with this narrative, but Rowan's is particularly thorny. It is not that knowledge is absent. But Rowan shows how the categories she uses are mostly managerial. Her ten days of initial training consisted of just one hour of information about mental health. Much more time was spent on learning how to perform bureaucratic tasks, such as record keeping and data protection. Rowan emerges more a bureaucrat than a clinician, who uses biomedical knowledge to achieve institutional goals. Diagnostic categories or ideas about symptoms play a role, but they are determined as much as they are determinative, acted upon as much as they are agential. Knowledge is, as Lakoff puts it, liquid (Lakoff 2005). For Lakoff, this meant that knowledge was shaped by the global networks that make up technoscience. In our account the forces operating on it are local and institutional. For Rowan, biomedical knowledge is a tool to get through the working day.

In a series of influential publications, the philosopher Ian Hacking analysed how mental healthcare changes its patients (Hacking 1995, 1998). In his memorable phrase, mental healthcare 'rewrites the soul' of patients, transforming them into something new (Hacking 1995). But when we look at Rowan's ethnography, something different emerges. When she works as a health professional, Rowan feels harried and constrained, her attention scattered, forced to respond to multiple pressures as best she can. Yet as a patient she remains in a stance of critique, even dissent, towards mental healthcare. It appears that it is as a clinician, rather than as a patient, that Rowan's soul is rewritten. And it is the institutions she works for that are doing the rewriting, rather than the behemoth of biomedicine.

This prompts the question: how is it that institutions have the capacity to rewrite our souls? And how does that help us understand the problems of mental healthcare that Rowan describes? Some ways of framing the relationship between mental healthcare and its institutional or organisational setting offer limited help in illuminating this process. For example, we may think of institutions as an external constraint. To use Weber's famous phrase, they might be an 'iron cage.' The idea here is that staff find their freedom to act limited by rules, routine and protocol. This suggests that staff aren't really changed. Their souls are untouched. Rather, a coercive institution prevents them from doing what they want. Such a framing has some purchase on Rowan's ethnography. It might be an adequate description of moments when Rowan wants to do one thing, but finds that she can't. She wanted to make tea for a patient on a ward, for example, but didn't have time. When working for Charity A, she exploits 'accountability gaps' to performatively pursue patient comment and criticism in the knowledge it will lead nowhere, because that is what is expected and to do otherwise would lead to being disciplined. It makes her feel compromised, forced by the institution to act against her better judgement.

But, for the most part, the institutional setting changes Rowan. In these moments, Rowan is not caged. Rather, her world is redefined, or remade, according to whether she is a staff member or a patient. The differences are subtle, even insidious. Concepts in the social science and humanities

literature like 'internalising values' or 'subjectification' do better in representing institutional effects on staff members because they show that the
changes go deep, into hearts and minds. A person who is subjectified is not
forced to do things they don't want to do. Rather, the things they want to do
are determined by forces external to themselves. But both these terms have
limitations too. They suggest that the effects are programmatic, the ordered
consequences of an ideological project. In a Foucauldian account, subjectification is ultimately a form of governmentality, a means by which the
state discursively disciplines its citizens. A theme of this book is that there
are reasons to resist simple, neat, orderly accounts of the world, however
appealing they might be. The world Rowan describes is haphazard and
messy. The various organisations she has worked for are not all the same and
the effects of their ways of organising are almost random in that they reflect
the play of multiple, uncoordinated factors. So we might want different analytic terms to describe the way Rowan's soul is rewritten. A further limitation
of 'internalising values' or 'subjectification' is that they suggest a clear, durable dividing line between inside and outside the person, such that a particular kind of practical, discursive, or disciplinary environment can lead to
matching substantial and long lasting changes on the inside. But Rowan's
ethnography reveals the changes to be unstable and impermanent. We see
Rowan move between stances, commitments and tastes. When she is a service user she actively hates people who, when they are colleagues, she
respects. Her subjectivity is not fixed but contextual and fleeting.

*

A more helpful way of drawing attention to the causal properties of institutions
is the notion of 'affordances.' James Gibson introduced the concept of affordances to try to break down the idea that discrete, bounded individuals
'interact' with their environment (Gibson 1977). Gibson saw the world as
more permeable and interpenetrating. He wanted to understand how humans
become attuned to their environment and how that enables particular forms of
life. At first, the idea of affordances was used to think through human
engagement with the material world, but subsequently the notion was extended. In a discussion of ethical affordances, Webb Keane suggests: 'Affordances are properties of the chair vis-a-vis a particular human activity' (Keane
2016: 28). A chair presents an opportunity for sitting. It does not compel you,
but it has limits: it cannot be eaten, or flown, or made into a scarf. If you are
tired, and see a chair in front of you, you may well find yourself sitting. The
hard limits and easy opportunities of the organisations where Rowan works
are at times obvious. Forms have to be completed in appointments irrespective
of the wishes of those present. On wards, allocations take up time and so limit
interaction with patients. There is an overlap in these instances with the notion
of the iron cage, in that Rowan retains a sense of what she wants to do, and

feels forced, or pressured, to behave otherwise. But it is preferable to see these as affordances because it suggests a continuity between hard limits and more subtle, interior effects.

The interior effects of institutional affordances can be profound. The relationship between people and chairs transforms the experience of being tired into being in need of a chair for a sit down. A tired person thinks of sitting. Seeing a chair might remind them of their fatigue. This seems to get close to how to capture the agency of the institutions Rowan works in, and how they get to rewrite Rowan's soul. What seems true, or important or valuable changes according to whether Rowan is a patient or a clinician. Rowan started out wanting to talk to patients. It seemed central to the job. And when she is a patient, she knows how important contact with staff can be. But when at work, how it feels to talk or listen to patients is transformed. It doesn't feel like the core of her working life, something humane, or compassionate. Instead, it feels burdensome, slightly pointless, additional or frivolous, a 'fun luxury.' This is the intimate power of affordances. Institutional affordances direct her attention, shape perceptions, and suggest priorities and strategies. Safeguarding might be seen as an extension of Rowan's initial desire to help. But practices around safeguarding occur in a setting where risk and responsibility are linked in a particular way. Like the tired person in the presence of a chair, as a member of staff, Rowan finds safeguarding to be a kind of exposure to responsibility occurring in a setting where responsibility can be dealt with by specific document entry practices. Helping a patient, and thinking about their interests and needs, blurs into assessing personal risk to reputational damage. Safeguarding becomes a performative exercise in which following procedures and producing documentation is a way of dealing with responsibility. Institutional affordances shape patients too.

One of the strengths of the notion of affordances is that it makes an association between features of Rowan's ethnography and the institutional setting without specifying the connecting pathways. This is helpful, because the pathways are difficult to conceptualise. They cross fundamental conceptual distinctions. Institutional affordances include ethics, ontology, affect and relationality, that is, what is right and wrong, real and unreal, how life feels and who should be trusted and who is other. Affordances include rules and regulations, hierarchies and procedures, KPIs and official forms. But they extend into the unspoken, the informal and even unnoticed. Interpersonal dynamics shape institutional affordances. The notion of a 'moral engine' can be seen as doing a similar conceptual job, trying to show how social situations (amongst other things) can give rise to moral intuitions that might not be deterministic, but nonetheless be felt to be authoritative or binding (Mattingley et al 2017). Rowan describes how 'ward culture' exerts a moral pressure. It points her towards the meritorious 'real work' activities and away from spending time with patients. At times, Rowan rejects these pressures. But they nonetheless colour her experiences of spending time with patients, giving it a particular affective quality, as a 'fun luxury'. Rather than being rewarded, or praised, therapeutic moments have to be 'stolen.' Attempts to help become tiny acts of institutional transgression. 'Real care' is imprudent, whilst not transgressing is prosocial, creating bonds of solidarity with colleagues.

Institutional affordances cannot be understood simply as changes of perspective, or of lived experience versus second-hand, theoretical knowledge. When reflecting on her working life and her life as a patient, Rowan is aware of her discomfort with forms and allocations. To extend Keane's metaphor a little, we might see Rowan's ethnography of her life as a clinician as a sequence of occasions in which she has felt tired and found herself sitting, whilst (mostly) retaining a sense of what not sitting might be like. But we might wonder if this would be the case for staff without her double life, not least as people go about their busy working lives. Over the years we might suspect that discomfort will recede, become unstable and patchy, and might even fade away completely, replaced by feelings of professionalism, of necessary emotional labour oriented towards patient health. It would be difficult to continue a career in mental healthcare without sometimes feeling that it helped. This points to the difficulties of introducing 'expertise by experience' into clinical care. Being a patient isn't just a matter of lived experience but of institutional positionality. For the most part, Rowan isn't able to translate the insights from her lived experience into additional competencies in her professional role, but, rather, jumps between the two. If there is a transfer of knowledge or expertise it appears to be the other way, from clinician to patient. In the final section of this chapter we see how Rowan's knowledge of clinical strategies contributes to her role as patient.

*

Rowan's ethnography shows that there is a considerable space between feeling coerced by hard institutional limits and the wholesale adoption of the organisational point of view. Affordances frequently take Rowan to a halfway point. There are many moments when she seems neither entirely sincere nor entirely insincere, where she is pressured into documentation she half believes in and half rejects, where scepticism, performativity, open mindedness and hoping for the best all merge. When Rowan assesses already known patients, she is trying to meet demographic targets. This is far from how she would like to deliver care, but, at the same time, she doesn't think it is wholly wasted: 'they won't gain much' but perhaps they will gain something. She ends up clustering patients without feeling entirely competent to do so.

Rowan's account of hair washing is particularly helpful in highlighting the grey area between wholly sincere belief and calculated, strategic performance. Rowan washed her hair at the prompting of a member of staff. She knew she was not getting better and was not ready for discharge, as did her wife. A second member of staff took a different view, and wrote in her medical notes that Rowan washing her hair showed she was beginning to get better and that it was time to plan her discharge. We don't know why the second member of staff took this view, and what motivated them. But we do know that the notes were untrue. Yet Rowan goes on to remark: 'I know why notes have to be believed.' When she is a clinician, she has to believe notes too. Had she been working on the ward at that moment, she would likely have believed the erroneous notes. It is necessary, part of her professional role. She might have pushed doubts from her mind, triaging her attention away from reasons to query the notes or ways to check their veracity, in order to focus on the pragmatics of the situation, the need to get the job done. The second clinician who used Rowan's freshly washed hair as evidence for discharge might have been wholly sincere. She might have looked at the hair, and at Rowan, and simply misjudged the situation. But, equally, she might have just had a chat with the ward manager and realised that they need to find a bed for an incoming patient. A desire to help, by accommodating a new patient, might have shaped perceptions of Rowan's health and the meaning of hair washing, imperceptibly nudging her into pragmatism. Or, perhaps, the staff member knew that Rowan had been prompted to wash her hair, but pushed it to the back of her mind and engaged in the emotional labour necessary to reach a settled view that made sense in notes.

The uncertainty and ambiguity surrounding the second clinician seems both irresolvable and entirely typical. Mental healthcare is a shadow world of ambiguity and compromise. Beliefs are only half believed, views are expressed but doubts and qualifications are withheld. Something confidently stated in an appointment might be mocked later on. Being a good clinician means being able and willing to be disingenuous. Professionalism means allowing contextual factors to shape, perhaps even trump, what look like straightforward truth claims.

All of this is concealed from patients. It is a kind of secret. It is a variety of what Taussig calls 'public secrets', that is 'something known by everyone but not easily articulable' (Taussig 1999: 216). The public secrets that Rowan describes are things that shouldn't or couldn't be said. Here, though, 'everyone' means all members of staff. The fault line between staff members and patients is so great that, in Rowan's words: 'neither side knows how much they are missing of the complete picture.' There are public secrets on both sides of the divide. But the degree to which the secrets are known, by whom, and, critically, when, remains both ambiguous and fluid. In a given situation, some members of staff are more 'in on the secret' than others. Cynicism jostles with naivety, tactics with honesty. As both insider and outsider, patient and clinician, it is not just that Rowan is alive to the blind spots and epistemic fallibilities of each role. Rather, she is both deceiver and deceived, simultaneously in and out of secrets, privy to understandings that she both knows and – at least in some sense – doesn't know.

This might sound dispiriting. As Graham Jones puts it 'the concept of secrecy has carried overwhelming negative, antisocial, and primitive connotations' (Jones 2014: 54). Surely it has no place in mental healthcare? Elizabeth Anne Davis' rich ethnography of mental healthcare in Modern Greece suggests reasons why the presence of secrecy and deception in mental healthcare might be something less than an emergency (Davis 2012). Davis stresses that mental healthcare encounters are intensely personal, relational and, thus, negotiated. Even if psychiatric encounters involve the application of knowledge, they are also necessarily pragmatic and situational, involving, like many other complex and consequential human encounters, strategy and performativity, confusion and uncertainty. In such a domain, bad faith and deceit play necessary roles. Matthew Carey has gone further, revisiting the reputation of lying and obfuscation as social forms and finding positive aspects (Carey 2017). Carey describes social life in the mountains of Algeria, where a great deal of everyday conversation is, apparently, highly unreliable. People just can't trust each other. Carey suggests that this creates a kind of social space between individuals, which plays out in positive ways as a 'radical respect for the moral and psychological autonomy of others' (ibid.: 31). Is this what is going on in NHS mental healthcare? In Rowan's ethnography, there are signs that secrecy works like Carey suggests, in that it allows clinicians a certain room for manoeuvre. But a key part of Carey's argument is that the space between people created by socially sanctioned dissembling is reciprocal. Everybody lies. This doesn't sound like mental healthcare, because clinicians expect patients to tell the truth. There is no reciprocity in assumptions about untrustworthiness and so none of the mutual respect that might arise from it. However, Carey's work might explain feelings of imbalance between clinician and patient in that the demand for honesty and openness that might undercut the autonomy of the individual is distributed unequally between clinician and patient. We might see a service-user's deception of her psychiatrist as gesture of autonomy, a way of enacting personal dignity.

The notion of secrecy highlights the different audiences at play in mental healthcare. Clinical appointments can appear intimate as if they take place in a sealed off, even liminal setting. But we can see that Rowan is seldom able to be purely attentive to a patient. Any semblance of separation or privacy is misleading. Rowan is never really alone with a patient. External audiences intrude, and they do so in a way that is concealed. The details that matter to Rowan when she is a patient - is the clinician attentive, do they understand - are not recorded and are, in effect erased. But clinical decisions, data gathering and signposting are all subject to scrutiny. Rowan might try to listen, but in the back of her mind she knows that whatever she records will be read by others. Institutional affordances loom in the background as the unmentionable elephant in the bureaucratised room.

Rowan's dual role suggests that the disjunction between staff voices and patient voices is, at least in part, created by the rhetorical work of staff. For staff members, it is appearances that matter, KPIs and other documentary traces. Part of the clinical role is to erase this, to make it appear as if care, and not the documentation of care, is the driving force. In the clinical world Rowan describes, concealment, even deception, are central. This is why when she writes from the perspective of a healthcare professional, her ethnography reads as disclosure. However truthful and constructive, Rowan's account also feels transgressive. She is telling us secrets. Telling the truth as a clinician necessarily means breaking the bonds of loyalty, letting her colleagues down.

The philosopher Harry Frankfurt regards bullshit as a form of insincerity (Frankfurt 2005). Bullshit is not lying. It may not even be false, although it often is. Bullshit is phony. The central quality of bullshit is that the bullshitter is not concerned with truth. She is not trying to get things right. Rather, in Frankfurt's words, she is 'trying to get away with something' (ibid.: 23). Bullshit is a variety of intentional misrepresentation, designed to produce an effect:.

> The bull-shitter may not deceive us, or even intend to do so, either about the facts or about what he takes the facts to be. What he does necessarily attempt to deceive us about is his enterprise. His only indispensably distinctive characteristic is that in a certain way he misrepresents what he is up to.
>
> *(ibid.: 54)*

In Rowan's ethnography there seems to be an element of bullshit both in the writing of notes and in the deliberations of team meetings that use notes. A lot of what Rowan does as a healthcare professional might, broadly, be characterised as an attempt to get away with something. Rowan attempts to conceal that the true enterprise of mental healthcare is 'to maintain my organisations funding and my salary,' by numerous acts of intentional misrepresentation and a continual focus not on getting things right, but in getting things done. When Rowan and her wife resist plans for her discharge, she remarks 'As a member of staff I understand why notes have to be believed... A service runs far more inefficiently if you cannot trust your colleagues.' Yet Rowan also explains how the notes are written with an emphasis on length not accuracy. They are not very believable notes. Their credibility appears to be domain specific, in that notes are more believable when viewed in a team meeting than they would be whilst being written.

Choosing to believe notes sounds like pretending to believe notes, or trying to believe them, perhaps by wilfully ignoring doubts. If staff choose to believe them in meetings, in the interests of efficiency, are they not acting as if they believe rather than genuinely, sincerely believing? If so, this is bullshit. Bullshitting in this case means staff are misrepresenting themselves, concerned not with the truth, but with pragmatic considerations. This is one instance, but we believe it is typical of a wider phenomenon. Making this claim seems shocking and surprising, but we believe it is familiar to those who work in mental healthcare. None of this is intrinsic to psychiatry, psychology or nursing, or any of the disciplines that make up mental healthcare. Most of the activity that Rowan describes in the section above could not be conducted in a spirit of candour. Evasion, tendentiousness, partiality and insincerity are key to getting the job done. It doesn't feel right to be thinking about secrecy or bullshit. They may not even feel real enough to be investigated. This is part of the institutional affordance. It is how the institutional setting erases itself. In Frankfurt's terms, the institutional setting of mental healthcare has introduced a lot of bullshit into the enterprise of psychiatry and then encourages staff members to bullshit about the bullshit.

Neither secrecy nor bullshit are intrinsic to psychiatry, psychology or nursing, or any of the disciplines that make up mental healthcare. What does it mean to deliver mental healthcare in a setting where sincerity – that is the opposite of bullshit – is difficult to achieve? How does bullshit impact on trust, attention, attunement, mutuality, affective investment? How does bullshit impact care? Quite what care is, and how it relates to the institutional affordances of mental healthcare institutions is a subject we return to in the next chapter. Here, we suggest that secrecy, multiple audiences and bullshit are likely to have some part in the story of why the care Rowan describes is so bad. Anthropologists are increasingly paying attention to the concept and phenomenology of care, puzzling over quite what care is and why experiences of healthcare often feel so empty and abrasive. In day-to-day life, it is a hallmark of rich relationships that they contain elements of sincerity. We sometimes differentiate between relationships that are 'genuine' or 'real' and those lesser relationships that are neither. Strong, or deep, or lasting relationships are built on mutual knowledge rather than deceit or misrepresentation. Rowan describes care that is strategic, performative, almost manipulative (ironically, these are charges laid against the patients said to have EUPD). Sincere disclosures from the patient are traded for phony responses. A patient who feels they are not really being heard, or that their distress is not really being understood are perhaps right. Not listening can take many forms. Suggesting Rowan should pray is a kind of not listening. In her monograph about health in the north of Canada, Lisa Stevenson describes a moment of real care: 'In such moments, we recognise the uniqueness/specificity of the being in front of us (that he or she could not be otherwise) and a specific (and necessarily reductive) identity is not what, at that moment, is demanded' (Stevenson 2014: 166). Such moments of unmediated, attentive encounter seem almost impossible in mental health institutions.

Thinking in terms of affordances helps us theorise the agency of mental healthcare organisations. It helps us understand how Rowan's soul became rewritten. But it doesn't determine the nature of the agency. Affordances can turn out badly, as they do here, by putting a shadow between Rowan's aspirations to care and the realities of her day to day work. But equally, they might turn out well. It looks reasonable to suspect the affordances of mental healthcare institutions are inimical to some of what we might hope care to be. Mental healthcare institutions are in this sense uncaring, even if the professionals who work in them have good intentions, and are people of integrity and talent.

But should we take Rowan's 'care vs KPI' dichotomy at face value? Is she not reifying bureaucracies, suggesting they have some unchangeable essence that is forever uncaring? Might these problems be mitigated within the current system? One way of developing this argument is to propose that current bureaucratic arrangements are unfocussed or wrongly directed, or problematic in various ways, but they could be improved such that they adequately represent the real work of care. In other words, the problem isn't KPIs themselves, but just the KPIs that Rowan currently finds herself working with. Might we even speculate that instruments like KPIs could be reformed such that they are the solution to the problems Rowan describes?

We argue that this is not likely to be the case. This is because, as we discussed in chapter one, the simplifications and reductive logics of bureaucratic working are not accidents. Nuance is a problem that KPIs rhetorically solve. KPIs work – if they do indeed work – because they distort and conceal. It isn't noise in the machine, it is how the machine works. Simplified working is part of how bureaucracies reassure. More nuanced KPIs, or more refined paperwork, might undermine the capacity of mental healthcare institutions to reassure because they would fail to exclude the truly problematic or alarming. As 'members of the public' we are all soothed by the performative accountability of bureaucratic institutions.

Even if it seems counterintuitive, bureaucracy has a kind of spiritual role. Removing simplification and obfuscation would ask more of the public. We would have to accept a world that is uncomfortably complex and uncertain, unpredictable and unknowable. Often, staff members seem aware, or half aware of these reductive practices. This is why they feel compromised, and give care that is insincere, directed to unseen audiences who consume the documents, rather than the service users who are physically present. If the mysteries of human suffering could truly be reduced to a half dozen disorders that come with evidence-based, effective treatments, the world would be a simpler, safer, and more hospitable place. Improving mental healthcare thus asks something of the public. It requires us to live with more anxiety about mental healthcare and to be more sceptical when presented with reassuring documentation. Critically, we may have to accept that distress is more complex, intractable and hard to treat than the institutions competing for public funds might have us believe.

The power of affordances

Writing ethnography is very different to the work I do as a frontline mental health professional. My views and opinions change and alter with the different settings. For example, when writing ethnography I very much agree that mental health is full of bullshit – but when working I only notice the worst excesses. Most of the time I am simply trying to get the best for my patient and that is my sole focus. At times I may be aware that my work is based on flimsy foundations, but there is no space for conscious awareness of bullshit when working. 'Attentional triage' pulls my focus away to getting a demanding job done.

Undeniably my 'world is redefined' by the context and task I am doing, in ways that 'are subtle, even insidious'. Working in the mental health sector 'transforms the experience' of helping someone. The way I respond to mental distress outside of work is very different to how I respond while working. For example, outside of work I am much more likely to be bluntly honest about the limitations of the mental health sector – something I could not do at work. The different affordances in different settings mean that my 'soul is rewritten' when working as a professional.

My colleagues are equally affected by affordances. My colleagues express different opinions when talking in the pub compared to discussions during team meetings. For example their views on personality disorder may wildly vary. In the pub we may all agree it is a flimsy diagnosis to the point of almost being meaningless. During team discussions they will make arguments based upon the symptoms associated with personality disorder, and assume the label is meaningful enough to predict client behaviour and treatment outcomes. These discussions are different again to how we would discuss personality disorder with a client, such as using much less pejorative language than either within the pub or team meeting. I suspect the thoughts are different as well as the language used, based upon the actions my colleagues take with clients compared to the actions decided upon within team meetings. For example they will be more sympathetic with a specific client in front of them.

The affordances my colleagues experience change over time as well as by situation. While significant service cuts were being made – and my colleagues were relatively disillusioned – they were willing to talk critically about our organisation and its practices. For example, we agreed that large numbers of assessments, without sufficient treatment was a bad thing. Similarly, some of my colleagues were receptive to the idea that our work involved bullshit. Several years later, with treatment services cut yet further, the same individual colleagues now speak positively about our organisation, and are more hostile to concepts such as bullshit. This suggests that 'over the years' my colleagues' discomfort has receded, and 'become unstable and patchy'. This discomfort also has been 'replaced by feelings of professionalism'.

The first part of this ethnography was written approximately fifteen months prior to this second section. At the time it was 'difficult to continue a career in mental healthcare without sometimes feeling that it helped'. Since then I have restructured my working patterns to only deliver interventions and perform tasks which feel meaningful. This means I experience the 'institutional setting' I work within very differently to when I wrote the first piece of ethnography. The institutional affordances I experience have changed dramatically. Intellectually I agree with my ethnography, but emotionally cannot quite believe it. I could not write it now. Clearly my 'subjectivity is not fixed but contextual and fleeting' based upon how I '"interact" with [my] environment' – 'what seems true, or important or valuable changes' based upon my role and 'engagement' with my environment.

Bullshit and the game of being a clinician

As a clinician my work 'is not concerned with the truth' – truth is less important than aiding my patient's recovery. I have no hesitation in being 'phoney' when it is required. However this does not make all my work 'bullshit'. Instead it means I have artifice and artificiality as part of my professional toolbox, ready to be deployed tactically when beneficial or required.

This artifice and artificiality can benefit my patients. It can be helpful that 'sincere disclosures from the patient are traded for phoney responses'. For example I am completely non-judgmental, even when clients have done terrible things or hold offensive extremist views. Similarly clients may describe horrific and shocking events. They do not need to see my emotional reaction, unless I tactically display part of it to build a therapeutic outcome.

When I choose to be artificial it is fundamentally 'sincere'. I want to help my patient. However at times the institutional setting 'exerts a moral pressure' in combination with 'hard limits' that makes artifice and artificiality feel necessary in contexts where I would prefer to be transparent. Sincerity transitions into insincerity as artifice and artificiality bleeds into bullshit.

Artifice and artificiality exists on a spectrum between interpersonal and therapeutic skill to outright lies. It can be expressed in words or through actions. At times it is clearly beneficial, while at others it is harmful.

Primarily my job is to care and listen, but it contains elements of the police officer and lawyer. To formulate a client's problems I gather evidence. I ask the same question in different ways. I do not take their first answer at face value. For example few patients disclose problems with their family immediately, and may initially insist their family is fine – but gradually disclose information suggesting the contrary. Skilfully I build a picture, and then create the opportunity for them to discuss it. Similarly a patient may report severe depression, but after more detailed questioning about their experiences, it may actually be the case they are experiencing mild depression - opening up services I can signpost them to.

After building a formulation, it can be my job to cross-examine a client's beliefs and thought patterns. This follows from some of the central ideas of CBT. Similarly I may employ motivational interviewing techniques to help a client alter their behaviour. This can border on manipulation, but is therapeutic when it is in line with a patient's stated objective. For example with an alcoholic decreasing their alcohol consumption. I am aware of conditioning with praise or attention, and have been known to refuse support when a team decision is to systematically not reward unhelpful behaviours. Sometimes this is necessary, often I am uneasy with doing so – certainly more so than my colleagues. I deploy interpersonal strategies such as the 'broken record' technique to enforce team decisions and organisational policies.

Ideally this would be my only professional artificiality, however the real world of limited resources and time create situations where the same skills are modified and used to essentially give bad news. For example if we cannot meet the needs of a client, I might try to persuade them that what is available will be sufficient. Multiple times I have tried to persuade individuals with significant mental health needs that a one-day managing stress workshop will be enough to help them. This insincerity rings hollow to me, but I try to justify it by pretending I am giving them hope. I claim to myself that I am trying to minimise their disappointment at a chronic lack of help by the mental health system.

I'm amazed how rarely my patients become angry at how blatantly lacking my suggestions are for ongoing support – particularly as at the start of any assessment I promise we'll end with a plan. Often my intensive listening allows me to understand my patient well enough to give them a meaningful and beneficial conversation – about half the time I can spin the situation enough that even without further support my patient feels like they have a way forward; even if quietly I know how much more they would gain if I could offer them any support. Perhaps one in ten or one in twenty I can help, but the other assessments end with an awkward explanation of funding cuts and under-resourced services.

I wonder if this is because I'm providing a 'moment of real care' where I 'recognise the uniqueness/specificity of the being in front of [me]'. I offer something rare and valuable, even while I am using artifice and artificiality to 'get away with' not offering a meaningful intervention beyond that individual conversation. I use that 'moment of real care' to help disguise the bullshit situation and my bullshit explanation as to why I cannot help.

The only outright lies I tell are to cover my managers and our organisation. I simply cannot tell my patients the truth – that we are a mismanaged inefficient organisation that could do a lot more but wilfully doesn't. When we cut our day services by half, I couldn't tell my clients how unnecessary it was. How we sat around in an empty building. That half our site-specific funding had been syphoned to HQ management salaries. I played my part in our phoney consultation, listening to plausible solutions suggested by patients, while knowing the outcome was already decided no matter how much I pretended to take their ideas on board.

There are hollow artificialities that are true yet also false. For example I have routinely recommended to clients that they contact their GP or in an emergency go to A&E. These are true facts, and the correct protocol. In theory an acutely ill mental health patient should attend A&E and receive helpful care. In reality most experienced professionals know this is not the case. I have done this while believing it would not positively affect their care and they might well have a very negative experience if they attended A&E.

In some cases I have done this knowing that my client will not take these options, but gains reassurance from believing support exists, while appreciating the fact I am taking their distress seriously enough to make recommendations. In other cases I make the recommendations knowing I have to in case something goes wrong (e.g. they commit suicide) while fearing they will follow my advice and their mental health will suffer as a result. Am I 'getting away with' covering my back at the expense of patient outcomes, or am I using artifice as part of an established protocol?

While working within a day hospital service I wrote weaponised notes. Each was written as part of a campaign to alter the response of other parts of the NHS trust. In one case I tried to emphasise a patient's need for ongoing support after discharge. In another our team believed our patient needed a hospital admission. As a strict policy we could only give our patients twelve sessions over six weeks. As a crisis service, we were meant to easily be able to escalate care as part of a stepped care model. In reality this was almost impossible – and in some cases our patients were due to be discharged from all services at the end of six weeks.

We hoped our notes might convince other parts of the NHS to change their minds, though it was opaque if we were ever successful. However even with these weaponised notes, a desire to manipulate other professionals was balanced against defensive practise. Some of us would be careful how we documented risk – we might express significant risk, but with mitigations suggesting we had done everything possible and without a smoking gun that might leave the organisation liable (eg. using the phrase 'a safety plan was discussed'). Whether the defensiveness was honest or to the benefit of our patient I don't know. I never lied, but often felt uneasy dancing around the level of unmanaged risk.

The game of being a patient

'Being a patient isn't just a matter of lived experience but of institutional positionality'. This means that patients encounter institutional affordances in the same way staff do. It is easy to imagine patients as passive, acted upon by staff. Patients receive treatment and interventions are delivered to them. But this is not the case. Patients are people, and people have aims and goals – even if they don't say them out loud. As a friend put it: 'Once you're in the game, you need to know how to play it'.

Different patients have different goals. A sectioned individual experiencing psychosis may want to be discharged without treatment. A detained person who is severely depressed may truly want to die. However these goals do not exist in a vacuum – they are constrained by the institutional setting. In the same way a staff member may want to talk to patients, but ends up completing bureaucratic tasks, so too may a patient want one thing but end up engaging with treatment instead. The effect of affordances on patients are no less 'subtle' or 'insidious' than their impact on staff. They 'direct [patients'] attention, shape perceptions, and suggest priorities and strategies'. They are equally contextual. In the context of talking to peers, a patient may not want medication - but then willingly take tablets at medication time. Similarly during ward-round a patient may have no intention of absconding, but when on leave decide to take the opportunity to try and escape. Patients' 'subjectivity is not fixed but contextual and fleeting'.

Affordances do not only affect patients in hospital. Community mental health teams and GPs are also institutions with their own affordances. For example one of my friends, who is a patient, adopts the strategy of never suggesting an idea to a doctor. Instead they say things to try and manoeuvre the professional into suggesting what they want, while making the professional believe it's the professional's own idea. They do this skilfully and have a conscious awareness of it being a necessary strategy to get the outcomes they want.

In a sense this is 'phoney', and might appear more concerned with outcomes than the truth. Staff reading this might think it sounds manipulative - an attempt 'to get away with' receiving support that might not otherwise have been offered. However I would disagree – this strategy is fundamentally sincere. Somebody wants help and is behaving in a way that is necessary to receive that help. Resources are so limited that an alternative strategy might not lead to help – even if in principle all involved would agree the help they are angling to receive is best practice. The affordance of the situation leaves the patient with little alternative – they are as constrained as the clinician who cannot behave as they would like. This strategy is closer to artifice and artificiality than bullshit.

Staff expect patients not to use strategies. In team meetings and discussions we do not discuss a client's aims or objectives. Patients are viewed as blank slates waiting for assistance with their recovery, in a form of stasis until we interact with them. We focus on their symptoms and what we can do, but only if the patient is suitably passive. If our patient tells us what they want, it is treated with suspicion. If we cannot – or will not – provide what they want, we become defensive. If a patient continues to advocate for what they want, we begin to view them as unreasonable. If they attempt to persuade us – or spell out the consequences of our inaction - they are labelled as manipulative. The more direct and eloquent they are, the more manipulative we call them.

Adopting a strategy is different to deploying bullshit. Nor is manipulation synonymous with bullshit. A patient trying to get help does not 'attempt to deceive us' about 'his enterprise'. They are not unconcerned with the truth - even if sometimes they might lie. However bullshit can be part of the strategy a patient adopts.

In contrast to the strategy of my friend aiming to receive more help, I also have friends who utilise strategies to receive less help – often in the context of hospital and the mental health act. Sometimes it involves straightforward lies – such as claiming symptoms have stopped when they have not. Sometimes it involves bullshit. My friends say what they think the psychiatrist wants to hear. They insincerely bluster around topics 'without concern for the truth'. They try to 'get away with' being how they are with minimal treatment. My friends have learned these strategies over time, moving from naive participants to skilled operators.

In the same way affordances take staff 'to a halfway point' where they are 'neither entirely sincere nor entirely insincere', so too do the affordances of being a patient take my peers to a halfway point with regards to their views on treatment. Most of my fellows on a ward 'half believe in and half rejects' the paradigms of mental health treatments. At times they will talk to nurses therapeutically, while at others vehemently deny any possibility of being ill. The affordance of talking to sympathetic staff changes their thoughts and feelings, as does the affordance of being bored on a ward with fellow patients. I see it as a staff member treating clients as well, particularly in relation to antipsychotic medication. The same patient will both agree that there is a need for medication and in a different context strongly disagree with their needing it – the only change is the context within which they are talking. This difference has been most striking when individuals I have treated have become friends while I have been detained on psychiatric wards. Patients are not self-contained boxes of personality waiting for staff contact - they are as affected by context and affordances as staff; even if most of my colleagues appear to be blind to this fact.

As a staff member '"ward culture" exerts a moral pressure' and changes my behaviour, shaping the affordances available. The same is true for patients. On a good, caring ward affordances exist for therapeutic contact and just enough compassion exists for most patients not to be overtly angry all the time. On a bad ward, with a culture of indifference and disrespect, there are no therapeutic affordances – but there is a greater pressure towards anger, shouting, and other challenging behaviours. I have seen this first hand as a contrast between poorly run wards that ended up chaotic and better-run wards that were settled. This pressure has also shaped my own behaviour, making my presentation on one ward unrecognisable to another.

For me, engaging with mental health services is mainly a battle of bullshit and counter-bullshit. From the minutiae of ward life, to major treatment decisions, bullshit pervades everything with rare exceptions. Doctors bullshit me by making unjustified pronouncements during ward rounds, confidently making statements which change from week to week. My psychological expertise lets me see the logical fallacies in what they are saying. Therefore I bullshit them back by pretending to engage with them, making it look like I want a therapeutic relationship, when really I just want to go home. This helps me to avoid *outcomes I don't want, such as looking uninsightful or ending up on depot medication. I do this by using pre-planned rules designed when I am well. For example one must always attend ward round no matter how pointless it feels.*

With nurses I face a daily war of bullshit. For example nurses obfusticate with giving me escorted leave, sending me in circular loops between different workers. On the leave form I write a false leaving time five minutes later than the clock, and lead my escorting nurse on a route that inevitably turns my thirty minute leave into at least forty minutes – distracting them with bullshit small talk so they don't realise. Nurses try to search my room, giving bullshit justifications. I bullshit back claiming its illegality, while knowing alternative justifications exist to make it legal. Nurses give phoney justifications for rules. I argue back, saying what I need to in order to win with no regard for the truth. Outside of being sectioned on a mental health ward I am scrupulously honest and moral. Being sectioned is hell and I do what I need to survive. Nurses become tools that I have to use in order to get what I need, and I bullshit them as much as is necessary to do so. I have no alternative affordances and therefore behave in ways that are entirely uncharacteristic for me.

This bullshit continues into the community, the spectre of the Mental Health Act hanging in the background. For occupational health checks and other pieces of life admin it is still important to appear insightful and the right kind of patient. In relation to staff we've already discussed 'how does bullshit impact care', but we should also ask how does patient bullshit impact care? For me it can be beneficial and self-protective – bad mental health care is worse than no mental health care. Bullshit is prophylactic against the negative consequences. 'A moment of real care' might require staff to 'recognise the uniqueness/specificity of the being in front of us', but for a patient perhaps it is safer to hide than risk misrecognition? Equally, if there's a good chance staff will just bullshit you, why not take the safe option of just bullshitting them first?

'Being a patient isn't just a matter of lived experience but of institutional positionality' and similar forces to those that act on staff also act on patients. Patients are constrained by institutions, and affordances shape the way patients think, feel, and behave in subtle but powerful ways. My colleagues appear blind to this, and the consequences it has. They see symptoms and expect cross-situational consistencies without being aware that a client's presentation can be hugely shaped by the institutional context they find themselves within – whether in the community or as an inpatient. Equally my friends who are patients are blind to the game of being a staff member. They do not recognise the subtle forces reshaping staff perspectives and behaviours.

CONCLUSION

This book grew out of frustration. I was frustrated by the lack of productive interdisciplinary working in mental health research and, at the same time, frustrated by a lack of progress in mental healthcare research. Looked at from within biomedicine, mental healthcare research is not advancing in the way other areas of health research advance. Every few years there are announcements of breakthroughs in mental healthcare, and suggestions of new treatments just round the corner, but then it all goes quiet. Some clinical researchers think we have made little or no progress in the last few decades. And while there is a lively literature in the humanities and social sciences on mental healthcare, it rarely seems to penetrate healthcare itself. Surely we need this research to actively engage with clinical research?

I felt that I had good reasons to find this impasse frustrating. Over several years as an anthropologist amongst mental healthcare professionals, I have been told again and again that care is not very good, that it helps some people some of the time, often in marginal ways, but leaves others stuck and that many continue to suffer. Some members of staff were more forthright, describing mental healthcare as shambolic, rigid, ineffective and self-regarding. These were claims I was familiar with because I have been a patient. I know first-hand that although some members of staff are excellent, and sometimes treatments help, it is altogether much less effective than we might wish. Biomedical research supports these doubts. For example, in a paper called 'More treatment but no less depression: The treatment-prevalence paradox' published in the journal *Clinical Psychology Review* Ormel et al, discuss why, although vastly more people are treated for depression, there also seems to be more depression (Ormel et al 2022). With newer treatments and reduced stigma, should we not expect depression to be declining? Instead, we find the reverse. Ormel et al ask the simple question:

DOI: 10.4324/9781003154235-8

why doesn't widespread treatment for depression reduce the incidence of depression? The answer, they suggest, is that: 'the published literature over-estimates short- and long-term treatment efficacy...[and] treatments are con-siderably less effective as deployed in "real world" settings' (ibid.: 1). Tellingly, they also think we need more research into the harm caused by care.

Versions of these concerns can be heard every day on NHS premises in off-the-record conversations between mental healthcare professionals (and between mental healthcare patients). Doubts about the effectiveness of treatments, the accuracy of trials data, and the overall effects of mental healthcare are not the reserve of dissidents or mavericks. They are shared by experienced, mainstream clinicians, as well as by experienced patients. Whilst mental healthcare is widely promoted, the lived reality of care falls short of expectations.

When I started out as a researcher, I assumed that mental healthcare sciences themselves were responsible for the failure of interdisciplinarity. I thought that psychiatrists, in particular, were too insular, prickly or insecure (perhaps, even, too unsophisticated) to engage with anthropologists and philosophers or historians. I now see it differently. It seems to me that social scientists have started out on the wrong foot, basing their work on the asso-ciation of knowledge and power. Even if they do not adopt all of Foucault's theory, they often work in the shadow of Foucault. Of course, working in this way can result in high quality research. But it inhibits interdisciplinary col-laboration because it produces descriptions of mental healthcare that aren't recognisable to mental health professionals. They just don't experience themselves that way. At the same time, research building on a nexus of power and knowledge captures some aspect of patient experience at the expense of others. In particular, it can erase patient agency. Whatever the strengths, Foucauldian approaches to mental healthcare have not been able to engage with biomedical or psychological sciences. This is reason enough to consider new directions.

This book explores these proposed new directions. We have attempted to remove assumptions about knowledge and power, and tried to think of mental healthcare in a fresh way. We have tried to attend to the experiences, opinions and priorities of those involved in mental healthcare. Our aim throughout has been to use the methods of the humanities and social sci-ences to address expressions of discontent from service users and providers, and to ask questions that connect to ongoing clinical research.

Miranda Fricker's work on epistemic injustice has shed new light on mental healthcare. Her ideas provide a fertile way of unpacking the asym-metries and inequalities of clinical relationships, suggesting that clinicians harm patients if they disbelieve them out of prejudice or if they deny them the expressive resources to make sense of their lives. There is something very valuable in how Fricker characterises unfavourable patient experiences as instances of being harmed, rather than, say, being dissatisfied. It is striking that some of the adverse effects of epistemic injustice outlined by Fricker resemble poor mental health: a decline in confidence, reduced agency and a loss of hope. Iatrogenic harm, whether it is unwanted effects of pharmaceuticals or the effects of epistemic injustice, often resembles the distress that mental healthcare sets out to address. But we don't draw on Fricker's work all that much in our ethnographic chapters. This is in part because, in the ethnography above, times when patients feel unheard, or misunderstood seem to arise not so much because they are disbelieved but because the institutional conditions make it difficult for clinicians to really listen. We are less worried about clinicians holding stereotyped or prejudicial view about patients than about the structural conditions in which they work.

Both patients and clinicians talk all the time about the institutional setting. Patients say that care is impersonal, standardised, like a production line. Clinicians talk about feeling constrained, coerced, and sometimes compromised by how care is organised. They say that KPIs have replaced caring, and that much of what they do is now data entry. There is a large critical literature on bureaucracy. Accountable bureaucracies emerge as being characteristic of our times. An accountable bureaucracy can be monitored and evaluated, can participate in markets, compete for tenders, even contribute to the engineering of social equity. They have certain common features that might cause concern in those interested in how best to organise mental healthcare. The literature makes clear that bureaucracy general is reductive, constraining, limiting. It works through simplification, through ignoring complexity or subtlety. When applied to some activities, not least finance where many of these approaches originate, this can be unproblematic. But in many complex real-world situations, the results are unpredictable. In some cases, such as higher education, work become redefined, transformed by measures and protocols and tick boxes. In other cases, such as state planning of agriculture, there can be dramatic failures, including famine.

There is a further concern. Many commentators find that deception is central to how bureaucracies work. Bureaucratic working means being concerned with appearances. As Weber understood in the late nineteenth century, bureaucracies are places of secrecy and the protection of those secrets can be, in Weber's words, fanatical. This insight reveals bureaucratic expertise to be a representational expertise, consisting of skills that have to do with documentation. A good bureaucrat is a person who is able to produce documentation that says the right thing, even if that comes at the cost of full sincerity, because that is how to get things done. This means that documentation is partial, edited in particular ways, not entirely open and honest.

This has two implications that are of particular concern. First, it means we should be careful about taking official reports at face value. We should expect evasion, even misrepresentation from people working in an accountable bureaucracy. This undercuts the value of many of the supposed goods of accountable bureaucracies: the creation of accurate and complete paper trails, the possibility of quality monitoring, a capacity to comprehensively implement policy. At very least, we propose a degree of scepticism towards official reports outlining the work of a bureaucratic institution. Second, problems might arise in situations where the setting of mental healthcare does not encourage and support honesty and sincerity. This is because therapeutic relationships are seen as the cornerstone of care. Clinicians need their patients to be sincere and honest. They need to create trusting relationships. But working in an accountable bureaucracy makes sincerity and honesty difficult to maintain. It falls against the grain of how accountable bureaucracies work. This isn't necessarily a problem. But it demands empirical investigation. We need to investigate how mental healthcare is organised and how it impacts on healthcare experiences, including relationships, communication and trust.

There is a more hopeful strand of research into bureaucracy. Several scholars have noted how officials often have a degree of personal freedom in how they follow the rules. This discretion enables work to be made more personal, tailored to individual cases, to be, potentially, more caring. At very least, discretion offers a breathing space between policy and patient. It appears, however, that the last couple of decades have seen increasing levels of managerialism in mental healthcare. Work is becoming more and more specified, protocolised, and controlled, leaving decreasing space for discretion. Looked at from some perspectives, this is a good thing. Evidence based medicine advances by constraining individual clinicians, replacing personal judgement that may be biased, or faulty, or poorly informed, with high quality research evidence. At very least, it is a way of making care defensible, predictable and uniform. But it limits time and space for that which can't be specified. In mental healthcare, we might think that there is a lot that can't be specified. Patients who have recovered sometimes talk of critical moments of mutual attention and understanding between clinician and patient, for example, that seemed hugely therapeutic, but are very difficult to really explain or unpack. Removing discretion from mental healthcare means closing the door on such moments, and relying on the specific effects of interventions, as demarcated in clinical trials.

So there is a kind of mismatch between what we know about accountable bureaucracies and what we want from mental healthcare. We need to recognise that certain goals, such as demanding that bureaucracies produce extensive accounts of what they do and why they do it, can stand in tension to other kinds of goals, such as making mental healthcare personalised, attentive, patient centred. Making progress towards one set of goals means sustaining losses regarding the other set of goals. Difficult choices must be made about what we value, how much uncertainty we can stand, how responsive to clinician and patient discontent we want to be.

Research has an essential role in negotiating these dilemmas and finding a way forward. But, as we worked together on this book, the nature of that research felt less obvious. Of course, the more science-like areas of medical research have a particular vision of what counts as valid knowledge production. There is a sense that they 'collect' data, in such a way that their methods are separable from their results, and that research findings gradually accumulate to answer questions, which ultimately lead to advances in knowledge and then improvements in mental healthcare itself. Ethnographic working looks rather different. The ethnographer doesn't try to erase himself or herself, but becomes a kind of research instrument, immersed in a social world, and learning from subjective responses just as much as from observations and questions. The resulting research is not strictly replicable, although it can be empirically challenged. It can look unrespectable. But I argued that the distance between scientific research and ethnography is rather smaller than it at first appears. Even in the best designed clinical trial, methods and results mingle such that results reflect not just independently existing features of the world, but are shaped by the kinds of questions asked. Equally, there is a potential for ethnographic work to be more directed towards clinical questions than it has been. These methods can work together. This is important, because interdisciplinary working demands an openness to other ways of understanding research.

In this book, we wanted to foreground the institutional setting as a key determinant of healthcare practice because this seemed to be a way of producing knowledge that might make sense to clinicians and patients and speak to existing clinical research. This means we have turned our attention in a certain direction and not others. Concerns about the corrupting influence of big pharma take a back seat, important though they are. And we don't look at the international networks of cooperation that tie instances of mental healthcare into global systems. Because we pay limited attention to official categories of knowledge, we side-step the many debates about the scientific validity or ontological status of diagnosis. In place of these lines of enquiry comes a focus on how to understand the impact of the institutional setting. We do not settle on a single theory or concept, but use several approaches to try to capture different aspects. The literature on bureaucracy suggests that ways of organising, regulating, monitoring are all highly impactful. It makes a strong case for investigating the causal influence of the institutional setting of mental health care. At very least, some patient discontent might be generated not by biomedical reason, or clinician prejudice, but by the institutional setting. Yet, in biomedical research, organisational impact tends to be ignored, as if healthcare organisations are inert vessels, without causal efficacy.

It isn't easy. Ethnographic approaches to investigating bureaucracy, indeed, probably any methodological approach to investigating bureaucracy, are difficult because bureaucracies are not places of candour. In the smoke and mirrors world of bureaucratic working, we can't rely on official documentation, or in what we are told on the record by mental health professionals. It isn't that everything we are told is false. Rather, everything we are told is partisan, selective, strategic, tendentious. Whether or not they mean it, or are even aware of it, a critical feature of working in an accountable bureaucracy is that it influences how a staff member sees the world and how they express themselves. The institutional stetting impacts what it feels right to say (to patient, to a family member of a patient, to a passing anthropologist) and what should be omitted.

Our solution is to create distance between our analysis and the documents produced by mental healthcare bureaucracies. We have been selectively sceptical, casting an agnostic eye on what, in other contexts, are high-status, authoritative forms of knowledge. Ideas like 'resilience,' 'mood,' 'bipolar disorder,' and 'evidence-based' need not to be taken at face value, but opened up and investigated. Our analysis focussed on why these terms are so beautifully suited to the documentary work of an accountable clinician, and what might result from this, for example when it comes to understanding patient experience. We have done this at length by contrasting clinical descriptions of distress with ethnography and auto-ethnography of distress. The problem is that enquiries like this feel transgressive. It is difficult to retain an agnostic or sceptical stance towards the kinds of knowledge produced by healthcare bureaucracies because, in other settings, we want to trust public institutions and the things they tell us. We want to trust a doctor who tells us that our test results are good, and that surgery isn't necessary (or that the test shows that tumour can be removed). It isn't just healthcare. We want to accept that institutions that do important public work, such as dealing with criminal justice, caring for children, dealing with finance and banking, protecting our borders, promoting international development, all do a decent job. We feel like we need to know that these organisations are safe, efficient and effective. We expect monitoring processes to be able to pick up on problems and, when necessary, provide an account of what went wrong, why it went wrong, and what steps have been taken to prevent it happening again.

In other words, we want to be reassured. Perhaps this is because we live in an anxious society, perhaps the contemporary world is neurotic. It could be that humans are insecure creatures. Whatever the reason, we seem to need Herzfeld's secular theodicy. And if, as private citizens we are believers, it is difficult to become sceptics when we conduct research. It takes emotional labour. It turns bad faith into a research asset. This is where collaborative ethnographic working seems to have special powers. Coproduction resists objectification. Because it brings trusting, open, respectful relationships into the writing process, collaborative ethnographic methods are resistant to the temptation to overlook the way organisations tidy away the mess of human lives. This makes the resulting analysis alert to the disingenuousness of bureaucratic working. You might even say that coproduction coproduces a kind of integrity.

Thinking through these methodological issues led us to reconceive what it was we are trying to do. We realised that we should think of our work not primarily as uncovering fresh data, something unknown, perhaps unsuspected. It might sound nonsensical, but we hope that much of our argument is familiar to many of our readers. We are looking for things people already know, but which the institutional setting encourages people to overlook, misconstrue, possibly even conceal. We deal with public secrets that, unless they are adequately conceptualised and framed, can't be included in larger interdisciplinary research. This approach keeps our analysis close to the way that mental healthcare patients and staff talk about their lives. Psychiatrists form the focus of many ethnographies of mental healthcare. But people receiving secondary mental healthcare, even if they spend time on a ward, find that contact with a psychiatrist is limited and infrequent. Most clinical relationships are formed with other professionals, such as social workers, nurses, health care assistants and occupational therapists. As a consequence, we broaden our focus from psychiatrists to all mental health professionals. We don't forget that patients have relationships with several bureaucracies. For many, the DWP looms larger than the NHS.

Claire's three jobs suggest a tension between clinical intuition, institutional pressure and actual practice that goes beyond both Mol's distinction between the logic of care and the logic of choice and Zacka's understanding of healthy tensions in bureaucratic working. Claire stresses that these tensions are not an abstract matter. They impact on the quality and effectiveness of care, and so on patient health. She suggests that the 'promotional aspect' of care based on data recording and KPIs is misleading, even duplicitous, and that services can only help some of the patients they see. Viv's institutionally expedient re-diagnosis is a remarkable example of actual practice starting out as reflecting clinical intuition, but seamlessly shifting in response to institutional demands. Rebecca and Giles think that Viv won't benefit from the kind of healthcare they provide because of her personality. They even fear that she might be harmed. But when Viv comes to the clinic and applies some carefully calibrated pressure, she is able to secure antidepressants. It isn't that staff change their minds about her distress, or her vulnerability to iatrogenic harm. Rather, they prioritise maintaining contact with her, for reason that have to do with how things look, for Claire's 'promotional aspect.' This emerges as being more important than their clinical views about Viv's health. The clinicians are slightly patronising towards Viv, seeing her as manipulative. But Viv just seems to have understood the situation she is in and secured the best result she can. If she is manipulative, she is not more so than the staff responsible for her.

Catriona Watson's account contains a lot of medical terms. She is 'bipolar', has experienced 'psychosis' and 'low mood.' She 'self-manages' her condition, and has benefitted from 'psychoeducation.' On good days she is 'euthymic.' It might sound as if she has been turned into a drone, assiduously internalising biomedical discourse. Sylvie Fainzang found that even those in rebellion against biomedicine reproduce key aspects of biomedical thinking and practice: 'The practice of self-medication is anchored in an internalisation of expert discourse' (Fainzang 2017: 84). But on closer inspection, Catriona is very different. She has not internalised expert discourse, but turned herself into an expert. Her bipolar is not the bipolar of her doctors. It is a beautiful opponent, a rat in her pocket, it makes her like a bird with bright plumage. Catriona's account of her moodscapes are rich, nuanced and multidimensional, incorporating bodily states, temporal impressions and subtle alterations in thinking. It becomes apparent that, to repurpose Lorna Rhodes' terms, patients as well as doctors can construct 'patchwork quilts' combining multiple theoretical strands. We might think Catriona is more creative than the doctors, because much of her account is homespun, organised around her experiences and her reflections on others with similar experiences. Rhodes' doctors are primarily motivated by their needs, which are mainly to discharge patients to clear beds for new arrivals. In contrast, Catriona's account is organised around self-understanding, and enables her to negotiate a non-bipolar world and manage her health. It would be of little use to a clinician. Catriona's engagements with the welfare bureaucracies are painful, because she is forced into partiality and evasion. This leads to moral injury. We might speculate that these injuries resemble harms done to clinicians when they engage with bureaucratic arrangements that conflict with their own views or values. Overall, by her own account, Catriona has benefitted from mental healthcare. In some ways, she has benefitted from mental ill health, too. She learned through experience, perhaps even triumphing over her distress and finding 'a life worth living.'

In my autoethnography, I try to reimagine my distress. For the medical team, it was simple. I was bipolar. This was the basis of many interventions, mostly pharmaceutical, delivered over a long and unhappy decade. My argument is not that this is wrong (or right) but that many other stories might be told. My personal trajectory can appear extreme and is probably unusual. I became worse whilst receiving care and became well by abandoning care. In my case, ignoring medical advice and discontinuing treatments led to improved health. If this makes me an outlier, that doesn't necessarily lessen the value of my ethnography. It might even be an advantage, because my life shows in stark form the limitations of the medical narrative. As my psychiatrist said of my recovery: 'science can't explain this.' We might imagine that there is a lot that goes on the clinic that isn't scientifically explicable, but it tends to be sidelined and left unnoticed. In contrast, my autoethnography highlights events that go beyond the limited expressive resources of contemporary biomedicine, demonstrating a need for other accounts. In a different universe, my psychiatrist might have gone on to say something like: 'Since science can't explain your recovery, I wonder if other disciplines, such as medical anthropology, might do better?' The chapter is an attempt to do just that. I present my distress as the effect of a habitus, a set of intuitions and commitments that structured my life project. As a young man, trying to make sense of the world, find a way forwards, and deal with some painful events, I developed a depressive habitus. It was poorly adopted to the world around me, and became painful, even disabling, but was hard to shake off. Once diagnosed, healthcare became entwined in a new habitus, in which change seemed impossible and care became part of the problem. I got better because I had an epiphany. Something happened to me that enabled me to redirect my life and start to make up for lost time. It isn't just that bipolar talk can't account for these changes, but the ideas, practices, relationships and treatments that are part of the world of bipolar harmed me, and inhibited much needed personal development.

For Hugh as well, mental health is connected to a point of discontinuity, a rupture in day to day living that facilitated personal change. A period of what his psychiatrists called florid psychosis stopped Hugh in his tracks. The doctors treated it as serious illness. But another reading is possible: that it allowed him to heal himself. Hugh's life had been lived as a kind of rebellion, in which human connection was a barrier to personal freedom. His years appear to have been divided between periods of intense, creative activity as a photographer, and periods of pallid, listless dissatisfaction at home with his family. Throughout, he was sealed off, boundaried (perhaps distanced is a better word) an autonomous individual who was immune to the risks and attachments of mundane living, in some sense unreachable. He seems almost solipsistic.

When he retired, things started to unravel. Hugh benefitted from admission and from the medications he was given. He still describes himself as bipolar. But his account of his life goes far beyond the world of mood disorders and medical interventions. In the lead up to a breakdown (or had it already begun?) he became a holy man, a renouncer, socially dislocated, apart from society. He had entered a state where human connection was almost eliminated. Thinking in psychiatric terms suggests that psychosis is a pathology to be treated. Hugh's account suggests it might also be a mode of action, a reboot, a way of being in the world that is expressive, symbolic, enacting the hidden logic of his values. Anthropologists write about how meaning effects can boost medical treatments. They are sometimes called placebo effects. But Hugh's experiences look as if he is staging his life as performance art, creating his own meanings. Admission helped Hugh, brought him to a needed place of safety. But admission and antipsychotic medication might be read in anthropological terms, as creating liminality, a space where the usual conditions of life are removed and personal change becomes possible. Hugh left behind an individualistic sense of self (that, perhaps unsettlingly, resembles the self of mental healthcare). Getting well-meant finding new human connections, new ways of relating to others. And it required new ways of narrating these experiences and putting them in the larger context of his life.

Rowan's positioning on the frontier between service provision and service use, where she is sometimes a patient and sometimes a professional, reveals something important about how the institution insinuates itself into staff and patients. She presents an alarming picture of a compromised mental healthcare service, underfunded and over-bureaucratised, in which the goals of account-ability dominate care. Form-filling and box-ticking occupy her attention and are the focus of her expertise. What Rowan regards as moments of real care have to be stolen, surreptitiously inserted in the gaps in the real work of documentation. Yet these documentary representations are, to use philosopher Harry Frankfurt's phrase, bullshit. This doesn't mean they are false. It means that they are phony. They are attempts to distract more than mislead, to get away with something, When Rowan deals with the extensive paperwork connected to safeguarding, for example, she is trying to show that all the correct procedures have been followed, that everything that should be done has been done. So the purpose of safeguarding procedures is to be able to produce documentation showing that responsibilities are discharged and no one can be found to be at fault. Safe-guarding might appear to be for patients (and other members of the public) but the people really being safeguarded are staff.

Rowan knows this, finds it obvious. But she mentions that some colleagues might not agree, that they might even be 'wilfully unaware' of it. Thinking of safeguarding as bullshit does not help a care worker get through their day. An 'attentional triage' emerges as part of what it means to be a mental health pro-fessional. When she is a member of staff Rowan finds she is inclined to believe medical notes. There is no other way of getting the job done. But when she is a patient she knows they are highly unreliable. Rowan's institutional positioning changes what seems likely, what seems important, even what seems real.

We use the concept of affordances to try to unpack this. The concept of affordances is designed to capture how humans become entwined with, and attuned to, their environment. In material terms, a chair has certain properties, such as that it can be sat upon. That chairs afford sitting can become entwined with the human experience of feeling tired. This means that feeling tired becomes an experience of wanting a sit down, and of being on the lookout for chairs. We extend this idea to the working environment of mental healthcare. We suggest that mental healthcare is flexible, but has certain properties that have subtle interior effects. These institutional affordances make interaction with patients feel wasteful, maybe a little self-indulgent, whilst documentation feels professional and virtuous. Entertaining doubts about medical notes feels unprofessional and disloyal whilst believing them is collegial and praiseworthy. These affordances are highly impactful. Staff members become strategic bull-shitters. But patients recognise this too. Patients know how to bullshit staff members. Interaction in clinical setting becomes a kind of game, in which par-ticipants shift between telling outright lies and engaging in sincere dialogue, most of the time finding themselves located in a grey area in between, neither wholly sincere not wholly insincere. It is clearly a highly complex and difficult to understand environment. The question is: how does it impact on the quality care? Is this the mental healthcare we want?

*

So what to do with all of this? Our ethnographic data suggest that organising mental healthcare as an accountable bureaucracy has important and complex effects. It shapes clinical practice and illness experience, and generates a way of describing distress that is narrow and limited. These effects are widely noticed, but are concealed, and excluded from much research. Yet they are likely to be deleterious to mental healthcare quality, including healthcare outcomes, costs, and safety. If the institutional setting of mental healthcare is an active agent, it demands further enquiry. This includes historical and comparative work on how mental healthcare institutions develop in different regulatory regimes (Armstrong & Hall 2023).

What might a reduction in the power and influence of bureaucratic accountability look like? We might anticipate less dissembling from clinicians and patients a fuller acceptance of the limitations of treatment and the harms of care. Relationships might become more open and, maybe, more therapeutic. Since institutional affordances shape clinical thinking such that they effectively generate knowledge, we might speculate that a change in the institutional conditions would lead to psychiatric and psychological knowledge beginning to change. The neat and tidy disease categories might become more fluid, and that care might be seen more holistically, with a better sense of the patient in their social world. Perhaps some categories, such as personality disorders, can't really survive outside particular bureaucratic settings.

A clinician who is less concerned about exposure to reputational damage is more likely to listen to unwelcome ideas, to take seriously alternative ways of narrating distress or conceptualising recovery. So the gulf between ethnographies of distress and medical notes could reduce.

A less bureaucratised work setting sounds like it might leave more space for kindness. Ballatt and Campling call for 'intelligent kindness' in healthcare, which they argue is strongly causally connected to health outcomes:

> Kindness…is a binding, creative and problem-solving force that inspires and focusses the imagination and goodwill. It inspires and directs the attention of people and organisations towards building relationships with people, recognising their needs and treating them well… kindness… assumes authenticity, where emotional response and behaviour are in tune and spring from generosity, empathy and openheartedness.
>
> *(Ballatt & Campling 2011: 16)*

These are lofty ambitions. But it is hard to imagine even the best funded mental healthcare service being run on generosity, empathy and openheartedness because are not the kinds of qualities that accountable bureaucracies can reliably produce. Procedures that make care transparent, that enable healthcare institutions to be monitored and to be capable of competing in market mechanisms pull in the opposite direction, making care less kind and more formulaic. If we take the institutional setting seriously, we need to think about how to deal with contradictions between care and institutional form.

One direction of travel might be to disaggregate aspects of mental health. For example, we might separate out the components of mental healthcare as we know it: support, responsibility, care, medical interventions, data recording, therapeutic relationships, (and more). We could recognise that even if they might all need to be present in some form, there may be tensions, even contradictions between them. In an ethnography of informal (and unregulated) drug rehab centres in Mexico where the treatment involves violence, Angela Garcia finds an unsettling connection between pain and recovery (Garcia 2015). She suggests that violence has redemptive possibilities. In a passage that speaks to some of the ethnography above, Garcia states:

> Constituted in and through violence, Padrino Fransisco's scars represented the 'truth' of his recovery. Shirt off, smoking, he explained: "It is what makes it so effective here. You feel like you are dying. When you go through your treatment here you feel your death. We make sure you feel it. We bring you this close."

> *(ibid.: 467)*

An accountable healthcare bureaucracy can't (and shouldn't) make you feel your death. Inflicting violence can never be part of the medical repertoire. And it is probably not for everyone anyway. But, it raises a concern. Inflicting violence might be a highly effective way of dealing with addiction, but we can never entertain such thoughts in the UK because it is inconstant with how we choose to organise mental healthcare. Perhaps the solution is to organise differently. If we want to respond to people's distress, we might need to escape the limitations imposed by our current organisational configurations. For example we might consider dividing mental healthcare into elements that are professionalised and run as accountable bureaucracies that take responsibility for patients and areas that are looser, more informal, that focus on connection, community, solidarity, caring, and so do not organise themselves around the forms of knowledge and practices of data recording that inhibit these processes.

People with lived experience have invaluable expertise. The future of mental healthcare organisations must draw on this expertise. But those who happily cooperate with services may not be the only ones who should be consulted. Sceptical patients, ex-patients and people who reject services altogether run support groups, community gardens, activist organisations and social forums outside mainstream mental healthcare to provide the kind of personal support that healthcare bureaucracies cannot. Different kinds of relationships appear possible when conducted outside an accountable bureaucracy. These groups might be exemplars, the inspiration of studies that might lead to real innovation in care. At present, there is a trend to open up biomedical mental healthcare so that external groups like this can make formal connections with NHS healthcare providers. It sounds exciting, a way of moving beyond stale, limited, pharmaceutical-based psychiatry, an example of joined-up thinking. But losing autonomy and joining larger structures means falling under the gravitational pull of bureaucratic organising. This risks losing the qualities that made the group therapeutic in the first place.

If we reduce the role of bureaucratic accountability, we reduce the reassurances the general public can receive about mental healthcare. It might be a price worth paying. We may have to learn to live with more uncertainty and anxiety regarding mental healthcare. When things go wrong, we may know less about it. If we are to have mental health provision that can meet popular aspirations, learn from lived experiences and benefit from interdisciplinary collaborative research, it is likely to be less bureaucratic. This may mean imposing constraints of accountability, or preserving aspects of care from bureaucratic influence. The future of mental healthcare may lie not in new interventions, but in new institutional forms.

BIBLIOGRAPHY

Aaslestad, Petter (2009) *The Patient as Text: The Role of the Narrator in Psychiatric Notes 1890–1990*. Oxford: Radcliffe.

Adams, Vincanne (2013) Evidence-Based Global Public Health: Subjects, Profits, Erasures. In Joao Biehl & Adriana Petryna (eds) *When People Come First: Critical Studies in Global Health* (pp. 54–90). Woodstock: Princeton University Press.

American Psychiatric Association (2013) *Diagnostic and Statistical Manual of Mental Disorders: DSM-5. Fifth edition*. Washington, DC: American Psychiatric Publishing.

Armstrong, Neil & John Hall (eds) (2023) The processes and context of innovation in mental healthcare: Oxfordshire as a case study. *History of Psychiatry*, special issue, 34. 1.

Ashworth, Jenn (2019) *Notes Made while Falling*. London: Goldsmiths Press.

Ballatt, John & Penelope Campling (2011) *Intelligent kindness: rehabilitating the welfare state*. London: Royal College of Psychiatrists.

Barrett, Robert J. (1996) *The Psychiatric Team and the Social Definition of Schizophrenia: An Anthropological Study of Person and Illness. Studies in Social and Community Psychiatry*. Cambridge: Cambridge University Press.

Behrouzan, Orkideh. (2016) *Prozak Diaries: Psychiatry and Generational Memory in Iran*. Stanford: Stanford University Press.

Bhugra, D. et al (2017) The WPA-Lancet Psychiatry Commission on the Future of Psychiatry. *Lancet Psychiatry*, Oct 4, 10: 775–818.

Bica, C. C. (1999) A therapeutic application of philosophy. The moral casualties of war: Understanding the experience. *International Journal of Applied Philosophy*, 13. 1: 81–92.

Bourdieu, Pierre (1977) *Outline of a theory of practice*. Cambridge: Cambridge University Press.

Bourdieu, Pierre (1990) *The Logic of practice*. Stanford: Stanford University Press.

Bowker, Geoffrey C. & Star, Susan Leigh (2000) *Sorting Things Out: Classification and Its Consequences*. Cambridge: The MIT Press.

Boyer, Dominic & George E. Marcus (2020) *Collaborative Anthropology Today: A Collection of Exceptions*. Ithaca: Cornell University Press.

Bradley, Bridget (2021) From biosociality to biosolidarity: the looping effects of finding and forming social networks for body-focused repetitive behaviours. *Anthropology and Medicine*, 28. 4: 543–557.

Bromley, Elizabeth (2019) Commentary: Questions from the Ground in Severe Mental Illness. *Ethos: Journal of the Society for Psychological Anthropology*, 47. 1: 108–114.

Buber, Martin (2019 [1923]) *I and Thou*. London: Bloomsbury.

Carel, H. H., & I. J. Kidd (2014) Epistemic injustice in healthcare: a philosophical analysis. *Medicine, Health Care and Philosophy*, 17. 4: 529–540.

Carey, Matthew (2017) *Mistrust: An Ethnographic Theory*. Chicago: HAU.

Carpenter-Song, E. (2009) Caught in the Psychiatric Net: Meanings and Experiences of ADHD, Pediatric Bipolar Disorder and Mental Health Treatment Among a Diverse Group of Families in the United States. *Culture Medicine and Psychiatry*, 33: 61–85.

Cavanaugh, J. R. (2016) Documenting subjects: Performativity and audit culture in food production in northern Italy. *American Ethnologist*, 43: 691–703.

Chan, D., & L. Sireling (2010) 'I Want to Be Bipolar'... a New Phenomenon. *The Psychiatrist*, 34: 103–105.

Charon, Rita (2006) *Narrative Medicine: Honoring the Stories of Illness*. Oxford: Oxford University Press.

Clare, Eli (2017) *Brilliant Imperfection: Grappling with Care*. Durham: Duke University Press.

Clarke, Simon & Colin Wright (2019) Tactical authenticity in the production of autoethnographic mad narratives. *Social Theory and Health*, 18: 169–183.

Cook, Jo (2016) Mindful in Westminster: The Politics of meditation and the limits of neoliberal critique. *HAU: Journal of Ethnographic Theory*, 6. 1: 141–161.

Crocq, Marc-Antoine (2013) Milestones in the History of Personality Disorders. *Dialogues in Clinical Neuroscience*, 15. 2: 147–153.

Crook, S. (2020). Historicising the 'Crisis' in Undergraduate Mental Health: British Universities and Student Mental Illness, 1944–1968. *Journal of the History of Medicine and Allied Sciences*, 75. 2: 193–220.

Darwall, Stephen (2006) *The second-person standpoint: morality, respect, and accountability*. Cambridge: Harvard University Press.

Davis, Elizabeth Anne (2012) *Bad Souls: Madness and Responsibility in Modern Greece*. Durham: Duke University Press.

Dresch, Paul (2000) Wilderness of Mirrors: Truth and Vulnerability in Middle Eastern Fieldwork. In Paul Dresch, Wendy James & David Parkin (eds) *Anthropologists in a Wider World*. New York, Oxford: Berghahn.

Du Gay, Paul (2000) *In Praise of Bureaucracy: Weber, Organization and Ethics. Organization, Theory and Society*. London: SAGE.

Estroff, Sue E. (1981) *Making It Crazy: An Ethnography of Psychiatric Clients in an American Community*. Berkeley; London: University of California Press.

Fabian, Johannes. (2014) Ethnography and intersubjectivity. *HAU: Journal of Anthropological Theory*, 4. 1: 199–209.

Fainzang, Sylvie (2017) *Self-Medication and Society Mirages of Autonomy*London: Routledge.

Flinders, Matthew, et al (2016) The politics of co-production: risks, limits and pollution. *Evidence and Policy*, 12. 2: 261–279.

Frankfurt, Harry G (2005) *On Bullshit*. Princeton: Princeton University Press.

Fricker, Miranda (2007) *Epistemic Injustice: Power and the Ethics of Knowing*. Oxford: Oxford University Press.

Foucault, Michel (2004) *Security, Territory, Population. Lectures at the College De France 1977–1978*. New York: Palgrave Macmillan.

Foucault, Michel (2008) *The Birth of Biopolitics. Lectures at the College De France 1978–1979*. New York: Palgrave Macmillan.

Garcia, Angela (2015) Serenity: Violence, Inequality, and Recovery on the Edge of Mexico City. *Medical Anthropology Quarterly*, 29. 4: 455–472.

Gay y Blasco, Paloma & Liria Hernández. (2020) *Writing Friendship: a reciprocal ethnography*. London: Palgrave Macmillan.

Goffman, Erving (1959) *The Presentation of Self in Everyday Life*. Garden City, NY: Doubleday.

Goffman, Erving (1963) *Stigma: Notes on the Management of Spoiled Identity*. Englewood Cliffs: Prentice-Hall.

Good, Byron J. (1994) *Medicine, Rationality and Experience*. Cambridge: Cambridge University Press.

Graeber, David (2015) *The Utopia of Rules: On Technology, Stupidity, and the Secret Joys of Bureaucracy*. New York: Melville House.

Hacking, Ian (1995) *Rewriting the Soul: Multiple Personality and the Sciences of Memory*. Princeton: Princeton University Press.

Hacking, Ian (1998) *Mad Travelers: Reflections on the Reality of Transient Mental Illness*. Charlottesville: University Press of Virginia.

Hammersley, Martyn & Paul Atkinson (2019) *Ethnography: Principles in Practice*. London: Routledge.

Hardon, Anita & Emilia Sanabria (2017) Fluid Drugs: Revisiting the Anthropology of Pharmaceuticals. *Annual Review of Anthropology*, 46. 1: 117–132.

Harrison, Stephen (2015) Street-Level Bureaucracy and Professionalism in Health Services. In Peter Hupe et al (eds) *Understanding Street-Level Bureaucracy*. Nashville: Polity.

Hazan, Haim & Esther Hertzog. (2012) Introduction towards a nomadic turn in anthropology. In Haim Hazan & Esther Hertzog (eds) *Serendipity in anthropological research: The nomadic turn*. Farnham, UK: Ashgate.

Herzfeld, Michael (1992) *The Social Production of Indifference: Exploring the Symbolic Roots of Western Bureaucracy*. Chicago: University of Chicago Press.

Heywood, Paolo (2018) *After Difference: Queer Activism in Italy and Anthropological Theory*. Oxford: Berghahn.

Illich, Ivan (1990) *Limits to Medicine: Medical Nemesis: The Expropriation of Health*. [*New ed.*]. London: Penguin.

Irving, Andrew (2017) *The Art of Life and Death: Radical Aesthetics and Ethnographic Practice*. Chicago: HAU Books.

Jackson, Michael (2013) *The Politics of Storytelling: Variations on a Theme by Hannah Arendt*. Copenhagen: Museum Tusculanum Press.

Jenkins, Janis H. (ed.) (2010) *Pharmaceutical Self: The Global Shaping of Experience in an Age of Psychopharmacology*. Santa Fe, New Mexico: School for Advanced Research Press.

Jenkins, Janice H. (2015) *Extraordinary Conditions Culture and Experience in Mental Illness*. Oakland: University of California Press.

Jenkins, Janis H. & Thomas J.Csordas (2020) *Troubled in the Land of Enchantment- Adolescent Experience of Psychiatric Treatment*. Berkeley: University of California Press.

Johnstone, Lucy (2019) Do you still need your psychiatric diagnosis? Critiques and alternatives. In J. Watson (ed.) *Drop the Disorder! Challenging the Culture of Psychiatric Diagnosis*. London: PCCS.

Keane, Webb (2016) *Ethical Life: its Natural and Social Histories*. Princeton: Princeton University Press.

Gennep, Arnoldvan (1960[1906]) *The Rites of Passage*. Chicago: University of Chicago Press.

Gibson, James J. (1977) The Theory of Affordance'. In R. Shaw &J. Bransford (eds) *Perceiving, Acting and Knowing: Towards and Ecological Psychology*. Hillsdale: Lawrence Erlbaum.

Jones, Graham (2014) Secrecy. *Annual Review of Anthropology*, 43: 53–69.

Kafka, Ben (2012) *The Demon of Writing: Powers and failures of writing*. New York: Zone Books.

Klein, Rudolf (2013) *The New Politics of the NHS: From Creation to Reinvention*. 7th edition. London: Radcliffe.

Kyratsous, M. & Sanati, A. (2017) Epistemic injustice and responsibility in borderline personality disorder. *Journal of the Evaluation of Clinical Practice*, 23: 974–980.

Lakoff, Andrew (2005) *Pharmaceutical Reason: Medication and Psychiatric Knowledge in Argentina*. Cambridge: Cambridge University Press.

Lassiter, Luke Eric (2005) Collaborative Ethnography and Public Anthropology. *Current Anthropology*, 46. 1: 83–106.

Lassiter, Luke Eric (2012) 'To fill the missing pieces of the Middletown puzzle': lessons from re-studying Middletown. *The Sociological Review*, 60: 421–437.

Lassiter, L. et al. (2004) *The Other Side of Middletown: Exploring Muncie's African American Community*. Lanham: AltaMira.

Lipsky, Michael (1971) Street-Level Bureaucracy and the Analysis of Urban Reform. *Urban Affairs Review*, 6. 4: 391–409.

Lipsky, Michael (2010) *Street-Level Bureaucracy: Dilemmas of the Individual in Public Services*. Updated edition. New York: Russell Sage Foundation.

Luhrmann, Tanya M. (2006) Subjectivity. *Anthropological Theory*, 6. 3: 345–361.

Luhrmann, Tanya M. (2007) Social Defeat and the Culture of Chronicity: Or, Why Schizophrenia Does so Well over There and so Badly Here. *Culture, Medicine and Psychiatry*, 31. 2: 135–172.

Luhrmann, Tanya M. (2008) 'The Street Will Drive You Crazy': Why Homeless Psychotic Women in the Institutional Circuit in the United States Often Say No to Offers of Help. *American Journal of Psychiatry*, 165. 1: 15–20.

Mahmood, Saba (2012 [2005]) *Politics of Piety: The Islamic Revival and the Feminist Subject*. Princeton: Princeton University Press.

Marcus, George E. (1997) The uses of complicity in the changing mis-en-scene of anthropological fieldwork. *Representations*, 59: 85–108.

Marcus, George E. (2001) From rapport under erasure to theaters of complicit reflexivity. *Qualitative Inquiry*, 7. 4: 519–528.

Martin, Emily (2007) *Bipolar Expeditions: Mania and Depression in American Culture*. Princeton, NJ; Oxford: Princeton University Press.

Mathur, Nayanika (2016) *Paper Tiger: Law Bureaucracy and the Developmental State in Himalayan India*. Cambridge: Cambridge University Press.

Mattingley, Cheryl (2010) *The Paradox of Hope Journeys through a Clinical Borderland*. Berkeley: University of California Press.

Mattingley, Cheryl et al (eds) (2017) *Moral Engines: Exploring the Ethical Drives in Human Life*. Oxford: Berghahn.

Mauss, Marcel (1985 [1932]) A Category of the Human Mind: the Notion of the Person; the Notion of the Self. In M. Carrithers et al (eds) *The Category of the Person*. Cambridge: Cambridge University Press.

McGoey, L. (2010) Profitable Failure: antidepressant drugs and the triumph of flawed experiments. *History of the Human Sciences*, 23. 1: 58–78.

McKnight, Rebecca et al (2019) *Psychiatry*. Fifth Edition. Oxford: Oxford University Press.

Mintzberg, Henry (1979) *The Structuring of Organizations: A Synthesis of the Research*. Englewood Cliffs, NJ; London: Prentice-Hall International.

Mintzberg, Henry & Alexandra McHugh, (1985) Strategy formation in an adhocracy. *Administrative Science Quarterly*, 30. 2: 160–197.

Moerman, Daniel (2002) *Meaning, Medicine and the 'Placebo Effect.'* Cambridge: Cambridge University Press.

Mol, Annemarie (2008) *The Logic of Care: Health and the Problem of Patient Choice*. London: Routledge.

Molendijk, Tine. (2018) Towards an interdisciplinary conceptualization of moral injury: From unequivocal guilt and anger to moral conflict and disorientation. *New Ideas in Psychology*, 51: 1–8.

Moncrieff, J. (2008) *The Myth of the Chemical Cure*. Basingstoke: Palgrave Macmillan.

Montgomery, Kathryn (2006) *How Doctors Think: Clinical Judgment and the Practice of Medicine*. New York; Oxford: Oxford University Press.

Mosko, M. (2010) Partible penitents: dividual personhood and Christian practice in Melanesia and the West. *Journal of the Royal Anthropological Institute*, 16: 215–240.

Mosse, David (2005) *Cultivating Development: An Ethnography of Aid Policy and Practice*. London: Pluto.

Muller, Jerry Z. (2018) *The Tyranny of Metrics*. Princeton: Princeton University Press.

Navaro-Yashin, Yael (2009) Affective spaces, melancholic objects: ruination and the production of anthropological knowledge. *Journal of the Royal Anthropological Institute*, 15. 1: 1–18.

Oliver, Kathryn, Anita Kothari & Nicholas Mays (2019) The dark side of coproduction: do the costs outweigh the benefits for health research? *Health Research Policy and Systems*, 17: 33.

Ormel, Johan et al (2022) More treatment but no less depression: The treatment-prevalence paradox. *Clinical Psychology Review*, 91: 1–17.

Palmer, V. J. et al. (2019) The Participatory Zeitgeist: an explanatory theoretical model of change in an era of coproduction and codesign in healthcare improvement. *Medical Humanities*, 45. 3: 247–257.

Parish, Steven M. (2014) Between Persons: How Concepts of the Person Make Moral Experience Possible. *Ethos*, 42. 1: 31–50.

Parsons, Talcott (1951) *The Social System*. London: Routledge & Kegan Paul.

Priebe, S., T. Burns, & T. K. J. Craig (2013) The future of academic psychiatry may be social. *British Journal of Psychiatry*, 202. 5: 319–320.

Rabinow, Paul (1996) *Essays on the Anthropology of Reason*. Princeton: Princeton University Press.

Ratcliffe, Matthew (2008) *Feelings of Being*. Oxford: Oxford University Press.

Reddy, William M. (2001) *The Navigation of Feeling: A Framework for the History of Emotions*. Cambridge: Cambridge University Press.

Rhodes, Lorna A. (1995) *Emptying beds: the work of an emergency psychiatric unit*. Berkeley; London: University of California Press.

Rivoal, Isabelle, & Noel B. Salazar (2013) Introduction: Contemporary ethnographic practice and the value of serendipity. *Social Anthropology/Anthropology Sociale*, 21. 2: 178–185.

Rose, Nikolas (2009) *The Politics of Life Itself: Biomedicine, Power, and Subjectivity in the Twenty-First Century*. Princeton: Princeton University Press.

Rose, Nikolas (2019) *Our Psychiatric Future: The Politics of Mental Health*. London: Polity.

Rose, Nikolas & Des Fitzgerald (2022) *The Urban Brain: Mental health in the vital city*. Princeton: Princeton University Press.

Rush, A. J. *et al.* (2003) The 16-Item Quick Inventory of Depressive Symptomatology (QIDS), clinician rating (QIDS-C), and self-report (QIDS-SR): a psychometric evaluation in patients with chronic major depression. *Biological Psychiatry*, Sep 1, 54. 5: 573–583. (Erratum in: *Biological Psychiatry*. Sep 1, 54. 5: 585.)

Sanati, A. & M. Kyratsous (2015) Epistemic injustice in assessment of delusions. *Journal of Evaluation in Clinical Practice*, 21. 3: 479–485.

Scheff, Thomas J. (1966) *Being Mentally Ill: A Sociological Theory*. London: Weidenfeld & Nicolson.

Scott, James C. (1998) *Seeing like a State: How Certain Schemes to Improve the Human Condition Have Failed*. New Haven; London: Yale University Press.

Shah. Alpa (2017) Ethnography? Participant observation, a potentially revolutionary praxis. *HAU: Journal of Ethnographic Theory*, 7. 1: 45–59.

Shay, J. (1994) *Achilles in Vietnam: Combat trauma and the undoing of character*. New York: Simon and Schuster.

Shore, Cris (2017) Audit Culture and the Politics of Responsibility: Beyond Neoliberal Responsibilization? In S. Trnka & C. Trundle (eds) *Competing Responsibilities: The Ethics and Politics of Contemporary Life*. Durham: Duke University Press.

Sinclair, Simon (1997) *Making Doctors: An Institutional Apprenticeship*. Oxford: Berg.

Stevenson, Lisa (2014) *Life Beside Itself: Imagining Care in the Canadian Arctic*. Oakland: University of California Press.

Strathern, Marilyn (1997) 'Improving Ratings': Audit in the British University System. *European Review*, 5. 03: 305–321.

Strathern, Marilyn (2000a) New Accountabilities: Anthropological Studies in Audit, Ethics and the Academy. In Marilyn Strathern (ed.) *Audit Cultures: Anthropological Studies in Accountability, Ethics and the Academy* (pp. 1–18). London, New York: Routledge.

Strathern, Marilyn (2000b) *Audit Cultures: Anthropological Studies in Accountability, Ethics, and the Academy*. London: Routledge.

Strathern, Marilyn (2000c) The Tyranny of Transparency. *British Educational Research Journal*, 26. 3: 309–321.

Sweeney, A. & P. Beresford (2020) Who gets to study whom: survivor research and peer review processes. *Disability & Society*, 35. 7: 1189–1194.

Taussig, Michael (1999) *Defacement: Public Secrecy and the Labor of the Negative*. Stanford: Stanford University Press.

Taylor, Charles (2007) *A Secular Age*. Cambridge: Harvard University Press.

Thornicroft, Graham (2006) *Shunned: Discrimination against People with Mental Illness*. Oxford: Oxford University Press.

Turner, Victor (1969) *The Ritual Process: Structure and Anti-Structure*. Chicago: Aldine.

Wahlberg, Ayo (2008) Above and beyond superstition– western herbal medicine and the decriminalizing of placebo. *History of the Human Sciences*, 21. 1: 77–101.

Weber, Max (2009) *From Max Weber: Essays in Sociology*. London: Routledge.

Whitehouse, Harvey (2021) *The Ritual Animal: Imitation and Cohesion in the Evolution of Social Complexity*. Oxford: Oxford University Press.

Whitley, Rob (2011) Social Defeat or Social Resistance? Reaction to Fear of Crime and Violence Among People with Severe Mental Illness Living in Urban 'Recovery Communities'. *Culture, Medicine, and Psychiatry*, 35. 4: 519–535.

Widiger, Thomas A. (2012) *The Oxford Handbook of Personality Disorders*. New York: Oxford University Press.

Williams, Oli et al (2020) Lost in the shadows: reflections on the dark side of co-production. *Health Research Policy and Systems*, 18. 43.

Woods, A., A. Hart & H. Spandler (2022) The Recovery Narrative: Politics and Possibilities of a Genre. *Culture Medicine and Psychiatry*, 46: 221–247.

Wright, Anthony G. (2012) Social Defeat in Recovery-Oriented Supported Housing: Moral Experience, Stigma, and Ideological Resistance. *Culture, Medicine, and Psychiatry*, 36. 4: 660–678.

Zacka, Bernado (2016) Adhocracy, security and responsibility: Revisiting Abu Ghraib a decade after. *Contemporary Political Theory*, 15. 1: 38–57.

Zacka, Bernado (2017) *When the state meets the street: Public service and moral agency*. Cambridge, MA: Harvard University Press.

Zeitlyn, David (2022) *An Anthropological Toolkit: Sixty Useful Concepts*. Oxford: Berghahn.

Zigon, Jarrett (2007) Moral breakdown and the ethical demand: A theoretical framework for an anthropology of moralities. *Anthropological Theory*, 7. 2: 131–150.

INDEX

Note: page numbers in italic type refer to Figures.